Vegan Diet for Weight Loss:

2 Books in 1:

Vegan Meal Prep & Vegan Keto. 100% Plant-Based Low Carb Recipes Cookbook to Nourish Your Mind and Promote Weight Loss Naturally. (21-Day Keto Plan Included)

Table of Contents

Vegan Meal Prep

Vegan Keto

Vegan Meal Prep

The Complete 100% Plant-Based Whole Foods Cookbook. Over 100 Recipes to Cleanse Your Body and Promote Weight Loss Naturally With a Low Carb Ketogenic Diet. (30-Day Keto Plan Included)

Introduction

I want you to use your imagination.

Imagine a world where there was no animal cruelty and death for the sake of having a meal or a new fur coat. Imagine a world where the climate and environment benefited because animal agriculture was a non-existent activity. Imagine a world where greenhouse gases were reduced because transportation of livestock and manufacturing plants for animal-based products were discontinued. Imagine a world where world hunger was eliminated by feeding crops to the less fortunate rather than wasting it on animals that were being farmed. Imagine a world where every single person led a healthy lifestyle and was free from the confines of obesity, disease, and the challenges of being overweight!

Such a world and an existence does not only have to live in your imagination, it can become your reality as well. Adopting a vegan lifestyle makes all these positive outcomes possible. There has been a lot of misinformation spread about what it means to be a vegan and live a vegan lifestyle. This book aims at clearing up this misunderstanding and showing you the many benefits not only to you but to the general global population for adopting veganism.

You can completely take control of your physical, emotional, and mental health by changing your diet and lifestyle. Going vegan gives you the tools to effectively control and manage your general health and well-being. Your body is a temple and you should treat it as such. Your general health and well-being is directly related to your diet and lifestyle. Eating animal-based products weigh you down and sap your energy. However, consuming green and plant-based foods allows your body to detoxify naturally while taking in the wholesome goodness that it needs. You body uses the nourishment from plant-based foods in an efficient manner by controlling fat deposits in your body and boosting the overall quality of your health. This green way of eating allows your internal body conditions to thrive and is often reflected in your outer appearance. Most vegans who practice the lifestyle consistently and appropriately exhibit fuller hair, healthier skin, and slimmer waistlines. They are at reduced risk of developing chronic diseases and are better able to control their mental and emotional health so that they can live generally happier and more fulfilled lives.

What you will learn in this book

Many people turn to veganism as a way to lose weight, but they will soon learn that there is a lot more to this diet and lifestyle than what they initially expected. Inside these pages, you will learn about:

- What it means to go vegan and why you should challenge the stereotypes that exist around this diet and lifestyle
- The difference between a vegan diet and a vegan lifestyle
- The benefits of veganism
- The ketogenic diet and how it relates to veganism
- How incorporating the ketogenic diet can enhance vegan eating
- Food to eat and avoid on the vegan diet
- Food to eat and avoid on the keto-vegan diet
- A 30-day vegan meal plan for vegan eating
- How to grocery shop to suit your vegan lifestyle
- How to meal prep and store food on a vegan diet
- Recipes for breakfast, lunch, dinner, desserts and more
- Much more!

This guidebook and cookbook combo is a powerful source of information that not only helps you transition into a vegan lifestyle but shows you what to eat and the vast variety of foods you have at your disposal. Eating healthy does not mean that you have to adopt a boring diet or that you have to make your taste buds suffer. A vegan diet can be rich in variety and flavor. This book is packed with over 125 recipes for breakfast, lunch, dinner, dessert, and everything in between to not only make this a healthy journey but a tasty one too! Also included is a detailed shopping list and information on the foods you should avoid and those that are good for you.

I want to take the opportunity to thank you for downloading this book. This book was written to give you maximum value with every word you read. Turn the page to learn how veganism can completely overhaul your life so that you not only improve your diet but also live a happier, healthier, and more fulfilled life every single day.

Chapter 1: What is Veganism

'Veganism' is the general term for a type of vegetarian diet. A vegan diet excludes the use of meat, eggs, dairy products, and all other ingredients derived from animals. This includes ingredients that have been processed using animal products like some types of wine and white sugar. This diet allows only allows the consumption of foods that are made from plants.

A vegan is someone who abides by these diet guidelines. The word 'vegan' also describes a food item.

Reasons someone might choose to go vegan include:

- Preventing death and cruelty to animals
- Wanting to lose weight
- Wanting to live a generally healthier lifestyle
- Reducing the toxic overload and the negative impact of animal agriculture on the climate and environment
- Aiding in the fight against world hunger by feeding crops to less fortunate human beings rather than farm animals.
- Allowing animals to live they way they were meant to live: free and in their own natural habitat.

There are three types of vegan diets:

- **Plant-based veganism:** Most people who choose this type of vegan diet do so for health reasons or to lose weight. They choose to avoid meat and dairy products. As a result, all saturated fats have been eliminated from the diet, hence promoting weight loss and general improved health. This diet is popular because it is easy for weight management, helps prevent chronic diseases such as heart disease and type 2 diabetes, and it leaves a lighter environmental footprint.
- **Raw veganism:** On this type of vegan diet, the practitioner chooses not to eat anything that has been cooked or heated up. Therefore, this diet mainly consists of vegetables, fruits, nuts, seeds, and grains. Again, this diet is chosen mostly for the health benefits. Others choose it for spiritual reasons believing that they are creating a new Eden or Garden of Life. There are different ways to practice raw veganism. The first follows an 80/10/10 rule which translates into 80% carbohydrates, 10% fat, and 10% protein consumption. The other type of raw vegan diet is loosely called "raw till 4" which includes eating raw food until 4 p.m. then having a cooked meal for dinner.
- **High Carb Low Fat (HCLF) veganism:** Just as the name suggests, practitioners of this type of veganism will consume large quantities of carbohydrates in the form of vegetables, fruit and grains and as little fat as possible. Practitioners may also choose to consume carbohydrates in the form of potatoes, rice, and pasta, and healthy fats in the form of avocados, seeds, and nuts. This is often the route that a newbie vegan will take as it allows for a smoother transition while eating a balanced healthy diet without as many restrictions as a plant-based vegan diet and a raw vegan diet.

For the sake of this book, we will be focusing on information and recipes that fit into the plant-based vegan diet.

Vegan vs. Vegetarian

'Vegan' and 'vegetarian' are two terms that are often used interchangeably and can be quite confusing to differentiate for a newly transitioning vegan. Even though both diets exclude the use of meat, they are *not* the same thing.

Vegetarians do not consume meat however, they do continue to consume dairy products like milk and eggs. On the other hand, vegans do not use any animal products or byproducts. To put it simply, vegetarians do not eat animals but may sometimes consume products that come from animals such as dairy or eggs, while vegans do not consume any animal products whatsoever.

There are different types of vegetarianism. There include:

- **Lacto-ovo vegetarianism:** This is the most common type of vegetarianism. Lacto-ovo vegetarians eat dairy products and eggs but avoid meat, poultry, and seafood.
- **Lacto vegetarianism:** Lacto-vegetarians consume dairy products but abstain from eggs, meat, poultry or seafood.
- **Ovo vegetarianism:** Ovo-vegetarians eat eggs but abstain from dairy products, meat, poultry or seafood.
- **Pesco vegetarianism:** This type of vegetarianism does not follow the rules exactly since pescatarians still eat fish and other seafood, but avoid poultry or meat.

Veganism also refers to a range of lifestyle choices that extend beyond your food choices such as the products your use, the materials your home and lifestyle products are made of, whereas vegetarianism is a purely dietary choice. Whatever the reason a vegan choses this diet, the fact remains that no animal products are consumed or purchased.

Is Veganism a Lifestyle or a Diet?

Most vegans extend their definition of veganism past just their choice of what to eat. This also extends to the products they use in their households and the things they choose to purchase for use. That is why the definition of veganism has been extended to include a way of life that excludes all forms of exploitation of and cruelty against animals as far as possible and practical. It is for this ethical reason that most people choose a vegan lifestyle.

Non-food products that most vegans choose not to use include leather, fur, wool, and cosmetic products that include animal ingredients or were tested on animals. They even opt against going to aquariums and zoos.

Many also choose to go vegan to help lighten the impact on the environment. Animal farming has many environmental implications such as deforestation to provide space for this activity, the diversion of plant products away from human beings to feed the livestock, transportation of animals hence releasing greenhouse gas into the atmosphere and many more. By going vegan, you are doing your part to help decrease the carbon footprint that humanity is leaving in addition to reducing deforestation and other actions that help the planet rather that place such a strain on it.

Therefore, if you are considering going vegan, take some time to ponder the fact that veganism is not just a change in your diet, but a lifestyle shift as well.

Benefits of Veganism

Apart from the obvious benefit of weight loss, there are many more additional health benefits to a vegan lifestyle and diet. They include:

- Obtaining high amounts of certain nutrients such as antioxidants, fiber, potassium, magnesium, folate, vitamin A, vitamin C, vitamin D, vitamin B, and vitamin E.
- Because of the decreased consumption of processed foods in the vegan diet, those on a vegan diet tend to have healthy blood sugar levels, improved kidney function, and higher insulin sensitivity which lowers the risk of the development of type 2 diabetes.
- Protection against certain cancers. Many cases cancer development can be traced back to a poor diet. Eating vegan has been shown to reduce the risk of several cancers such as colorectal cancer. This decrease is due to the consumption of legumes on a regular basis. The consumption of soy products can protect against some types of breast cancer. Eliminating the consumption of animal products also helps reduce the risk of colon, breast, and prostate cancer.
- Being at low risk of developing heart disease. Consumption of fruits, vegetables, legumes, whole grains, and nuts on a vegan diet reduces your chances of developing heart disease and improve cardiovascular function.
- Helps decrease inflammation within the body. Raw foods are rich in probiotics and antioxidants which help decrease the symptoms of rheumatoid arthritis including pain joint, swelling, and morning stiffness.

The lifestyle benefits of transitioning to a vegan diet include:

- A significant decrease in deforestation which minimizes the toxic overload and usage of global resources, and protects the environment. A lot of resources are used to ensure that factory farmed animals are fed (even if it's the unhealthiest of feeds) and to maintain the upkeep of other products. These resources can be better diverted toward further bettering our agricultural practices to help alleviate world hunger and manufacture more natural and sustainable alternatives.
- Increasing the awareness of animal welfare. Animal farming often involves cruelty against animals, not to mention death. Adopting a vegan lifestyle can eliminate cruelty and death toward animals.
- Using natural products. In addition to getting rid of animal-based ingredients and animal testing in cosmetic products, adopting a vegan lifestyle means getting rid of the use of synthetic products such as parabens, sulfates, and phthalates, all of which have been linked to abnormalities in growth and development, reproductive and neurological issues. Using natural vegan beauty products eliminates this risk in addition to making you look your best.
- Supporting better fashion choices. The sale of fashion products that include the use of leather, wool, silk, and suede all involve animal welfare issues. By choosing

fashion and lifestyle products that were produced with plant-based materials to mimic leather, 'pleather' or vegan leather, you also support animal welfare rights.
- Saving the bees by forgoing the use of honey and using plant-based sweetener alternatives such as a maple syrup, coconut sugar, dates, and stevia.
- Saving the seas and oceans by reducing or eliminating the use of plastics, harmful toxins, and pesticides.
- Eliminating the use of fertilizer and herbicide to manufacture crops to feed factory farmed livestock, and becoming more sustainable by living a more nature-friendly lifestyle.

What You Need to Know Before You Go Vegan

Often what makes a lifestyle shift and a diet change difficult is not knowing where to start. This section is dedicated to helping you clear the clutter and make this transition easier for you. While you may have gotten the general gist that a vegan diet and lifestyle entails eating less meat and more vegetables, you may be confused as to where to start and exactly what that means. Here are a few tips that will help make your switch to a vegan diet easy, hassle-free, and healthy so that you can get started with as little fuss as possible.

Embrace The Variety and Tastiness That Vegetable Bring to a Meal

People often get hung up on what they cannot eat on a vegan diet rather than what they can eat. A tasty meal does not have to include animal-based products as the main ingredient. Vegetables can be the star of the show and they can earn that spotlight with vigor and deliciousness. They are full of vitamins and minerals that help keep your calorie count in check so that your waistline benefits in addition to all the other health advantages. They are often rich in fiber as well so that you feel full and satisfied with every meal.

Eat More Variety

Being vegan does not mean that your diet consists of reaching for carrots every single day. There are thousands of options available to you in the form of veggies and fruits. You can switch things up by adding whole grains such as brown rice quinoa and beans to the equation. There are also many ways to prepare your vegetables and fruits such as sautéing, stir frying, frying, roasting, baking, barbequing, stewing, and more.

Get Rid Of Refined Grains and Choose Whole Grains

Foods such as white bread or pasta made with refined grains are high in carbohydrates and contribute to weight gain and the development of other chronic diseases. Often times, when grains undergo the refining process, they are stripped of essential nutrients such as iron and vitamin B. Swap your favorite refined carb food choice for whole grain options such as quinoa, kamut, spelt, buckwheat, amaranth, whole grain pasta, brown rice, and wild rice which are rich in minerals and vitamins. Whole grains also offer extra fiber to help you lose weight faster and help you feel fuller quicker.

Use Plant-Based Options to Get Your Proteins

Most people are familiar with obtaining protein from animal sources such as meat, cheese, and eggs but there are plenty of vegan sources that offer protein such as soy, beans, lentils, chickpeas, textured vegan protein (TVP), tofu, and tempeh. Nuts and seeds such as almonds, walnuts, pumpkin seeds, and chia seeds also help supplement your diet with protein. You do not have to suffer a protein deficiency just because you choose a vegan diet. There are plenty of plant-based options to supplement your diet with this much-needed nutrition.

Get Your Omega-3s

Omega-3 fatty acids are important for brain development, eye development and heart health. Popular sources of these fatty acids include fatty fish such as salmon, sardines, and tuna. However, you can supplement your diet with this omega-3 nutrition from plant-based sources such as chia seeds, hemp seeds, walnuts, canola oil, soy, flax seeds, and soy milk to name a few.

Be Wary Of Vegan Products on Store Shelves

Not everything that promises to be vegan-friendly actually is. Many vegan options such as vegan cookies on grocery shelves are laden with fat products that are not good for your waistline. Try to stick with as many raw options such as dried fruit, nuts, and vegetables as possible. It is, of course, okay to indulge in the occasional store bought snack. Just do not simply pick up a product because the word 'vegan' is slapped on the packaging. Do your research and be conscious of the food choices you make.

Ensure You Get Your Vitamin D

Popular products for obtaining vitamin D include canned fish like salmon and sardines and fortified dairy products such as yogurt and milk. However, you can also obtain vitamin D from vegan sources such as fortified non-dairy milk (nut and grain milks) and fortified juices like orange juice. Some mushrooms also provide vitamin D because they have been exposed to and absorbed UV light. Additionally, you can take a natural vitamin D supplement. You can, of course, simply go outside and absorb vitamin D straight from nature's best source, which is the sun.

Ensure That You Pump Up On Your Iron

Animal products like chicken are popular sources of iron. However, vegans do not have to worry about iron deficiency since it can be sourced from leafy green vegetables like spinach, kale, Swiss chard, broccoli, lentils, legumes, and beans. Ensure that you stock up on vitamin C-rich foods which helps with the absorption of iron.

Go At Your Own Pace

While some people are able to transition to veganism overnight, this is not the right approach for everyone. It is okay to make small changes to your everyday life and diet one step at a time and adjust accordingly. You can start by removing dairy or meat one day a week and building from there. For example, start with meatless Mondays and then work your way to doing this three times a week, until you completely eliminate meat from your diet.

Keep Learning

Just as with everything else, veganism can have a steep learning curve. Adopt a growth mindset and approach this lifestyle with curiosity so that you continue to learn and adapt to new information every single day.

Chapter 2: Keto Veganism

The ketogenic diet is a low-carb, high-fat, and moderate-protein diet. Even though this diet originated in the 1920s as a treatment for epilepsy, it has gained a lot of popularity since then because of its many health benefits including its powerful effect on weight loss.

At first glance, the ketogenic diet does not seem to have a lot in common with the vegan diet. Why? Because the ketogenic diet relies on the consumption of high-fat, high-protein ingredients, which are often derived from animal-based sources while vegans are on the opposite end of the spectrum. Even though the ketogenic diet is often associated with consuming animal foods and their byproducts, it can be adapted to fit plant-based diets such as the vegan diet. Vegan diets exclude the consumption of all animal products and by-products, which can make it quite challenging to eat a low-carb diet. However, with careful planning and consideration, vegans can reap the benefits of adopting the ketogenic diet.

What is the Ketogenic Diet?

This is also called the keto diet for short. The ketogenic diet relies on a process called ketosis, hence the name. The body needs energy to perform all functions, even those that you are not aware of. Carbohydrates are the body's main source of energy because it is the easiest to convert to the few will let the body needs. However, it is easy to consume excessive carbohydrates and this excess has very serious health implications such as excessive weight gain, cardiovascular diseases, the development of type 2 diabetes, and more.

The ketogenic diet forces the body to rely on a different source of energy, namely fat deposits. This is facilitated by the process of ketosis: a metabolic process that allows the body to gain energy from fat rather than the use of carbohydrates. This process occurs when fat cells are turned into molecules known as ketones in the liver. These ketones are then used by the body as fuel. Ketosis can only occur if there is a limited amount of carbohydrates and therefore, blood sugar. Sugars are simple forms of carbohydrates. Limited blood sugar only occurs during conditions such as starvation, fasting, pregnancy and the ketogenic diet.

While on the ketogenic diet, a person consumes less than 50 grams of carbohydrates per day. This limitation forces the body to seek out fat molecules to facilitate the process of ketosis.

When the body derives energy from burning fat, weight loss is a natural effect. This occurs for several reasons including feeling fuller and satisfied because of the higher consumption of fat and protein, the consumption of fewer calories and a reduction in appetite due to fewer carbs being consumed. This effect is magnified if the practitioner implements an exercise regimen in conjunction with the ketogenic diet.

What is the Vegan Keto Diet?

The vegan keto diet is a sub diet of both the ketogenic diet and vegan diet. It gives the practitioner the best of both worlds.

The ketogenic diet comprises of consuming more healthy sources of fat. This generally comprises of 75% of dietary intake. Most ketogenic dieters turn to a high-fat animal products such as dairy and meat to get to consume this amount of fat. However, this is not the only option because vegans can achieve ketosis too by relying on high-fat plant-based sources such as avocados, seeds, nuts, and coconut oil. The vegan keto diet is a low-carb, high-fat, and moderate protein diet that excludes the use of animal-based products while following the vegan principle of consuming plant-based products only.

Benefits of the Vegan Keto Diet

There are several health benefits associated with both the vegan and ketogenic diets. When these two diets are combined, a lot of these benefits are compounded, which include:

- Lowered risk of the development of chronic health conditions such as type 2 diabetes, certain cancers, and heart disease.
- Improved blood sugar regulation and fat metabolism due to elevated levels of a protein called adiponectin.

- Lowered risk of developing high blood pressure and high cholesterol.
- Improved and quicker weight loss and easier weight management.
- Improved emotional and mental health due to elevated moods and lowered risk for the development of mental diseases such as depression.

Foods That Should Be Avoided On the Vegan Keto Diet

- Poultry and meat
- Dairy products
- Eggs
- Seafood and fish
- Animal-based ingredients
- Fruits. These are a natural source of sugar and should be limited except for the consumption of berries.

The following products can still be consumed but they need to be in limited quantities:

- Starches and grains, including bread, pasta, rice, baked goods, cereals, and grains.
- Drinks with added sugar such as soda, fruit juices, smoothies, chocolate milk, and sports drinks.
- Sweeteners such as brown sugar and maple syrup.
- Legumes and beans such as chickpeas, kidney beans, and black beans.
- Starchy vegetables such as potatoes, squash, beets, and peas.
- High carb alcoholic beverages such as wine and beer.
- High-carb sauces and condiments such as sweetened salad dressings and barbecue sauce.
- Highly processed foods.

Foods That You Can Eat On The Vegan Keto Diet

- Oils including MCT oil, avocado oil, olive oil, coconut oil, and nut oil.
- Coconut products such as coconut milk, unsweetened coconut, and coconut cream.
- Nuts and seeds such as chia seeds, flax seeds, pistachios, cashews, macadamia nuts, pumpkin seeds, almonds, and walnuts.
- Nut and seed butters such as peanut butter, almond butter, cashew butter, and sunflower butter.
- Vegan protein sources such as tofu and tempeh.
- Avocados in the form of whole avocados and guacamole.
- Berries such as raspberries, strawberries, blackberries, and blueberries. These should be consumed in moderation.
- Condiments such as salt, pepper, spices, lemon juice, fresh herbs, and nutritional yeast.

- Vegan full fat 'dairy' products such as vegan butter, cashew cheese, vegan cream cheese, and coconut yogurt.
- Non-starchy vegetables such as zucchini, broccoli, cauliflower, peppers, mushrooms, and dark, leafy green vegetables.

While there are limitations to the keto vegan diet, ensuring that it is carefully planned can be extremely beneficial for the practitioner and enhance a vegan lifestyle.

Chapter 3: What to Eat on the Vegan Diet

Foods to Avoid on the Vegan Diet

On a vegan diet, you should avoid consuming any animal foods or foods that contain ingredients that were derived from animals. The list of foods to avoid on a vegan diet include:

- Poultry and meat. This includes organic meat, wild meat, chicken, turkey, duck, quail, beef, lamb, pork, veal, etc.
- Eggs. This can be from any animals including chickens, fish, ostriches, etc.
- Seafood and fish. This includes all types of fish and seafood including shrimp, squid, crab, lobster, mussels, anchovies, scallops, etc.
- Dairy products. This includes cheese, butter, cream, yogurt, milk, etc.
- Bee products. This includes honey, royal jelly, bee pollen, etc.
- Animal-based products. This list includes fish derived omega-3 fatty acids, animal derived vitamin D3, whey, lactose, egg white albumen, gelatin, shellac L-cysteine, casein, etc.

This list is pretty extensive but there are still some surprising foods that you may not realize are not vegan friendly. This list includes:

- Milk chocolate. Cocoa itself is vegan but milk, milk products, whey, and casein are often added to chocolate.
- Wine and beer. A gelatin-based substance which is derived from fish is often used as a clarifying agent in the manufacture of wine and beer.

- Sugar. Table sugar, which is made from sugar beets or sugarcane, is both completely fine to use. However, some sugars are processed with bone char, which is used in the refining process to help whiten sugar. Bone char is not vegan-friendly.
- Sugary snacks. Some of your favorite candies like gummies and marshmallows contain gelatin, which is derived from animals, and hence not vegan-friendly.
- Red processed foods. Some foods such as yogurt, fruit juices, soda, and candy contain an ingredient called carmine (otherwise known as red dye), which is derived from an insect.
- Non-dairy creamers. Some of these contain a milk-based derivative called sodium caseinate.
- Worcestershire sauce. Traditional recipes for this include anchovies. Note that there are vegan-friendly options available.
- Bread. Many common bread options include egg, butter, milk and other animal by-products in the ingredient list. Luckily, there are bread recipes available which do not contain such ingredients.
- Omega-3 fortified products. Ensure that the packaging for your omega-3 fortified purchases do not contain fish-based ingredients like sardines, anchovies, and tilapia.

Foods to Eat on the Vegan Diet

This list includes plant and plant-based products such as:

- Fruits and vegetables
- Whole grains, cereals, and pseudo-cereals such as spelt, quinoa, and teff—all of which are high-protein options that are also great sources of complex carbs, B vitamins, and several minerals such as zinc, iron, potassium, to name a few, and fiber.
- Fermented and sprouted plant foods. This includes pickles, kimchi, Ezekiel bread, miso, natto, and tempeh.
- Nutritional yeast. This is a great protein supplement you can include in dishes as a substitute for cheese given its cheesy flavor.
- Seeds such as chia seeds, flax seeds, and hemp seeds which are good sources of protein and omega-3 fatty acids.
- Nuts and nut butters are great sources of fiber, magnesium, zinc, selenium, vitamin E, and iron. The unroasted and unblanched varieties are best.
- Legumes such as lentils, beans, and peas are great protein sources and increase nutrient absorption.
- Plant-based protein replacements. This includes tofu, tempeh, and seitan. They make great replacements for meat, fish, poultry, and eggs in recipes.
- Calcium-fortified plant milks and yogurts. These are a great replacement for milk and yogurt and help provide the recommended daily supplement of calcium. Try

to get versions that have been fortified with vitamin B12 and D when possible.

Some vegans we find it difficult to ensure that they get adequate supplies of all nutrients required daily. Therefore, supplements can be taken to fortify the vegan diet. Supplements include EPA and DHA, which are omega-3 fatty acids which can be sourced from algae oil, Iron, vitamin D, vitamin B12, calcium, zinc and iodine, which can also be supplemented by adding 1/2 teaspoon of iodized salt to your diet.

Eating Out on a Vegan Diet

Eating out on any diet can be challenging and the same can be said for eating out as a vegan. The way to make this as stress-free as possible for you is to plan ahead. To make this process easier for you, here are a few tips that you can employ while eating out:

- Try to find the restaurant menu online beforehand so that you can determine if there are any vegan options available.
- You may try calling ahead to arrange a special vegan dish with the chef.
- At the restaurants, you can simply ask the staff about any vegan options available before you get seated so that you can know if this restaurant is the right choice for you.
- Try ethnic restaurants such as Mexican, Thai, Indian, Middle-Eastern, and Ethiopian cuisine because they tend to have several natural vegan-friendly options.
- At a restaurant, try to identify the vegetarian options on the menu and ask if any dairy or egg products can be removed to make the dish vegan-friendly.
- If there are no vegan meal options, order several vegan appetizers or side dishes to make up a meal.
- Also check out the new vegetarian and vegan restaurants within your neighborhood. With the widespread awareness of leading a plant-based lifestyle gaining traction each day, there are always newer pure vegan and vegetarian restaurants also popping up everywhere you go!

Chapter 4: Meal Plan and Preparation

30-Day Vegan Meal Plan

Below is a typical example of what one month's worth of meals would look like for someone who is a vegan. There are also keto vegan meals included within this meal plan. Most of the recipes for these can be found later on in this book. Each day includes breakfast, lunch, dinner, and two snacks/dessert meals.

Day 1

Breakfast: Chia Breakfast Pudding

Lunch: Cauliflower Fried Rice

Dinner: Cauliflower Alfredo

Snack 1: Banana-Berry Blast Cauliflower Smoothie

Snack 2: Baby Carrots dipped in Chickpea Hummus

Day 2

Breakfast: Mixed Berry Smoothie Bowl

Lunch: Keto Open-faced Hummus Sandwich

Dinner: Black Bean Quinoa Dinner

Snack 1: Coconut Cacao Bites

Snack 2: Keto Sugar-free Oatmeal Cookies

Day 3

Breakfast: Blueberry Chia Smoothie

Lunch: Creamy Keto Butternut Squash Soup

Dinner: Kung Pao Broccoli Dinner

Snack 1: Nutty Keto Crackers

Snack 2: Guacamole and gluten-free, dairy-free tortilla chips

Day 4

Breakfast: Strawberry Oats Smoothie

Lunch: Vegan BLT Sandwich

Dinner: Vegan Spicy Thai Noodles

Snack 1: Almond Coconut Keto Crackers

Snack 2: Vegan Chocolate Chip Cookies

Day 5

Breakfast: Maple Citrus Salad with Coconut Flakes

Lunch: Veggie Pita Pizza

Dinner: One Pot Keto Veggie Soup

Snack 1: Dried Berries

Snack 2: Almond Coconut Keto Crackers

Day 6

Breakfast: Sweet Potato and Black Bean Burritos

Lunch: Black Bean Salad

Dinner: Keto Zucchini Lasagna

Snack 1: Zucchini Brownies

Snack 2: Apple Cinnamon Chips

Day 7

Breakfast: Peanut Butter Strawberry Smoothie

Lunch: Jackfruit Veggie Tacos

Dinner: Keto Red Pepper Curry

Snack 1: Kale Chips

Snack 2: Raw Banana Pudding

Day 8

Breakfast: Breakfast Oatmeal Smoothie

Lunch: Sauteed Veggies in Spicy Garlic Chilli Sauce

Dinner: Easy Vegan Chili Soup

Snack 1: Almond Granola

Snack 2: Vegan Chocolate Ice-Cream

Day 9

Breakfast: Blueberry Banana Muffins

Lunch: Raw Mushroom Walnut Lettuce Wraps

Dinner: Mashed Cauliflower

Snack 1: Trail Mix

Snack 2: Mixed Berry Sorbet

Day 10

Breakfast: Sweet Potato Porridge Bowl

Lunch: Avocado Arugula Salad

Dinner: Lentil Rice Dinner

Snack 1: Cranberry Protein Bar

Snack 2: Peanut Butter Chocolate Marble Cake

Day 11

Breakfast: Green Apple Avocado Smoothie

Lunch: Keto Avocado Kale Salad

Dinner: Quinoa Lentil Chili

Snack 1: Vegan Chocolate Pudding

Snack 2: Vegan-Friendly Crackers and Almond Butter

Day 12

Breakfast: Mushroom Bacon Over Toast

Lunch: Spaghetti Squash with Mushroom and Tomatoes

Dinner: Tofu Veggie Dinner

Snack 1: Sweet Potato Chips

Snack 2: Coconut Vanilla Macaroons

Day 13

Breakfast: Tofu Avocado Toast

Lunch: Asian Coleslaw

Dinner: Whole Roasted Cauliflower

Snack 1: Sliced Banana Slathered With Peanut Butter

Snack 2: Apple Pie Smoothie

Day 14

Breakfast: Apple Buckwheat Pancakes

Lunch: Keto Broccoli Fried Rice

Dinner: Crispy Quinoa Cakes with Chickpea Hummus

Snack 1: Almond Butter over Apple Slices

Snack 2: Baked Pear

Day 15

Breakfast: Mediterranean Chickpeas on Toast

Lunch: Stuffed Tomatoes

Dinner: Black Bean Soup

Snack 1: Gingerbread Bites

Snack 2: Cashew Cream over Sliced Pear

Day 16

Breakfast: Ginger Cinnamon Waffles

Lunch: Tomato Sandwiches

Dinner: Spicy Vegan Mac and Cheese Dinner

Snack 1: Ants on a Log with Cashew Butter and Chopped Dates

Snack 2: Cashew Butter Stuffed Dates

Day 17

Breakfast: Easy Vegan French Toast

Lunch: Zucchini Noodle Salad

Dinner: Black Bean Burgers with Garlic Tahini Sauce

Snack 1: Ants on a Log With Peanut Butter and Cranberries

Snack 2: Peanut Butter Stuffed Dates

Day 18

Breakfast: Artichoke Spinach Quiche

Lunch: Quinoa Veggies Chopped Salad

Dinner: Black Bean Meatloaf

Snack 1: Cinnamon Raisin Granola

Snack 2: Peanut Butter Tortilla Roll-Ups

Day 19

Breakfast: Exotic Kale Smoothie

Lunch: Spinach Mushroom Tofu Wraps

Dinner: Mushroom Wraps with Chipotle Sauce

Snack 1: Cut Veggies and Chickpea Hummus

Snack 2: Vegan Banana Bread

Day 20

Breakfast: Tofu Scramble 'Eggs'

Lunch: Vegan Spring Rolls

Dinner: Creamy Broccoli Pasta

Snack 1: Sliced Celery and Roasted Carrot Hummus

Snack 2: Vegan Lemon Tart

Day 21

Breakfast: Tempeh Sweet Potato Scrambled 'Eggs'

Lunch: Quinoa Edamame Salad

Dinner: Slow Cooker Lentil Sloppy Joes

Snack 1: Tofu Chocolate Cheesecake

Snack 2: Beet Chips

Day 22

Breakfast: Chickpea Onion Omelette

Lunch: Mushroom Pecan Burgers

Dinner: Bell Peppers Stuffed with Black Bean, Corn and Sweet Potato

Snack 1: Peanut Butter Smoothie

Snack 2: Vegan Barry Bar

Day 23

Breakfast: Keto Vanilla Pancakes

Lunch: Zucchini Noodles in Avocado Sauce

Dinner: Sesame-Orange Ginger Chickpea Quinoa Stir-Fry

Snack 1: Vegan Doughnut

Snack 2: Kale Spinach Smoothie

Day 24

Breakfast: Keto-Friendly Vegan Cauliflower Hash Browns

Lunch: Roasted Red Pepper Sandwich

Dinner: Coconut Milk Lentil Curry

Snack 1: Fresh Mixed Berries

Snack 2: Peanut Butter Energy Balls

Day 25

Breakfast: Simple Coconut Keto Vegan Pancakes

Lunch: Grilled Eggplant Wraps

Dinner: Quinoa Beet Burgers

Snack 1: Mixed Nuts

Snack 2: Orange Beet Smoothie

Day 26

Breakfast: Keto Vegan Pumpkin Muffins with Coconut Glaze

Lunch: Potato Fritters with Almond Dipping Sauce

Dinner: Chickpea Curry over Coconut Brown Rice

Snack 1: Vegan Yogurt with Granola

Snack 2: Pretzels

Day 27

Breakfast: Keto Coconut Pecan Porridge

Lunch: Mexican Chopped Salad

Dinner: Tofu Cashew Coconut Curry

Snack 1: Sweet Potato Fries

Snack 2: Celery Sticks and Peanut Butter

Day 28

Breakfast: Almond Granola served with Almond Milk

Lunch: Vegan Greek Pasta Salad

Dinner: Sweet Potato Corn Chowder

Snack 1: Banana Chips

Snack 2: Vegan Sugar Cookies

Day 29

Breakfast: Vegan Fried 'Egg'

Lunch: Barbecue Tempeh Wraps

Dinner: Cauliflower Chickpea Curry

Snack 1: Berry Blast Smoothie

Snack 2: Zucchini Chips

Day 30

Breakfast: Strawberry Coconut Chia Pudding

Lunch: Grilled Corn Salad

Dinner: Roasted Butternut Squash Pasta

Snack 1: Vegan Strawberry Muffin

Snack 2: Vegan Bagel with Peanut Butter

How to Grocery Shop for Vegan and Keto Vegan Eating

One of the best things about cooking for yourself is having complete control over what goes into your body. Great vegan eating is based on finding great quality ingredients. Here is a shopping list to help getting you started right in your vegan cooking journey. If you are practicing the keto vegan diet, simply eliminate the items below based on the information provided on that diet.

Fruits (fresh, dried, and frozen)

Apples, citrus fruits such as limes, lemons, and oranges, berries such as cranberries, strawberries, blueberries and blackberries, pears, cherries, mangos, kiwis, grapes, grapefruit, dragon fruit, cantaloupe, bananas, papayas, pineapple, plums, pomegranates, watermelon, apricots, dates, raisins, peaches, nectarines, honeydew, current, figs, dried apple slices, banana chips, guava, and prunes.

Nuts and Seeds

Almonds, cashews, Brazil nuts, hazelnuts, macadamia nuts, pumpkin seeds, sunflower seeds, flax seeds, walnuts, pine nuts, peanuts, pecans, and hemp seeds.

Nut and Seed Butters

Peanut butter, almond butter, cashew butter, hazelnut butter, and tahini.

Vegetables (Fresh, frozen and canned)

Broccoli, cauliflower, cabbage, sweet potatoes, yellow potatoes, green leafy vegetables such as spinach, kale, bok choy and collards, onions, squash, tomatoes, arugula, asparagus, bean sprouts, beets, bell peppers, cucumber, corn, celery, garlic, ginger, green onion, green beans, jalapeno peppers, lettuce, mushrooms, parsnips, radishes, snow peas, snap peas, yam, turnip, pureed pumpkin, roasted red peppers, and avocado.

Beans and Legumes

Chickpeas, black eyed peas, Lima beans cannellini beans, black beans, kidney beans, Pinto beans, refried beans, soy products such as miso, tempeh, tofu, edamame, and lentils.

Baking Substitutes

You do not have to give up on your favorite kicks, cookies or other big treats because you go vegan. Here are some alternatives that will make your baked goods a whole lot healthier and tastier:

- Dairy substitutes include unsweetened almond milk, coconut milk or soy milk.

- Buttermilk is a common ingredient used in baking. Substitute by adding one tablespoon of lemon juice to one cup of non-dairy milk.
- Butter can be swapped for canola oil coconut oil or vegetable oil
- Popular egg substitutes include flaxseed. One tablespoon of ground flaxseed mixed with three tablespoons of water can be used to substitute one egg. Simply mix these two ingredients and allow it to sit for 10 minutes. Applesauce and mashed bananas are also great substitutes for eggs.

Dairy Alternatives

Almond milk, soy milk, hemp milk, rice milk, cashew milk, cashew yogurt, almond yogurt, oat milk, hemp milk, flax milk, vegan cheese, vegan cream cheese, and coconut yogurt.

Grains

Quinoa, tortillas, popcorn, whole grain pasta, whole grain cereal, gluten-free rolled oats, buckwheat, steel cut oats, whole grain bread, wild rice, brown rice, bulgur, barley, millet, amaranth, and seitan.

Sweeteners

Maple syrup, molasses, coconut sugar, agave nectar, stevia, date syrup, and rice syrup.

Spices

Cumin, coriander, cayenne pepper, salt, black pepper, cinnamon, rosemary, oregano, parsley, celery seed, cilantro, curry powder, garlic powder, onion powder, nutmeg, paprika, red pepper flakes, basil, dill, sage, Italian seasoning, turmeric, chili powder, thyme, lemongrass, clove, bay leaf, chamomile, star anise, peppermint, saffron, and spearmint.

Oils and Fats

Olive oil, canola oil, avocado oil, coconut oil, sesame oil, vegan butter, vegan margarine, and flaxseed oil.

Other ingredients

Liquid aminos, vegan chocolate chips, vanilla extract, cocoa, vegan mayo, olives, dark chocolate, organic cane sugar, mustard, salsa, lemon juice, lime juice, white vinegar, balsamic vinegar, soy sauce, baking powder, baking soda, cornstarch, apple cider vinegar, nutritional yeast, applesauce, hummus, tea bags.

Preparing and Storing Food

The idea of meal prepping and storing your prepped food can seem daunting and overwhelming. It might feel like you need lots of free time and lots of fancy kitchen equipment to get it done but that is far from the truth. Any and every one can meal prep so that they can reap the benefits, which include:

- Ensuring that a minimal amount of time is spent in the kitchen.
- Creating better productivity and efficiency because you do not have to spend time every day thinking about what you need to prepare to cook.
- Sticking to a healthy lifestyle and diet since you no longer reach for unhealthy foods stemming from chronic exhaustion or a lack of willpower.
- Keeping the cost of groceries down.
- Reducing food wastage.

Meal prepping is perfect for:

- People who work full time and need daily breakfast, lunch, dinner, and snacks on the go.
- People who are single and do not want to prepare single meal portions for themselves all the time.
- Parents who want to send their children to school with healthy meals.
- Students who would like to eat something in between classes or do not have access to a kitchen regularly.
- Anyone who wants their meals more readily available.
- Vegans who do not want to fall off the wagon due to inconvenience or lack of motivation.
- People who are on a budget or are looking for a way to reduce food wastage.

There are a few guidelines to help you get started on your vegan meal prepping and storage:

- Plan out your recipes. You can do this weekly or monthly. This allows you to also prepare a concise shopping list so that you buy exactly what you need and do not waste money on food that will not be eaten.
- If you are a newbie vegan, start with the foods that you know and like. It is a great experiment however, you should start slowly, with foods and combos that you know while pairing them with individual new ingredients you would like to try out.
- Make your own condiments. Many store bought condiments are not vegan or ketogenic friendly. Therefore, the best option is to make your own condiments and sauces with ingredients that you know. These can usually be kept in the refrigerator for up to a week. You can find tasty sauce and condiment recipes in Chapter 5.
- Make use of frozen produce. This can include frozen fruits and vegetables, which are usually cheap, fresh, and packed with a lot of nutrition. They also keep labor down to a minimum since no trimming or chopping is required and last longer

since they are stored in the freezer.

- Freezer versus refrigerator storage. Typically food stored in the refrigerator needs to be eaten within three days, whereas food stored in the freezer lasts for up to six to eight months. If you store food in the freezer, be sure to take it out a day before so that you can eat it when you need to. Also, mark your food containers with dates to keep track of their expiry date.

- Be careful with high protein foods to avoid food poisoning. Plant-based foods generally have lower the risk of food poisoning compared to animal-based foods. However, bacteria thrives in protein-rich foods. Therefore, be sure to take extra care when storing and reheating these.

- Be sure to always thoroughly reheat foods to avoid food poisoning. Never eat something that has just warmed as it may be in the food danger temperature zone where bacteria can thrive. Food that has been reheated needs to be extremely hot in the middle.

- Never place warm food in the refrigerator. Allow food to cool completely before placing it in the refrigerator or freezer because you risk raising the internal temperature of the fridge which puts this item and other foods at risk for spoiling.

- Defrost foods in a timely manner. Foods that have been frozen should be defrosted in the refrigerator or at room temperature before being eaten, typically at least 24 hours before consumption.

- Use proper storage containers. These should be BPA-free, microwavable, and dishwasher safe. Ziploc style bags are also great for storing food in the refrigerator and freezer and can be reused multiple times.

- Make use of cooking equipment. These are optional, however stocking your kitchen with the following equipment can make your cooking adventures in the kitchen more efficient and simplify your life. The rice cooker is great for cooking rice and other grains such as quinoa and oatmeal. It cuts down on your cooking time and ensures that your rice and pasta will done perfectly instead of being overcooked or undercooked. The slow cooker is another great time-saving and economical appliance that allows you to cook bigger portions, which then allows you to have leftovers you can either consume later on in the week or freeze a partial portion. There is also the instapot, which can take the place of a pressure cooker, sauteing pan, yogurt maker, rice cooker, and steamer. It allows you to cook grains, beans, vegetables, and more, quickly, which saves you time and energy.

Chapter 5: Sauce and Condiment Recipes

Chickpea Hummus

Nutritional Information:

Total fat: 3.2g

Cholesterol: 0mg

Sodium: 351mg

Total carbohydrates: 15.3g

Dietary fiber: 4.1g

Protein: 4.7g

Calcium: 65mg

Potassium: 202mg

Iron: 2mg

Vitamin D: 0mcg

Time: 15 minutes

Serving Size: 6

Ingredients:

- 2 cans 15 oz. chickpeas, rinsed and drained

- Juice of 1 large lemon
- 3 garlic cloves
- 2 teaspoon ground cumin
- ¼ cup vegetable broth
- 2 teaspoon liquid aminos
- 1 cup Kalamata olives
- 1 roasted and chopped bell pepper

Directions:

1. Blend all the ingredients in a high-performance blender until a thick paste is achieved.
2. Serve as a dip with fresh chopped veggies and vegan chips.

5-Minute Spinach Ranch Dressing

Nutritional Information:

Total fat: 1.6g

Cholesterol: 0mg

Sodium: 11mg

Total carbohydrates: 2.3g

Dietary fiber: 0.4g

Protein: 3.3g

Calcium: 66mg

Potassium: 124mg

Iron: 1mg

Vitamin D: 0mcg

Time: 5 minutes

Serving Size: 8

Ingredients:

- 2 cups fresh spinach, washed and dried
- 1 12-oz. bag soft tofu
- 2 teaspoon garlic powder
- 2 teaspoon onion powder
- 1 tablespoon white wine vinegar
- 1 tablespoon chopped chives
- 1 tablespoon chopped dill
- 1 tablespoon chopped parsley

- Salt and pepper to taste

Directions:

1. Place the spinach, tofu, white wine vinegar, garlic powder, and onion powder into a high-performance blender and blend until it's a creamy texture.
2. Transfer the creamy mixture to a medium bowl and stir in remaining ingredients. Mix well.
3. This can be stored in an airtight container for up to 3 days and is great as an oil-free dressing, a dip for fresh cut veggie or as a sandwich spread. Serve chilled.

Keto Butternut Squash Hummus

Nutritional Information:

Total fat: 9g

Cholesterol: 0mg

Sodium: 131mg

Total carbohydrates: 17.5g

Dietary fiber: 4.9g

Protein: 5.9g

Calcium: 39mg

Potassium: 291mg

Iron: 2mg

Vitamin D: 0mcg

Time: 15 minutes

Serving Size: 8

Ingredients:

- ½ cup butternut squash, cubed
- 2 garlic cloves with skin on
- 2 garlic cloves, peels and minced
- 1 tablespoon peanut butter
- 1 tablespoon lemon juice
- 1 cup chickpeas, rinsed and drained
- 3 tablespoon olive oil
- ½ cup chopped parsley
- ¼ teaspoon ground cinnamon
- ½ teaspoon ground cumin
- Salt and pepper to taste

Directions:

1. Preheat your oven to 400 degrees F and place a rack in the middle of the oven.
2. Place the butternut squash and unpeeled garlic cloves on a baking tray and drizzle with 2 tablespoons of olive oil and salt and pepper to taste. Toss to combine the ingredients.
3. Bake for 20 minutes or until the butternut squash is fork tender and the garlic is golden brown. Remove from the oven and let cool for at least 5 minutes.
4. Remove the peel from the roasted garlic and add to a food processor with the butternut squash, minced garlic, lemon juice, chickpeas, peanut butter, remaining olive oil, salt and pepper to taste, parsley, cinnamon, and cumin.
5. Blend this mixture until it is smooth and creamy. Scrape down the sides of the food processor as needed and add more olive oil if the mixture is too thick.
6. Serve immediately with fresh cut veggies or chips. This mixture can also be refrigerated and stored in an airtight container for up to 5 days.

Orange Olive Vinaigrette

Nutritional Information:

Total fat: 10.1g

Cholesterol: 0mg

Sodium: 119mg

Total carbohydrates: 0.8g

Dietary fiber: 0g

Protein: 01g

Calcium: 1mg

Potassium: 15mg

Iron: 0mg

Vitamin D: 0mcg

Time: 5 minutes

Serving Size: 10

Ingredients:

- ¼ cup of orange juice
- ½ cup olive oil
- 1 teaspoon pitted kalamata olives, minced
- 2 teaspoon shallots, minced
- ½ teaspoon salt

Directions:

1. Pour all of the ingredients into a mason jar. Cover and shake to blend.
2. Serve over your favorite salads. Can be refrigerated for up to 3 days. If the oil solidifies, let the dressing thaw at room temperature for at least 30 minutes before using the dressing.

Lime- Infused Cumin Vinaigrette

Nutritional Information:

Total fat: 10.1g

Cholesterol: 0mg

Sodium: 1mg

Total carbohydrates: 1.3g

Dietary fiber: 0.1g

Protein: 0.1g

Calcium: 3mg

Potassium: 20mg

Iron: 0mg

Vitamin D: 0mcg

Time: 5 minutes

Serving Size: 10

Ingredients:

- ¼ cup lime juice
- ½ teaspoon crushed cumin seeds, toasted
- ½ cup olive oil
- 2 teaspoon shallots, minced

Directions:

1. Pour all the ingredients into a mason jar. Cover and shake well to blend. Can be refrigerated for up to 3 days.

4-Ingredient Vegan Mayonnaise

Nutritional Information:

Total fat: 20.2g

Cholesterol: 0mg

Sodium: 37mg

Total carbohydrates: 0.8g

Dietary fiber: 0.1g

Protein: 0.4g

Calcium: 3mg

Potassium: 15mg

Iron: 0mg

Vitamin D: 0mcg

Time: 5 minutes

Serving Size: 5

Ingredients:

- 1 teaspoon apple cider vinegar
- ½ cup unrefined sunflower oil
- ¼ cup unsweetened soy milk
- Salt to taste

Directions:

1. Ensure that sunflower oil and soy milk are both at room temperature. Add all the ingredients, except for the oil, to a blender and blend for 5 seconds.
2. Gradually added oil and continue to blend the mixture. Slowly increase the speed of the blender from low to high until mixture thickens. If the mixture is too thick, add more milk. If the mixture is too runny, add more oil. Blend again until the mayonnaise reaches the desired consistency.
3. Serve with salads and sandwiches. Mayonnaise can be stored for up to 4 days in an airtight container in the refrigerator.

Creamy Cashew Sauce

Nutritional Information:

Total fat: 10.3g

Cholesterol: 0mg

Sodium: 127mg

Total carbohydrates: 5.8g

Dietary fiber: 0.6g

Protein: 2.7g

Calcium: 12mg

Potassium: 115mg

Iron: 1mg

Vitamin D: 0mcg

Time: 5 minutes

Serving Size: 6

Ingredients:

- ¾ cup raw cashews
- ¼ cup parsley
- ½ cup water
- ½ teaspoon soy sauce
- 1 tablespoon olive oil
- 1 tablespoon lemon juice
- ¼ teaspoon salt

Directions:

1. Add all the ingredients to a blender. Blend until a smooth consistency is achieved. Scrape down the sides of the blender if necessary.
2. Use as a sauce and condiment with sandwiches and salads. Dressing can be refrigerated in an airtight container for up to 5 days.

Vegan Nacho Cheese Sauce

Nutritional Information:

Total fat: 6.6g

Cholesterol: 0mg

Sodium: 240mg

Total carbohydrates: 6.6g

Dietary fiber: 1.5g

Protein: 4g

Calcium: 12mg

Potassium: 182mg

Iron: 2mg

Vitamin D: 0mcg

Time: 20 minutes

Serving Size: 10

Ingredients:

- 1 cup raw cashews
- ¼ cup nutritional yeast
- 2 cups water
- 1 ½ tablespoon lemon juice
- 1 teaspoon salt
- ¼ teaspoon chili powder
- ½ teaspoon garlic powder
- ½ teaspoon onion powder
- ¼ teaspoon paprika

Directions:

1. In a medium bowl, cover the raw cashews with boiling water and set aside for 15 minutes.
2. Drain the cashews and add to a blender. Also add lemon juice, one and a half cup of water, yeast, onion powder, garlic powder, paprika, chili powder, and salt. Blend until a smooth consistency is achieved.
3. Add the mixture to a medium saucepan. Boil over medium heat and whisk constantly until mixture thickens and begins to bubble.
4. Add the remaining water based on how thick or thin you want the sauce to be. Add more salt to taste if necessary.
5. Enjoy with chips, over steamed veggies or over a baked potato. Sauce can be refrigerated for up to 3 days in an airtight container. Reheat cheese sauce on the stove again, adding water as necessary.

Almond Dipping Sauce

Nutritional Information:

Total fat: 21.8g

Cholesterol: 0mg

Sodium: 126mg

Total carbohydrates: 5.8g

Dietary fiber: 3g

Protein: 5.1g

Calcium: 37mg

Potassium: 247mg

Iron: 2mg

Vitamin D: 0mcg

Time: 5 minutes

Serving Size: 5

Ingredients:

- ½ cup raw almonds
- 3 tablespoons nutritional yeast
- ¼ cup lemon juice
- ½ cup water
- 2 tablespoons olive oil
- ¼ cup grapeseed oil
- 2 garlic cloves
- ½ teaspoon cumin
- ½ teaspoon chili powder
- ¼ teaspoon cayenne pepper
- ¼ teaspoon paprika
- ¼ teaspoon ground coriander
- ¼ teaspoon salt

Directions:

1. Add all the ingredients to a blender and blend on low speed for 1 minute.
2. Turn the speed to high and blend for an additional 2 minutes or until mixture is smooth in consistency.
3. Store in an airtight container and refrigerate for up to 3 days. Can be used as a topping for salads or a dipping sauce for veggies.

Spicy Vegan Peanut Sauce

Nutritional Information:

Total fat: 14g

Cholesterol: 0mg

Sodium: 146mg

Total carbohydrates: 10.6g

Dietary fiber: 2g

Protein: 5.6g

Calcium: 5mg

Potassium: 42mg

Iron: 0mg

Vitamin D: 0mcg

Time: 5 minutes

Serving Size: 4

Ingredients:

- 3 tablespoons natural creamy peanut butter
- 1 ½ tablespoon water
- 1 tablespoon rice wine vinegar
- ½ tablespoon sesame oil
- ½ tablespoon lime juice
- ½ tablespoon of soy sauce
- 1 teaspoon agave
- 1 garlic clove, minced
- ½ teaspoon fresh ginger, minced
- ½ teaspoon garlic chili sauce (*see recipe below*)

Directions:

1. Add all the ingredients to a blender and blend until a smooth consistency is achieved.
2. Serve on sandwiches, salads, and as a dip for cut veggies. Sauce can be stored in an airtight container in the refrigerator for up to 5 days.

Spicy Garlic Chili Sauce

Nutritional Information:

Total fat: 0g

Cholesterol: 0mg

Sodium: 532mg

Total carbohydrates: 2.9g

Dietary fiber: 0.3g

Protein: 1g

Calcium: 8mg

Potassium: 49mg

Iron: 0mg

Vitamin D: 0mcg

Time: 5 minutes

Serving Size: 4

Ingredients:

- 1 tablespoon garlic, chopped
- ½ teaspoon ginger chopped
- 3 red chilies, stems removed
- ¼ cup low sodium soy sauce
- 1 tablespoon white vinegar
- ½ teaspoon maple syrup

Directions:

1. Combine all ingredients in a blender and blend to a smooth consistency. Sauce can be stored in an airtight container in the refrigerator for up to 5 days. Great for use in salads and stir fries.

Vegan Garden Pesto Sauce

Nutritional Information:

Total fat: 10.9g

Cholesterol: 0mg

Sodium: 45mg

Total carbohydrates: 1.6g

Dietary fiber: 0.8g

Protein: 0.8g

Calcium: 25mg

Potassium: 79mg

Iron: 1mg

Vitamin D: 0mcg

Time: 5 minutes

Serving Size: 10

Ingredients:

- ¼ cup pistachios
- 1 ½ teaspoon miso
- 1 cup cilantro
- 1 cup basil leaves
- ½ cup parsley
- ¼ cup mint leaves
- 1 garlic clove, chopped
- 2 teaspoons lemon juice
- ½ cup olive oil
- Salt and pepper to taste

Directions:

1. Add all of the ingredients except lemon juice, olive oil, salt, and pepper to a food processor. Pulse for 10 seconds. Scrape down sides of bowl if necessary.
2. While the processor is running, drizzle in the olive oil and lemon juice. Season with salt and pepper. Pulse for 5 more seconds.
3. Sauce can be refrigerated in an airtight container for up to 2 days. Great when served with pasta and vegetables.

Roasted Garlic Aioli

Nutritional Information:

Total fat: 5.6g

Cholesterol: 0mg

Sodium: 24mg

Total carbohydrates: 2.2g

Dietary fiber: 0.2g

Protein: 0.4g

Calcium: 11mg

Potassium: 31mg

Iron: 0mg

Vitamin D: 0mcg

Time: 50 minutes

Serving Size: 5

Ingredients:

- 3 bulbs of garlic
- 1 tablespoon olive oil
- 1 cup vegan mayo (*see recipe above*)
- 4 teaspoons lemon juice
- 1 tablespoon of parsley, finely chopped
- Salt and pepper to taste

Directions:

1. While leaving the head of the garlic cloves intact, peel off as much of the outer layer as possible. Cut off the top of the garlic head to expose as many of the garlic cloves as possible.
2. Wrap each garlic head in a small amount of foil. Place on a baking sheet and bake for 40 minutes until the exposed garlic cloves look slightly brown and can be easily pierced by a knife.
3. Remove the garlic from oven and let cool for at least 8 to 10 minutes. Remove and discard the foil. Separate the garlic cloves.
4. Add the garlic cloves, mayo, salt, and lemon juice to a blender. Blend until a thick creamy mixture is attained. Transfer the mixture to a bowl.
5. Taste and add more lemon juice or salt if desired. Add olive oil and whisk for 15 seconds. Combine the black pepper and chopped parsley.
6. Can be used as a sandwich spread or vegetable dip. Can be refrigerated in an airtight container for up to 3 days.

Vegan Chipotle

Nutritional Information:

Total fat: 0.3g

Cholesterol: 0mg

Sodium: 137mg

Total carbohydrates: 7.8g

Dietary fiber: 1.2g

Protein: 1.5g

Calcium: 15mg

Potassium: 175mg

Iron: 0mg

Vitamin D: 0mcg

Time: 25 minutes

Serving Size: 10

Ingredients:

- 3 cups cauliflower florets
- 1 dried chipotle pepper, tops and seeds removed
- 1 cup vegetable broth
- 1 tablespoon dried cherries, finely chopped
- 1 tablespoon garlic, chopped
- ¼ cup shallot, chopped
- 1 tablespoon Dijon mustard
- 2 tablespoons lime juice
- 1 teaspoon white wine vinegar
- 1 teaspoon of soy sauce
- 2 teaspoons paprika

Directions:

1. Place cauliflower florets in a steamer basket over a pot with 1 inch of water. Steam for 10 minutes or until the cauliflower a fork tender
2. While the cauliflower is steaming, place a medium-sized pot over medium heat. Add the chipotle pepper. Stir constantly for 2 minutes or until the pepper becomes fragrant.
3. Add enough water to completely cover the pepper. Add cherries. Bring this to a boil and simmer for 4 minutes. Turn off the heat and allow to cool for 5 minutes. Strain the mixture in a colander. Add liquid to a blender.
4. Add steamed cauliflower and all other ingredients to the blender. Blend until a smooth consistency is achieved.

Mango Salsa

Nutritional Information:

Total fat: 0.9g

Cholesterol: 0mg

Sodium: 85mg

Total carbohydrates: 30.6g

Dietary fiber: 4.2g

Protein: 2.4g

Calcium: 35mg

Potassium: 544mg

Iron: 1mg

Vitamin D: 0mcg

Time: 10 minutes

Serving Size: 2

Ingredients:

- 1 mango, chopped
- 1 cup cherry tomatoes, chopped
- 1 spring onion, chopped
- 1 jalapeno, deseeded and finely chopped.
- 2 teaspoons of lime juice
- Salt to taste

Directions:

1. Mix all the ingredients in a bowl well.
2. Refrigerate for at least 1 hour so that the flavors marinade well. Salsa can be served with chips, salad, tacos or on top of bean dip or beans. Can be refrigerated in an airtight container for up to 3 days.

Chapter 6: Breakfast Recipes

Chia Breakfast Pudding

Nutritional Information:

Total fat: 12.9g

Cholesterol: 0mg

Sodium: 52mg

Total carbohydrates: 27.3g

Dietary fiber: 11.7g

Protein: 7g

Calcium: 269mg

Potassium: 315mg

Iron: 3mg

Vitamin D: 0mcg

Time: 8 hour 15 minutes

Serving Size: 2

Ingredients:

- 2 tablespoons chia seeds
- 2 teaspoons maple syrup

- ½ cup unsweetened almond milk
- ½ cup banana, sliced
- ¼ teaspoon vanilla extract
- ¼ teaspoon ground cinnamon
- 1 tablespoon unsalted roasted pistachios, chopped
- A pinch of ground cardamom
- A pinch of ground cloves

Directions:

1. Add chia seeds, maple syrup, almond milk, vanilla extract, cinnamon, cardamom, and cloves to a small bowl. Mix well. Cover and refrigerate for at least 8 hours. This can be refrigerated for up to 3 days. Ideally, this is done overnight so that the pudding can be eaten for breakfast.
2. When it is time to serve, mix well. Divide the pudding mixture into 2 and place into 2 serving bowls. Top with the banana slices and chopped pistachios.

Mixed Berry Smoothie Bowl

Nutritional Information:

Total fat: 10.3g

Cholesterol: 0mg

Sodium: 49mg

Total carbohydrates: 39.1g

Dietary fiber: 11.7g

Protein: 5.3g

Calcium: 196mg

Potassium: 552mg

Iron: 2mg

Vitamin D: 0mcg

Time: 10 minutes

Serving Size: 2

Ingredients:

- 1 cup frozen mixed berries
- 1 large banana, peeled
- ½ cup unsweetened almond milk
- ¼ cup pineapple chunks
- 1 teaspoon chia seeds

- ¼ cup kiwi, sliced
- 1 tablespoon toasted almonds, sliced
- 1 tablespoon unsweetened coconut flakes

Directions:

1. Add the banana, mixed berries, and almond milk to a blender. Blend to a smooth consistency
2. Put the smoothie into a bowl and top with the pineapple chunks, kiwi slices, almond slices, coconut flakes, and chia seeds.
3. Serve immediately.

Blueberry Banana Muffins

Nutritional Information:

Total fat: 5.9g

Cholesterol: 0mg

Sodium: 101mg

Total carbohydrates: 27.5g

Dietary fiber: 3.8g

Protein: 3.1g

Calcium: 74mg

Potassium: 321mg

Iron: 1mg

Vitamin D: 0mcg

Time: 30 minutes

Serving Size: 12

Ingredients:

- 1 cup fresh blueberries, chopped
- 2 ripe bananas, mashed
- ⅓ cup maple syrup
- 2 teaspoon coconut oil, melted
- ⅓ cup coconut sugar
- ⅓ cup coconut flour
- ¾ cup of almond milk
- 1 teaspoon apple cider vinegar
- 2 cups oat flour
- 1 tablespoon cornstarch

- 3 teaspoons baking powder
- ½ teaspoon salt
- 1 tablespoon flax meal
- 1 teaspoon vanilla extract

Directions:

1. Preheat your oven to 350 degrees F.
2. Prepare a muffin tin by lining it with 12 paper liners.
3. Combine the almond milk and apple cider vinegar in a small bowl. Set aside.
4. In a large bowl, combine almond flour, oat flour, cornstarch, baking powder, and salt. Whisk well to ensure the dry ingredients are thoroughly combined.
5. Add the mashed bananas, maple syrup, coconut oil, vanilla extract, flax meal, and almond milk mixture to a medium bowl. Stir to combine.
6. Add wet mixture to dry ingredients and stir to thoroughly combine. Fold in blueberries and coconut sugar.
7. Pour batter into prepared muffin tin. Bake for 20 minutes or until the top of the muffins are golden brown and firm.
8. Remove the muffins from the oven and allow to cool before serving. Can be stored in the refrigerator or at room temperature in an airtight container for up to 4 days.

Sweet Potato Porridge Bowl

Nutritional Information:

Total fat: 10.3g

Cholesterol: 0mg

Sodium: 33mg

Total carbohydrates: 32.9g

Dietary fiber: 6.1g

Protein: 3.9g

Calcium: 18mg

Potassium: 679mg

Iron: 4mg

Vitamin D: 0mcg

Time: 1 hour 30 minutes

Serving Size: 2

Ingredients:

- 1 large sweet potato

- 1 small ripe banana, mashed
- 2 tablespoons pecans, chopped
- 2 tablespoons dried cranberries
- Cinnamon to taste

Directions:

1. Preheat your oven to 375 degrees F.
2. Wash and dry sweet potato. Poke holes around the entire surface of the sweet potato several times. Wrap sweet potato in aluminum foil and bake for an hour and 20 minutes or until a fork easily pierces through the entire sweet potato.
3. Cool for at least 5 minutes then peel and discard the skin.
4. Add the peeled potato to a medium bowl along with the ripe banana and cinnamon. Likely mash the mixture.
5. Top with dried cranberries and chopped pecans, and serve immediately. Can be stored overnight in the refrigerator and reheated for later consumption.

Almond Granola

Nutritional Information:

Total fat: 10.7g

Cholesterol: 0mg

Sodium: 194mg

Total carbohydrates: 13.5g

Dietary fiber: 2.8g

Protein: 4.4g

Calcium: 30mg

Potassium: 71mg

Iron: 1mg

Vitamin D: 0mcg

Time: 1 hour

Serving Size: 12

Ingredients:

- 1 cup raw almonds
- 4 cups gluten-free oats
- ½ cup coconut sugar
- ¼ cup canola oil
- 1 teaspoon of salt

- 1 teaspoon vanilla extract
- ½ cup sunflower seeds

Directions:

1. Preheat your oven to 350 degrees F.
2. Prepare 2 baking sheets by lining them with parchment paper.
3. In a large bowl, combine coconut sugar, canola oil, vanilla extract, and salt.
4. Add the rest of the ingredients to the bowl and toss to ensure that the almonds and oats are coated well. Divide the granola mixture between the two prepared baking sheets. Spread out into even, thin layers on the baking sheets.
5. Bake for 20 minutes or until the mixture is golden brown on the top and crisp.
6. Remove from the oven and let cool completely before serving with fresh fruit, with dairy-free milk such as almond milk, over vegan ice cream or as a snack. Can be stored at room temperature in an airtight container for up to 2 weeks.

Mushroom Bacon Over Toast

Nutritional Information:

Total fat: 6.7g

Cholesterol: 0mg

Sodium: 62mg

Total carbohydrates: 39.6g

Dietary fiber: 7.2g

Protein: 6.7g

Calcium: 52mg

Potassium: 1062mg

Iron: 3mg

Vitamin D: 63mcg

Time: 45 minutes

Serving Size: 6

Ingredients:

For mushroom bacon

- 1 ½ cup dried mushrooms, finely chopped
- 1 teaspoon maple syrup
- ⅛ teaspoon garlic powder
- ⅛ teaspoon onion powder

- ½ teaspoon paprika
- Salt and pepper to taste
- Olive oil to drizzle

For toast

- 6 slices almond bread (or any other gluten-free, dairy-free bread preferred)
- ½ cup chickpeas hummus (see recipe *Chapter 5: Sauce and Condiment Recipes: Chickpea Hummus*)
- 18 cherry tomatoes
- ½ cup fresh parsley chopped
- Salt and pepper to taste
- Olive oil to drizzle

Directions:

1. To prepare mushroom bacon, preheat your oven to 375 degrees F.
2. Prepare a baking sheet by lining it with parchment paper.
3. Place the finely chopped mushroom pieces on the baking sheet in a single layer. Drizzle with olive oil and season with salt and pepper.
4. Bake for 15 minutes. Remove from the oven and carefully toss mushrooms over. Return to oven to bake for 15 more minutes or until the mushrooms are browned and crispy.
5. Remove the mushroom pieces from the oven and place in a large bowl. Blot with a paper towel to remove the excess oil. Toss with maple syrup, garlic powder, onion powder and paprika. Return to the baking sheet and bake for 5 more minutes to caramelize the mushrooms.
6. Remove from the oven and set aside.
7. To arrange the toast, prepare 2 more baking sheets with parchment paper. Place the bread pieces on one and tomatoes on the other. Place this on the bottom and top racks of the oven for the last 10 minutes that the mushroom pieces of bacon are baking. Remove when the slices of toast are golden brown and the tomatoes blister and soften.
8. Spread the desired amount of hummus on each piece of toast. Add the blistered tomatoes, mushroom bacon bits, parsley, salt, and pepper. Drizzle with olive oil and serve.

Tofu Avocado Toast

Nutritional Information:

Total fat: 29.1g

Cholesterol: 0mg

Sodium: 16mg

Total carbohydrates: 28.1g

Dietary fiber: 6.3g

Protein: 8.5g

Calcium: 144mg

Potassium: 475mg

Iron: 2mg

Vitamin D: 0mcg

Time: 15 minutes

Serving Size: 2

Ingredients:

- 4 extra firm 1/2-inch thick slices of tofu, drained and patted dry
- 2 tablespoons olive oil
- ¼ teaspoon turmeric
- 2 slices almond bread (or any other gluten-free, dairy-free bread of your choice)
- ½ small avocado, sliced
- ½ cup chives, sliced
- Salt and pepper to taste

Directions:

1. Mix the turmeric, salt, and pepper in a small bowl and rub each piece of tofu with this mixture.
2. Heat a skillet over medium heat. Add olive oil to the skillet and fry tofu slices until golden brown on each side.
3. Once the tofu is cooked, assemble the sandwiches by toasting the bread then layering with the tofu and chives. Sprinkle with salt and pepper, and serve.

Apple Buckwheat Pancakes

Nutritional Information:

Total fat: 10.8g

Cholesterol: 0mg

Sodium: 473mg

Total carbohydrates: 22.3g

Dietary fiber: 3.7g

Protein: 3.5g

Calcium: 63mg

Potassium: 330mg

Iron: 2mg

Vitamin D: 0mcg

Time: 1 hour

Serving Size: 10

Ingredients:

- 1 ¾ cups buckwheat flour
- 2 tablespoons coconut sugar
- 2 teaspoons salt
- 2 teaspoons of baking powder
- 2 teaspoons ground cinnamon
- ½ teaspoon vanilla extract
- 1 ¼ cup almond milk + 2 tablespoons
- 1 tablespoon ground flaxseed
- 3 tablespoons water
- 2 tablespoons coconut oil, melted
- 1 cup Royal Gala apples, peeled and finely chopped
- Maple syrup to serve

Directions:

1. Create an egg substitute by mixing the ground flax seeds with water. Let it rest for 5 minutes.
2. Whisk together the buckwheat flour, coconut sugar, baking powder, salt and cinnamon. Mix the egg substitute with almond milk and gently fold this mixture into the dry ingredient mixture. Do not over mix the batter. Let the mixture rest for 15 minutes
3. After 15 minutes, fold in 2 more tablespoons of almond milk, coconut oil, and chopped apples.
4. Heat a non-stick frying pan over medium heat. Spread coconut oil over the surface of the frying pan with a paper towel.
5. Use a measuring cup, scoop ¼ cup of pancake batter into the heated frying pan.
6. Cook for 2 minutes or until bubbles start to form on the top. Flip the pancake over with a spatula and cook for 2 more minutes.
7. Repeat until all the pancakes have been cooked. In between pancakes, rub the same paper towel on the pan if more oil is needed.
8. To serve the pancakes, drizzle with maple syrup.

Mediterranean Chickpeas on Toast

Nutritional Information:

Total fat: 9.2g

Cholesterol: 0mg

Sodium: 21mg

Total carbohydrates: 56.31g

Dietary fiber: 11.4g

Protein: 12.4g

Calcium: 64mg

Potassium: 685mg

Iron: 4mg

Vitamin D: 0mcg

Time: 35 minutes

Serving Size: 8

Ingredients:

- 2 cups chickpeas, cooked
- 2 large tomatoes, skinned and diced
- 2 tablespoons olive oil
- 3 tablespoons water
- ½ cup shallots, finely diced
- 2 large garlic cloves, finely diced
- ½ teaspoon cumin
- ½ teaspoon sweet paprika
- Sugar to taste
- Salt and pepper to taste
- 8 slices almond bread (or any other gluten-free, dairy-free bread of your choice)
- Fresh parsley chopped to garnish

Directions:

1. Over medium heat, heat up some olive oil in a medium-sized frying pan. Add shallots and fry until almost translucent. Add the garlic and fry until the shallots are completely translucent and the garlic is soft.
2. Add all the spices to the pan and mix. Fry for 2 more minutes. Stir constantly.
3. Add the diced tomatoes and water to the pan. Simmer on low heat until the sauce has thickened.

4. Add the cooked chickpeas and cooked until warmed by the sauce. Season with sugar, salt, and pepper and remove from heat.
5. Serve the chickpeas over toasted bread. Sprinkle with parsley.

Ginger Cinnamon Waffles

Nutritional Information:

Total fat: 13g

Cholesterol: 0mg

Sodium: 159mg

Total carbohydrates: 11.6g

Dietary fiber: 1.3g

Protein: 1g

Calcium: 99mg

Potassium: 384mg

Iron: 1mg

Vitamin D: 0mcg

Time: 20 minutes

Serving Size: 6

Ingredients:

- 4 tablespoons coconut sugar
- 2 teaspoons ground ginger
- 1 ½ teaspoon ground cinnamon
- 2 teaspoons baking powder
- ¼ teaspoon baking soda
- ¼ teaspoon salt
- 1 cup coconut milk
- 1 tablespoon apple cider vinegar
- 1 ½ tablespoon coconut oil, melted
- 2 tablespoons molasses

Directions:

1. Grease and preheat your waffle iron according to manufacturer's instructions. If you do not have a waffle iron, you can use a non-stick frying pan and make these into pancakes.
2. Add the coconut flour, coconut sugar, ginger, cinnamon, salt, baking powder, baking soda and flax seeds to a large bowl and stir well to combine.

3. In another large bowl, combine coconut milk, apple cider vinegar, coconut oil and molasses. Mix well.
4. Fold in wet mixture into the dry ingredients and mix with a wooden spoon until just combined. There will be a few small lumps which is fine. Do not over mix the mixture.
5. Pour mixture into the waffle iron and cook on medium temperature until steam stops coming out of the side of the waffle iron. If you are using this batter to make pancakes, cook over medium heat until bubbles form on the top then flip and cook for 1 more minute.
6. Serve immediately. Can be stored in the refrigerator for a few days or freezer for a few weeks. Warm in a toaster before serving.

Easy Vegan French Toast

Nutritional Information:

Total fat: 12.1g

Cholesterol: 0mg

Sodium: 10mg

Total carbohydrates: 31.3g

Dietary fiber: 3.4g

Protein: 3g

Calcium: 10mg

Potassium: 264mg

Iron: 1mg

Vitamin D: 0mcg

Time: 35 minutes

Serving Size: 6

Ingredients:

- 6 slices of day-old almond bread (because the bread is lightly dried out at this age, it will hold its shape better)
- 1 large banana
- ¾ cup coconut milk
- 1 tablespoon maple syrup plus more for topping
- 1 tablespoon canola oil
- ½ teaspoon cinnamon
- 1 teaspoon vanilla extract

Directions:

1. Add peeled the banana, coconut milk, vanilla extract, cinnamon, and maple syrup to a blender and blend into a smooth consistency. Pour this mixture into a shallow, wide bowl in which slices of bread will fit.
2. Heat the canola oil in a non-stick frying pan over medium heat. When the pan is hot, dip a slice of bread into the banana batter. Coat both sides and place the bread in the hot pan and fry for 2 minutes on each side or until golden brown.
3. Serve the French toast with maple syrup, fruit or any other desired vegan topping.

Artichoke Spinach Quiche

Nutritional Information:

Total fat: 4.5g

Cholesterol: 0mg

Sodium: 215mg

Total carbohydrates: 16.6g

Dietary fiber: 5.1g

Protein: 8.6g

Calcium: 94mg

Potassium: 466mg

Iron: 3mg

Vitamin D: 0mcg

Time: 1 hour 20 minutes

Serving Size: 8

Ingredients:

- 1 14-oz can artichokes, drained and chopped with any hard pieces removed
- 2 cups fresh spinach
- ½ cup onion, chopped
- 2 garlic cloves, minced
- 1 teaspoon dried basil
- ½ teaspoon turmeric
- ¼ teaspoon salt
- ¼ teaspoon pepper
- 1 teaspoon Dijon mustard
- 14-oz soft tofu
- ⅓ cup nutritional yeast
- 1 tablespoon olive oil

- 1 tablespoon lemon juice
- Oil spray
- 2 large gluten-free, dairy-free tortillas

Directions:

1. Preheat your oven to 350 degrees F.
2. Prepare your pie plate by spraying it with the oil spray. Arrange the tortillas so that they cover the bottom and sides of the pie plate. Rip the tortillas in half if necessary.
3. Bake the tortillas for up to 15 minutes. Check at 5 minute intervals to ensure that the tortillas have remained in place and are not bubbling. Break any bubbles that form.
4. Heat the olive oil in a large pan over medium heat. Add onions and cook for 5 minutes or until the onions become translucent. Add garlic and cook for 2 more minutes. Add the spinach and cook until the leaves become wilted. Take the vegetable mixture off the heat.
5. Add the tofu, nutritional yeast, lemon juice, and spices to a food processor and pulse until smooth. Add artichokes and vegetable mixture to a food processor and pulse 20 times or until thoroughly mixed.
6. Pour mixture into the pie pan and bake for 45 minutes.
7. Allow to cool and serve.

Tofu Scramble 'Eggs'

Nutritional Information:

Total fat: 6.5g

Cholesterol: 0mg

Sodium: 420mg

Total carbohydrates: 47.2g

Dietary fiber: 12.3g

Protein: 23.1g

Calcium: 214mg

Potassium: 1159mg

Iron: 6mg

Vitamin D: 63mcg

Time: 30 minutes

Serving Size: 6

Ingredients:

- 2 tablespoons nutritional yeast
- 1 teaspoon ground cumin
- ¼ teaspoon garlic powder

- ¼ teaspoon of onion powder
- ¾ teaspoon turmeric
- 1 teaspoon of salt
- 1 454g block firm tofu
- 1 tablespoon olive oil
- 1 ½ cup button mushrooms, sliced
- 2 cups of black beans, drained and rinsed
- 1 red bell pepper, chopped
- 2 garlic cloves, minced
- ½ cup yellow onion, chopped

Directions:

1. Combine all the spices in a bowl.
2. Heat a large skillet over medium heat and add olive oil. Once the oil is hot, add the mushrooms, bell pepper, garlic, and yellow onion. Saute for 10 minutes or until the veggies begin to brown.
3. Add the tofu block and break it apart with a spoon until it obtains a scrambled texture with lots of chunks.
4. Stir in the spice mixture and black beans. Cook for 5 more minutes.
5. Serve with your favorite gluten-free, dairy-free bread, and sliced avocado.

Tempeh Sweet Potato Scrambled 'Eggs'

Nutritional Information:

Total fat: 13.8g

Cholesterol: 0mg

Sodium: 242mg

Total carbohydrates: 17.8g

Dietary fiber: 2.1g

Protein: 12.2g

Calcium: 93mg

Potassium: 476mg

Iron: 4mg

Vitamin D: 0mcg

Time: 20 minutes

Serving Size: 4

Ingredients:

- 1 8-oz package tempeh, crumbled
- 1 small sweet potato, finely diced

- 2 tablespoons olive oil
- ½ cup onions, diced
- 2 garlic cloves, minced
- 1 red bell pepper, diced
- 1 tablespoon soy sauce
- ½ tablespoon lemon juice
- 1 tablespoon maple syrup
- 1 tablespoon smoked paprika
- 1 tablespoon ground cumin

Directions:

1. In a large skillet over medium heat, heat the olive oil. Add a sweet potato and saute for 5 minutes or until lightly browned.
2. Add onion and saute until the onion becomes softened or about 5 minutes.
3. Add garlic and saute for 1 more minute. Add tempeh and saute until browned.
4. Add the bell pepper, soy sauce, cumin, paprika, lemon juice, and maple syrup. Saute for 2 more minutes.
5. Serve alongside toasted gluten-free, dairy-free bread or on a tortilla. Can be topped with avocado slices, scallions, and hot sauce.

Chickpea Onion Omelette

Nutritional Information:
Total fat: 15.7g

Cholesterol: 0mg

Sodium: 32mg

Total carbohydrates: 20.8g

Dietary fiber: 5.5g

Protein: 6.4g

Calcium: 242mg

Potassium: 604mg

Iron: 7mg

Vitamin D: 0mcg

Time: 5 minutes

Serving Size: 2

Ingredients:
- 3 tablespoon chickpea flour
- ½ cup onion, chopped
- 8 tablespoon water
- 2 tablespoons olive oil

- ½ cup fresh dill, chopped
- Salt and pepper to taste

Directions:

1. Whisk chickpea flour, salt, and pepper will in a medium bowl.
2. Add water and whisk until a creamy butter is formed.
3. Add chopped onions and chopped dill. Mix well.
4. Over medium heat, heat olive oil in a non-stick frying pan. Once the oil is heated, scoop the batter into the pan and spread it around with a spoon so that it forms a round omelette.
5. Cook for 3 minutes. Flip the omelette and cook for 2 more minutes.
6. Remove from the heat and allow to cool for a few minutes. Serve warm alongside your favorite gluten-free, dairy-free bread.

Keto Vanilla Pancakes

Nutritional Information:

Total fat: 17.4g

Cholesterol: 34mg

Sodium: 37mg

Total carbohydrates: 16.g

Dietary fiber: 3.4g

Protein: 11g

Calcium: 78mg

Potassium: 325mg

Iron: 3mg

Vitamin D: 0mcg

Time: 15 minutes

Serving Size: 2

Ingredients:

- ¼ teaspoon vanilla extract
- ½ scoop vanilla protein powder
- ¼ cup oat flour
- 1 teaspoon coconut sugar
- 1 tablespoon ground flax seed
- ¼ teaspoon baking powder
- ½ cup coconut milk

Directions:

1. Grease and preheat your waffle iron according to manufacturer's instructions.

2. In a large bowl, add the oat flour, vanilla protein powder, sugar, and ground flax seed. Mix well.
3. In a medium bowl, add the flaxseed, baking powder, vanilla extract and ¼ cup of coconut milk. Whisk well and let sit for 5 minutes so that the mixture gels up.
4. Add the wet mixture to the dry ingredients. Pour in the remaining coconut milk as well. Stir so that a thick batter is formed.
5. Cook according to your waffle irons manufacturer instructions until all the batter is used up. Can be frozen for up to two weeks in an airtight container or stored in an airtight container in the refrigerator for a few days. To reheat, simply toast in a toaster, top up with your favorite toppings and enjoy!

Keto-Friendly Vegan Cauliflower Hash Browns

Nutritional Information:

Total fat: 1.3g

Cholesterol: 0mg

Sodium: 203mg

Total carbohydrates: 8.8g

Dietary fiber: 2.5g

Protein: 2.4g

Calcium: 18mg

Potassium: 186mg

Iron: 1mg

Vitamin D: 0mcg

Time: 1 hour

Serving Size: 6

Ingredients:

- 2 cups cauliflower florets
- ¼ cup chickpea flour
- 1 tablespoon cornstarch
- 1 teaspoon coconut oil
- ⅓ cup onion chopped
- ½ teaspoon garlic powder
- ½ teaspoon salt
- 2 tablespoons water (if needed)

Directions:

1. Preheat your oven to 400 degrees F.
2. Prepare a baking sheet by lining it with parchment paper and brushing the parchment paper with coconut oil.

3. Add the cauliflower and onion to a food processor and pulse until a crumbly texture is achieved. Transfer this mixture to a large bowl.
4. Add the chickpea flour, cornstarch, garlic powder, salt, and water. Only add water if the batter is not moist enough to be pliable. Most times, the moisture from the cauliflower is sufficient. Stir and mix well.
5. Divide this batter into 6 equal portions and shape into 3 x 2 inch patties.
6. Place the patties on the prepared baking sheet and bake for 40 minutes. Turn halfway through the baking process.
7. Allow the hash browns to sit on the baking sheet for 10 minutes after removing from the oven so that they get firmer. Serve with your favorite keto vegan dipping sauce.

Simple Coconut Keto Vegan Pancakes

Nutritional Information:

Total fat: 10.3g

Cholesterol: 0mg

Sodium: 13mg

Total carbohydrates: 4.2g

Dietary fiber: 2g

Protein: 1.9g

Calcium: 28mg

Potassium: 117mg

Iron: 1mg

Vitamin D: 0mcg

Time: 25 minutes

Serving Size: 8

Ingredients:

- 1 tablespoon coconut flour
- 1 cup unsweetened coconut milk
- 1 tablespoon unsweetened almond butter
- 1 tablespoon ground flaxseed
- ½ teaspoon baking powder
- Canola oil for frying

Directions:

1. In a small bowl, combine almond butter and coconut milk.
2. In a medium bowl, combine the rest of the ingredients.
3. Pour the milk mixture into the dry ingredients and thoroughly mix. Allow the batter to sit for 5 minutes so that the flaxseed can form a gel and the coconut flour

can absorb the water. If this step is skipped, the pancakes will fall apart once cooked.

4. Heat a nonstick frying pan over medium heat. Add the canola oil and spoon the batter into the pan once the oil has heated. Spread the batter around so that it forms 4 inch pancakes.
5. Cook for up to 5 minutes or until the pancakes flip easily and bubbles form on the top. Cook for another 2 minutes or until the underside becomes golden brown.
6. Serve by topping with coconut cream, vegan butter or fresh berries.

Keto Vegan Pumpkin Muffins with Coconut Glaze

Nutritional Information:
Total fat: 16.7g
Cholesterol: 2mg
Sodium: 14mg
Total carbohydrates: 4.5g
Dietary fiber: 1.6g
Protein: 7.7g
Calcium: 94mg
Potassium: 88mg
Iron: 2mg
Vitamin D: 0mcg
Time: 25 minutes
Serving Size: 12
Ingredients:
- ½ cup pumpkin puree
- ½ cup coconut oil, melted
- ½ cup almond flour
- 2 scoops vanilla protein powder
- ½ cup natural peanut butter
- 1 teaspoon baking powder
- 1 tablespoon ground cinnamon
- ¼ cup coconut butter
- ¼ cup of almond milk
- 1 teaspoon stevia powder
- 2 teaspoons lemon juice

Directions:

1. Preheat your oven to 350 degrees F.
2. Prepare a muffin tin with 12 muffin liners.

3. In a large bowl combine almond flour, vanilla protein powder, baking powder, and ground cinnamon. Mix well.
4. Add the pumpkin puree, melted coconut oil, and peanut butter to the dry ingredients. Mix well to incorporate the wet ingredients.
5. Equally distribute this batter into muffin tin. Bake for 15 minutes or until an inserted toothpick comes out clean of the center.
6. Transfer to a wire rack and allow to cool completely.
7. Once the muffins have cooled, prepare the coconut glaze by combining the coconut butter, almond milk, stevia powder, and lemon juice. Mix well. Pour the glaze over the muffins and allowed to firm. Can be kept in an airtight container at room temperature for up to 2 days. Can be frozen in an airtight container for up to one week.

Keto Coconut Pecan Porridge

Nutritional Information:
Total fat: 39.2g
Cholesterol: 0mg
Sodium: 94mg
Total carbohydrates: 19.2g
Dietary fiber: 12g
Protein: 12.9g
Calcium: 268mg
Potassium: 331mg
Iron: 4mg
Vitamin D: 0mcg
Time: 15 minutes
Serving Size: 3
Ingredients:
- ¼ cup coconut milk
- ¾ cup unsweetened almond milk
- ¼ cup roasted almond butter
- 1 teaspoon MCT oil
- 2 tablespoons chia seeds
- 2 tablespoons hemp seeds
- ½ teaspoon ground cinnamon
- ¼ cup pecans, chopped
- ½ cup unsweetened coconut flakes, toasted

Directions:

1. Over medium heat, add coconut milk, almond milk, almond butter, and MCT oil to a small saucepan and bring to a simmer. Once the mixture becomes hot, remove from the heat.
2. Add chia seeds, hemp seeds, chopped pecans, cinnamon and toasted coconut. Mix and allow to sit for 10 minutes.
3. Spoon the porridge into 2 serving bowls. Can be served cold or hot. Before serving, top with more toasted coconut flakes, and enjoy!

Chapter 7: Lunch Recipes

This is a mixture of strictly vegan and keto vegan recipes. All Keto vegan recipes will include the word 'Keto' in the title.

Cauliflower Fried Rice

Nutritional Information:

Total fat: 40.6g

Cholesterol: 0mg

Sodium: 1019mg

Total carbohydrates: 39.2g

Dietary fiber: 11.2g

Protein: 14g

Calcium: 147mg

Potassium: 1153mg

Iron: 5mg

Vitamin D: 0mcg

Time: 25 minutes

Serving Size: 2

Ingredients:

- 5 cups cauliflower florets
- 3 tablespoons peanut oil, divided into 1 tablespoon and 2 tablespoons
- 3 scallions, sliced
- 1 tablespoon grated fresh ginger
- 1 tablespoon minced garlic
- ½ cup diced red bell pepper
- 1 cup trimmed and halved snow peas
- 1 cup shredded carrots
- ⅓ cup unsalted roasted cashews
- 3 tablespoons reduced-sodium soy sauce
- 1 tablespoon toasted sesame oil

Directions:

1. Pulse the cauliflower florets in a food processor for about 2 minutes or until it resembles rice. Set aside.
2. Place a large skillet over high heat and heat 1 tablespoon peanut oil. Add the scallions, ginger and garlic, and saute until the scallions have softened. This should be less than 1 minute. Add the bell pepper, snow peas, and carrots. Saute until the carrots are tender or for about 3 minutes. Transfer this mixture to a plate and set aside.
3. Add the remaining peanut oil to the skillet and heat. Add the cauliflower rice and saute until softened or for 2 minutes. Return the vegetable mixture and remaining ingredients of cashews, soy sauce, and sesame oil to the skillet.
4. Serve warm.

Keto Open-faced Hummus Sandwich

Nutritional Information:

Total fat: 17.2g

Cholesterol: 0mg

Sodium: 293mg

Total carbohydrates: 26.6g

Dietary fiber: 5.7g

Protein: 7.5g

Calcium: 100mg

Potassium: 105mg

Iron: 2mg

Vitamin D: 0mcg

Time: 5 minutes

Serving Size: 2

Ingredients:

- 1 large slice almond bread
- 4 tablespoons chickpea hummus (See recipe *Chapter 5: Sauce and Condiment Recipes: Chickpea Hummus*)
- 4 small baby plum tomatoes, sliced in half
- 1 cup arugula
- 1 tablespoon toasted sesame seeds
- Olive oil and salt for topping

Directions:

1. Spread the chickpea hummus over the almond bread.
2. Top the hummus with plum tomato slices and arugula.
3. Sprinkle with toasted sesame seeds and finish by drizzling with olive oil and salt.
4. Slice in half and serve immediately.

Creamy Keto Butternut Squash Soup

Nutritional Information:

Total fat: 16g

Cholesterol: 0mg

Sodium: 522mg

Total carbohydrates: 14.8g

Dietary fiber: 3.6g

Protein: 5.7g

Calcium: 77mg

Potassium: 5971mg

Iron: 3mg

Vitamin D: 0mcg

Time: 1 hour 15 minutes

Serving Size: 6

Ingredients:

- 1 lb butternut squash
- 1 ½ cup coconut milk
- 4 cups vegetable broth
- 2 tablespoons avocado oil

- 6 garlic cloves, minced
- 2 tablespoons fresh thyme
- ½ teaspoon cinnamon
- ⅛ teaspoon nutmeg
- Salt and pepper to taste

Directions:

1. Preheat your oven to 400 degrees F.
2. Prepare a baking sheet by lining it with parchment paper.
3. Cut a butternut squash in half lengthwise and remove the seeds. Place the two halves open side up on baking sheet. Drizzle with 1 tablespoon of the avocado oil. Sprinkle with salt and pepper. Flip the 2 halves over, face down.
4. Roasted butternut squash in the oven for 50 minutes or until it is fork tender.
5. About 30 minutes into the roasting process, heat the remaining avocado oil in a large pot over medium heat. Add minced garlic, thyme, cinnamon, and nutmeg and saute for about 1 minute or until it becomes fragrant.
6. Add the coconut oil and vegetable broth to the pot and simmer for 20 minutes or until the squash is completely cooked.
7. Scoop the squash out of the shells and place into the soup. Puree to a smooth consistency with an immersion blender.
8. Serve warm. Makes for an especially nourishing meal on snowy and rainy days.

Vegan BLT Sandwich

Nutritional Information:

Total fat: 23.7g

Cholesterol: 0mg

Sodium: 1045mg

Total carbohydrates: 63.7g

Dietary fiber: 18.5g

Protein: 36.4g

Calcium: 21mg

Potassium: 350mg

Iron: 4mg

Vitamin D: 0mcg

Time: 1 hour 45 minutes

Serving Size: 8

Ingredients:

- 24 thin slices tempeh (serves as the bacon in the BLT sandwiches)
- ¼ cup liquid aminos
- ½ cup of water
- 2 tablespoons apple cider vinegar
- 1 teaspoon coconut sugar
- ½ teaspoon ground cumin
- ½ teaspoon paprika
- Olive oil

To arrange sandwich

- 16 slices almond or coconut bread
- 2 ripe avocados
- Thick slices of 1 tomato
- 8 leaves iceberg lettuce
- Vegan mayonnaise

Directions:

1. In a small saucepan, combine the liquid aminos, apple cider vinegar, coconut sugar, cumin, paprika, and water. Bring to a boil over medium heat. Allow to boil for no more than 2 minutes then turn off the heat
2. Arrange the tempeh slices in a single layer in a casserole dish and pour the liquid aminos marinade over the top. Shake the casserole dish slightly to ensure that all the slices are coated with the marinade. Cover and allow to marinate for at least one hour. Overnight works best.
3. Preheat your oven to 300 degrees F.
4. Prepare a baking sheet by lining it with parchment paper and brushing the parchment paper with olive oil.
5. Drain the tempeh slices and arrange them in a single layer on the prepared baking sheet. Brush the top of the slices with olive oil.
6. Bake for 15 minutes or until the slices a slightly brown on the edges. Flip the slices and bake for 10 more minutes or until the slices become crisp.
7. Allow the slices to cool slightly before using.
8. To arrange the sandwiches, lightly toast the bread slices. Spread one side of the sandwich with vegan mayonnaise once this has been done.
9. Slice the avocado and arrange slices on top of the vegan mayonnaise-slathered bread slices.
10. Arrange the tempeh slices, tomato slices, and lettuce over. Top with the other slice of bread.
11. Serve immediately.

Veggie Pita Pizza

Nutritional Information:

Total fat: 1.2g

Cholesterol: 0mg

Sodium: 817mg

Total carbohydrates: 31.4g

Dietary fiber: 6.7g

Protein: 6.5g

Calcium: 65mg

Potassium: 667mg

Iron: 4mg

Vitamin D: 97mcg

Time: 20 minutes

Serving Size: 2

Ingredients:

- 1 pita bread
- ⅛ teaspoon dried basil
- ⅛ teaspoon dried oregano
- 1 cup tomato sauce

Toppings

- 3 mushrooms, sliced
- ⅛ cup chopped yellow onions
- ⅛ cup chopped green peppers
- ⅛ cup chopped scallions

Directions:

1. Preheat your oven to 300 degrees F.
2. Prepare a small baking sheet by lining it with parchment paper.
3. Cut the pita bread in half, separating it into two circles.
4. Spread tomato sauce over each circle. Sprinkle with the basil and oregano. Arrange the toppings next.
5. Bake for 10 minutes. Alternately, this can be heated in a toaster oven for 5 minutes at 250 degrees F.
6. Serve warm.

Black Bean Salad

Nutritional Information:

Total fat: 14.1g

Cholesterol: 0mg

Sodium: 706mg

Total carbohydrates: 51.7g

Dietary fiber: 17.7g

Protein: 15.9g

Calcium: 89mg

Potassium: 981mg

Iron: 4mg

Vitamin D: 97mcg

Time: 10 minutes

Serving Size: 4

Ingredients:

- 2 16-oz cans of black beans, drained and rinsed well
- 2 cup fresh corn
- 1 large tomato, chopped
- ½ cup yellow onion, chopped
- 1 cup pecans, chopped
- ¼ cup cilantro chopped
- Juice and zest of 1 small lime
- Balsamic vinegar to taste

Directions:

1. To a large bowl, add the black beans, corn, tomato, yellow onion, and pecans, and mix well.
2. Add the cilantro, juice and zest of the lime and balsamic. Mix again.
3. Can be served alone or as a side to a sandwich or meal.

Jackfruit Veggie Tacos

Nutritional Information:

Total fat: 9.5g

Cholesterol: 0mg

Sodium: 167mg

Total carbohydrates: 29g

Dietary fiber: 6.1g

Protein: 4.6g

Calcium: 49mg

Potassium: 4361mg

Iron: 1mg

Vitamin D: 0mcg

Time: 20 minutes

Serving Size: 8

Ingredients:

- 1 10-oz package jackfruit
- 8 corn tortillas, warmed
- 1 ripe avocado, chopped
- ¼ cup plain unsweetened almond milk
- 2 tablespoons olive oil
- 3 tablespoons lime juice
- ½ teaspoon salt
- 1 medium tomato, diced
- ¼ cup fresh cilantro, chopped
- 2 tablespoons onion, diced
- 1 tablespoon jalapeno pepper, diced
- 1 cup salt-free pinto beans, rinsed
- 1 cup romaine lettuce, shredded

Directions:

1. Add the avocado, almond milk, 2 tablespoons of lime juice, and ¼ teaspoon of salt into a blender. Blend until a creamy consistency is reached. Scrape down the sides of the blender if necessary
2. In a medium bowl, combine the remaining lime juice, 1 tablespoon of olive oil, the remaining salt, tomato, cilantro, onions, and jalapeno. Combine well.
3. Heat up the remaining olive oil in a large nonstick skillet over. Add the jackfruit and pinto beans and cook for up to 3 minutes or until heated through. Stir occasionally.
4. Serve the pinto beans and jackfruit in corn tortillas topped with the avocado mixture and lettuce.

Sauteed Veggies in Spicy Garlic Chili Sauce

Nutritional Information:

Total fat: 3.4g

Cholesterol: 0mg

Sodium: 40mg

Total carbohydrates: 25.7g

Dietary fiber: 5.5g

Protein: 5.3g

Calcium: 63mg

Potassium: 613mg

Iron: 3mg

Vitamin D: 63mcg

Time: 15 minutes

Serving Size: 2

Ingredients:

- ½ cup red bell peppers, chopped
- ½ cup green bell peppers, chopped
- ½ cup yellow bell peppers, chopped
- 1 red onion, chopped
- ½ cup white mushrooms, sliced
- 1 cup broccoli florets
- ½ cup baby corn, chopped
- ½ cup sugar snap peas
- ¼ cup leeks, sliced
- 1 teaspoon sesame seeds
- 1 teaspoon of olive oil
- 2 tablespoons spicy garlic chili sauce (See recipe *Chapter 5: Sauce and Condiment Recipes: Spicy Garlic Chili Sauce*)
- 1 1/2 cup water
- 5 basil leaves

Directions:

1. Heat the olive oil in a large, nonstick skillet over medium heat. Add the sesame seeds and basil leaves and saute for 10 seconds.
2. Add leeks and red onions and saute for 1 minute.
3. Add all bell peppers and saute for 1 minute.

4. Add the rest of the vegetables and saute for 2 minutes.
5. Add the water and garlic chili sauce. Stir. Cover the pot and cook for 4 minutes.
6. Can be served as is or over rice.

Raw Mushroom Walnut Lettuce Wraps

Nutritional Information:

Total fat: 40.4g

Cholesterol: 0mg

Sodium: 133mg

Total carbohydrates: 39.5g

Dietary fiber: 9.7g

Protein: 19.8g

Calcium: 74mg

Potassium: 938mg

Iron: 6mg

Vitamin D: 151mcg

Time: 3 hours 15 minutes

Serving Size: 5

Ingredients:

- 3 cups mushrooms, roughly chopped
- 3 tablespoons liquid aminos
- 2 tablespoons maple syrup
- 1 teaspoon apple cider vinegar
- 2 cups walnuts
- 4 cups water
- 1 cup quinoa, cooked
- ½ teaspoon cumin
- ½ teaspoon smoked paprika
- ½ teaspoon coriander
- ½ teaspoon chipotle powder
- ⅓ cup parsley, chopped
- 1 cup cherry tomatoes, quartered
- 1 small avocado, sliced
- 5 large butter lettuce leaves
- Salt and pepper to taste

Directions:

1. Mix liquid aminos, maple syrup, and apple cider vinegar in a small bowl.
2. Place mushroom pieces in a medium sealable bowl. Pour the maple syrup mixture over the mushrooms. Seal the bowl and shake so that the mushrooms are coated with the mixture.
3. Place the bowl in the refrigerator and let marinade for 3 hours. Shake occasionally to coat mushrooms.
4. While the mushroom marinade, cover the walnuts in water and let soak for 3 hours.
5. Drain and rinse the walnuts. Place in a food processor. Pulse until a chunky texture is achieved.
6. Add the marinated mushrooms and parsley to the food processor. Pulse until the mushrooms and parsley are well incorporated.
7. Stir in all spices, quinoa, salt, and pepper.
8. To assemble wraps, place the mixture in the lettuce leaves. Top with tomatoes pieces and avocado slices.
9. Sprinkle with salt and pepper. Serve.

Avocado Arugula Salad

Nutritional Information:

Total fat: 14.7g

Cholesterol: 0mg

Sodium: 123mg

Total carbohydrates: 8.6g

Dietary fiber: 5.1g

Protein: 1.7g

Calcium: 17mg

Potassium: 418mg

Iron: 1mg

Vitamin D: 0mcg

Time: 10 minutes

Serving Size: 6

Ingredients:

- 2 large ripe, firm avocados, diced into large chunks
- ½ cup baby arugula, roughly chopped
- ¼ cup red onions, diced
- 1 cup cherry tomatoes, halved

- 1 cup grape tomatoes, halved
- 6 basil leaves, thinly sliced
- 2 tablespoons orange olive vinaigrette (See receipe *Chapter 5: Sauces and Condiments: Orange Olive Vinaigrette*)

Directions:

1. Place all the avocado pieces, arugula, onions, tomatoes, and basil leaves in a large bowl.
2. Toss with vinaigrette and serve. Squeeze fresh lemon juice over the avocado chunks if you plan to serve later. This prevents the avocado from turning brown.

Keto Avocado Kale Salad

Nutritional Information:

Total fat: 5.8g

Cholesterol: 0mg

Sodium: 56mg

Total carbohydrates: 4.2g

Dietary fiber: 1.9g

Protein: 1.2g

Calcium: 27mg

Potassium: 197mg

Iron: 1mg

Vitamin D: 0mcg

Time: 15 minutes

Serving Size: 4

Ingredients:

- 10 Tuscan kale leaves
- 2 teaspoons of olive oil
- 2 teaspoons of sesame oil
- 1 teaspoon fresh ginger, grated
- 1 garlic cloves, grated
- A pinch of salt
- ½ cup snow peas, chopped
- 1 ripe avocado, cliced
- ⅓ cup scallions, shopped
- 1 teaspoon lemon zest

- 2 teaspoons balsamic vinegar
- 2 teaspoons liquid aminos

Directions:

1. Wash, rinse, and dry the kale leaves. Remove the stems with a knife. Slice the kale leaves into small pieces.
2. Add the kale pieces to a large bowl. Add the olive oil, sesame oil, ginger, garlic, and salt. Toss and ensure the kale leaves are thoroughly coated.
3. Add all the remaining ingredients and toss again. Refrigerate for 5 minutes and serve chilled.

Spaghetti Squash with Mushrooms and Tomatoes

Nutritional Information:

Total fat: 11.5g

Cholesterol: 0mg

Sodium: 19mg

Total carbohydrates: 10.4g

Dietary fiber: 1.2g

Protein: 2.4g

Calcium: 32mg

Potassium: 321mg

Iron: 1mg

Vitamin D: 42mcg

Time: 60 minutes

Serving Size: 6

Ingredients:

- 1 spaghetti squash
- 1 cup mushrooms, sliced
- 2 cups tomatoes, diced
- 4 garlic cloves, minced
- ¼ cup onions, chopped
- ¼ cup pine nuts, toasted
- 1 tablespoon fresh basil, finely chopped
- 3 tablespoons olive oil
- Salt and pepper to taste

Directions:

1. Wash and dry the spaghetti squash. Cut into two halves. Pierce the spaghetti squash with a knife several times. Place the spaghetti squash in a shallow baking dish which has about 1 inch of water and bake for up to 45 minutes or until it is soft enough to pierce with the knife easily.
2. When the squash is cool enough to handle, scoop out the seeds and stringy bits. Shred with a fork and set the spaghetti strands aside.
3. Heat olive oil in a nonstick skillet over medium heat. Add onions and mushrooms and saute for 4 minutes.
4. Add garlic and saute for 2 minutes or until fragrant. Do not let garlic brown.
5. Add tomatoes and cooked spaghetti squash. Cook and stir until the squash is hot and vegetables are evenly distributed.
6. Remove from heat. Toss with fresh basil and pine nuts. Season with salt and pepper. Serve warm.

Asian Coleslaw

Nutritional Information:

Total fat: 3.8g

Cholesterol: 0mg

Sodium: 93mg

Total carbohydrates: 11.7g

Dietary fiber: 3.1g

Protein: 2.4g

Calcium: 50mg

Potassium: 302mg

Iron: 1mg

Vitamin D: 0mcg

Time: 15 minutes

Serving Size: 10

Ingredients:

- 6 cups red cabbage, thinly sliced
- 6 cups green cabbage, thinly sliced
- ¾ cup shallots, sliced
- 1 cup cilantro, roughly chopped
- 2 cups carrots, shredded
- 1 teaspoon sesame oil

- 1 tablespoon olive oil
- 1 tablespoon maple syrup
- 1 tablespoon apple cider vinegar
- 2 teaspoons of soy sauce
- 1 tablespoon rice wine vinegar
- 2 tablespoons of almond butter
- 1 garlic clove, minced
- ½ teaspoon of ginger, grated
- ¼ teaspoon cayenne pepper
- Juice and zest of one small lime
- Salt and pepper to taste

Directions:

1. To make Asian coleslaw dressing, place olive oil, sesame oil, maple syrup, apple cider vinegar, soy sauce, rice wine vinegar, almond butter, garlic, ginger, cayenne pepper, juice and zest of lime, salt, and pepper in a small blender, and blend until a smooth consistency is achieved.
2. Place the remaining ingredients in a large bowl. Pour the dressing into the bowl. Mix thoroughly.
3. Refrigerate for at least one hour for the flavors to marinade. Serve chilled.

Keto Broccoli Fried Rice

Nutritional Information:

Total fat: 3.5g

Cholesterol: 0mg

Sodium: 95mg

Total carbohydrates: 10g

Dietary fiber: 3.6g

Protein: 3.9g

Calcium: 66mg

Potassium: 437mg

Iron: 1mg

Vitamin D: 0mcg

Time: 15 minutes

Serving Size: 3

Ingredients:

- 4 cups broccoli florets
- 1 tablespoon avocado oil
- 1 tablespoon liquid aminos
- 1 ½ teaspoon sesame oil
- 1 tablespoon garlic ,finely chopped
- ¼ cup cilantro, chopped
- 2 tablespoons scallions chopped
- 2 teaspoons of lime juice
- ½ teaspoon ginger, grated
- Sliced almonds for topping
- Salt and pepper to taste

Directions:

1. Add the broccoli florets to a food processor and pulse until a rice-like texture is achieved. Scrape down sides of bowl if necessary.
2. Add olive oil to a nonstick skillet and place over medium heat. Add riced broccoli and garlic, and saute for 1 minute.
3. Add liquid aminos, sesame oil, salt, and pepper. Saute for 2 more minutes or until the broccoli achieves a bright green color but is not mushy.
4. Turn off the heat and add ginger and lime juice. Stir to infuse flavors.
5. Top with scallions, cilantro and sliced almonds. Serve.

Stuffed Tomatoes

Nutritional Information:

Total fat: 5g

Cholesterol: 0mg

Sodium: 52mg

Total carbohydrates: 50.5g

Dietary fiber: 12.5g

Protein: 15.5g

Calcium: 126mg

Potassium: 1455mg

Iron: 5mg

Vitamin D: 0mcg

Time: 50 minutes

Serving Size: 6

Ingredients:

- 6 large beefsteak tomatoes
- ¼ cup red onion, diced
- 1 bell pepper, diced
- 1 tablespoon olive oil
- 4 garlic cloves, minced
- 1 block extra firm tofu, pressed
- 1 ½ cup cooked black beans, rinsed and drained
- 1 ½ cup corn, rinsed and drained
- 2 tablespoons tomato paste
- 2 tablespoons chili powder
- 1 teaspoon smoked paprika
- 1 teaspoon cumin
- 1 tablespoon lime juice
- ½ cup fresh cilantro, chopped
- Salt and pepper to taste

Directions:

1. Preheat your oven to 400 degrees F.
2. Add olive oil to a large nonstick skillet. Place over medium heat. Saute onions and bell peppers until the onions become translucent. Add garlic, chili powder, paprika, cumin, and tomato paste. Saute for 3 minutes.
3. Add tofu and mix. Cover the pan and cooked for 10 minutes on low heat. Stir occasionally.
4. As the filling cooks, cut the tops of the tomatoes and scoop out the seeds and guts. Sprinkle each tomato with salt and pepper to season.
5. After the 10 minutes are up, remove the lid and add black beans and corn. Stir and cook until this becomes warm.
6. Remove the filling from the heat. Add cilantro and lime juice. Stir to combine.
7. Stuff the tomatoes with good feeling and arrange the tomatoes on a casserole dish.
8. Bake for 15 minutes or until the tomatoes are blistered. Serve warm. Leftovers can be reserved in the refrigerator or freezer.

Tomato Sandwiches

Nutritional Information:

Total fat: 17.9g

Cholesterol: 2mg

Sodium: 300mg

Total carbohydrates: 61.9g

Dietary fiber: 6.4g

Protein: 8.5g

Calcium: 45mg

Potassium: 635mg

Iron: 2mg

Vitamin D: 0mcg

Time: 5 minutes

Serving Size: 2

Ingredients:

- 2 medium heirloom tomatoes
- 4 vegan cheese slices
- 4 slices almond bread (or any gluten-free, dairy-free bread that you prefer)
- Pesto sauce(see recipe *Chapter 5: Sauces and Condiments: Vegan Garden Pesto Sauce*)
- 4 lettuce leaves

Directions:

1. Slice the tomatoes.
2. To assemble sandwiches, layer lettuce, tomato slices, and vegan cheese on one slice of bread. Drizzle with pesto sauce. Top with another bread slice. Repeat with the remaining slices of bread. Can be served cold or pressed like a normal grilled cheese sandwich and served warm.

Zucchini Noodle Salad

Nutritional Information:

Total fat: 27.7g

Cholesterol: 0mg

Sodium: 927mg

Total carbohydrates: 20.2g

Dietary fiber: 7.6g

Protein: 19.7g

Calcium: 55mg

Potassium: 567mg

Iron: 1mg

Vitamin D: 0mcg

Time: 35 minutes

Serving Size: 4

Ingredients:

- 2 zucchinis
- 3 carrots
- 1 cup spinach, thinly sliced
- 3 tablespoons soy sauce
- ¼ cup natural smooth peanut butter
- ¼ cup peanuts roughly chopped
- 2 tablespoons lime juice
- 1 tablespoon maple syrup
- ¼ cup cilantro finely chopped
- Water

Directions:

1. Using a spiralizer, spiralize the zucchini and carrots into noodles. Add the spiralized noodles and the sliced cabbage to a large bowl.
2. Place peanut butter in a small microwave safe bowl and microwave for 20 seconds. Stir to achieve a smooth consistency.
3. Add lemon juice, maple syrup, and soy sauce to peanut butter. Whisk to combine. Add water if needed to achieve a smooth salad dressing-like consistency.
4. Add peanut sauce, peanuts, and cilantro to veggie noodles. Toss to combine.
5. Refrigerate for 30 minutes and serve chilled.

Quinoa Veggie Chopped Salad

Nutritional Information:

Total fat: 17.6g

Cholesterol: 0mg

Sodium: 22mg

Total carbohydrates: 51.5g

Dietary fiber: 6.3g

Protein: 12.7g

Calcium: 58mg

Potassium: 735mg

Iron: 5mg

Vitamin D: 0mcg

Time: 25 minutes

Serving Size: 6

Ingredients:

- 2 cups quinoa, cooked
- 1 red bell pepper, chopped
- 1 carrot, chopped
- 1 medium cucumber, chopped
- 1 cup arugula
- 1 cup cherry tomatoes, halved
- ½ cup pumpkin seeds
- 1 cup corn
- ½ cup white balsamic vinegar
- 1 tablespoon maple syrup
- ¼ cup olive oil
- 1 tablespoon lemon juice
- 1 garlic clove, grated
- Salt and pepper to taste

Directions:

1. Combine quinoa, bell pepper, carrots, cucumber, tomatoes, corn, arugula, and pumpkin seeds in a large bowl.
2. To make balsamic vinaigrette, whisk together white balsamic vinegar, garlic, lemon juice, maple syrup, salt, and pepper. Slowly drizzle in olive oil while continuously whisking.
3. Pour white balsamic vinaigrette over the chopped salad. Toss to combine and refrigerate for 30 minutes. Serve chilled.

Spinach Mushroom Tofu Wraps

Nutritional Information:

Total fat: 11.3g

Cholesterol: 0mg

Sodium: 781mg

Total carbohydrates: 32.8g

Dietary fiber: 2g

Protein: 9.9g

Calcium: 74mg

Potassium: 230mg

Iron: 2mg

Vitamin D: 126mcg

Time: 50 minutes

Serving Size: 4

Ingredients:

- 1 block firm tofu
- 2 cups mushrooms, sliced
- ½ cup spinach, frozen
- ½ cup cherry tomatoes
- ½ teaspoon curry powder
- ½ teaspoon turmeric
- 2 teaspoons canola oil
- ½ teaspoon salt
- 2 vegan tortillas
- 4 tablespoon chickpea hummus (See recipe *Chapter 5: Sauces and Condiments: Chickpea Hummus*)

Directions:

1. Add canola oil to a medium skillet and place over medium heat. Crumble the tofu and add to skillet. Scramble.
2. Add turmeric, salt, and curry powder. Mix well so that tofu gets an evenly distributed yellow color. Saute for 3 minutes.
3. Add sliced mushrooms and spinach and cook for 10 minutes.
4. To arrange tortillas, warm tortillas in a pan then spread 2 tablespoons of hummus on the tortilla. Top with tofu mixture and tomatoes. Fold wrap and serve.

Vegan Spring Rolls

Nutritional Information:

Total fat: 2.4g

Cholesterol: 0mg

Sodium: 67mg

Total carbohydrates: 17.2g

Dietary fiber: 1.6g

Protein: 2g

Calcium: 22mg

Potassium: 113mg

Iron: 1mg

Vitamin D: 0mcg

Time: 10 minutes

Serving Size: 8

Ingredients:

- 8 rice paper wrappers
- 8 lettuce leaves
- 1 red bell pepper, thinly sliced
- 1 cup red cabbage, thinly sliced
- 2 medium carrots, thinly sliced
- ¼ cup fresh cilantro, chopped
- ¼ cup fresh basil, chopped
- 3 oz rice noodles, cooked
- Almond dipping sauce for dipping (See recipe *Chapter 5: Sauces and Condiments: Almond Dipping Sauce*)

Directions:

1. To soften the rice papers, fill a large bowl with warm water and dip each rice paper into it for 5 to 10 seconds. Do not hold the rice paper in there longer because it will break apart.
2. Layer the rice papers on a flat surface.
3. Beginning at one end of one rice paper, layer veggies by starting with lettuce and adding cabbage, bell peppers, carrots, rice noodles, cilantro, and basil on top. Gently fold the rice paper so that the veggies are tucked inside.
4. Serve immediately with almond dipping sauce. Can be wrapped in plastic wrap and refrigerated to preserve for a later serving.

Chapter 8: Dinner Recipes

Cauliflower Alfredo

Nutritional Information:

Total fat: 9.5g

Cholesterol: 0mg

Sodium: 156mg

Total carbohydrates: 71.3g

Dietary fiber: 13.5g

Protein: 19.8g

Calcium: 62mg

Potassium: 210mg

Iron: 6mg

Vitamin D: 0mcg

Time: 30 minutes

Serving Size: 4

Ingredients:

- 2 cups cauliflower florets
- 8-oz pack whole wheat fettuccine
- ½ cup vegetable broth
- ¼ cup plain unsweetened almond milk
- 2 tablespoons olive oil
- 1 teaspoon yellow mustard
- 2 garlic cloves
- ¼ cup parsley, chopped
- Salt and pepper to taste

Directions:

1. Add the cauliflower florets and garlic to a steamer basket that has been fitted over a large saucepan which contains 1 inch of water. Cover the steamer basket. Bring the water to a boil and allow the cauliflower and garlic to steam until very tender or about 10 minutes.
2. While the cauliflower is steaming, bring water to a boil in a large saucepan over medium heat. Cook the fettuccine according to the package instructions. Drain well and return the pasta to the pot. Drizzle some olive oil and mix well to ensure pasta doesn't stick together.
3. Transferred the garlic and cauliflower to a blender. Add vegetable broth, almond milk, olive oil, yellow mustard, salt and pepper. Blend until smooth and creamy consistency is achieved. Pour this mixture over the pasta and toss to coat.
4. Top with parsley and serve.

Black Bean Quinoa Dinner

Nutritional Information:

Total fat: 5.6g

Cholesterol: 0mg

Sodium: 233mg

Total carbohydrates: 40.8g

Dietary fiber: 8.1g

Protein: 11.4g

Calcium: 56mg

Potassium: 727mg

Iron: 3mg

Vitamin D: 0mcg

Time: 15 minutes

Serving Size: 6

Ingredients:

- 1 cup quinoa
- ¼ teaspoon salt
- 1 cup black beans, rinsed and drained
- ½ cup hummus
- ½ medium avocado diced
- 4 tablespoons pico de gallo
- 2 tablespoons fresh cilantro, chopped
- 1 tablespoon lime juice

Directions:

1. Rinse quinoa in a fine mesh sieve over running water until the water runs clear.
2. Allow the quinoa to drain then transfer to a medium-sized pot. Add 2 cups of water and salt and bring to a boil over high heat. Cover and reduce the heat to medium and simmer until all the water is absorbed by the quinoa. This should take no more than 20 minutes. Turn off the heat and set the pot aside for 5 minutes. Uncover the pot and fluff the quinoa with a fork.
3. Combine the quinoa and black beans in a large bowl.
4. Stir the hummus and lime juice in a small bowl. If the hummus mixture is too thick, add a small amount of water until you reach the desired consistency. Pour hummus over the quinoa and black beans. Top with avocado, pico de gallo, and cilantro, and enjoy!

Kung Pao Broccoli Dinner

Nutritional Information:

Total fat: 9.5g

Cholesterol: 0mg

Sodium: 218mg

Total carbohydrates: 13.9g

Dietary fiber: 1.7g

Protein: 2.3g

Calcium: 49mg

Potassium: 235mg

Iron: 1mg

Vitamin D: 0mcg

Time: 40 minutes

Serving Size: 4

Ingredients:

- 4 cups broccoli florets
- 1 red bell pepper, chopped
- 1 yellow bell pepper, chopped
- 2 scallions, sliced
- 1 teaspoon crushed red pepper
- 1 teaspoon fresh ginger, minced
- 1 tablespoon of garlic, minced
- ½ cup unsalted roasted peanuts
- ⅓ cup water
- 2 tablespoons balsamic vinegar
- 1 tablespoon hoisin sauce
- 2 teaspoons low-sodium soy sauce
- 2 teaspoons of sesame oil
- 2 tablespoons peanut oil
- 2 teaspoons cornstarch
- ½ teaspoon Chinese five-spice powder

Directions:

1. Whisk the water, balsamic vinegar, hoisin sauce, soy sauce, sesame oil, cornstarch and five spice powder in a small bowl. Set aside.
2. Over medium heat, heat the peanut oil in a large nonstick skillet. Add the broccoli florets and all bell peppers. Saute for about 6 minutes or until the veggies are tender crisp.
3. Add scallions, crushed red pepper, ginger, and garlic. Saute for another 30 seconds.
4. Reduce the heat to low. Add the sauce mixture and cook for 30 more seconds so that the sauce thickens.
5. Remove from the heat and stir in peanuts. Serve warm.

Vegan Spicy Thai Noodles

Nutritional Information:

Total fat: 15.7g

Cholesterol: 0mg

Sodium: 1352mg

Total carbohydrates: 22.7g

Dietary fiber: 5.2g

Protein: 28.7g

Calcium: 680mg

Potassium: 677mg

Iron: 6mg

Vitamin D: 0mcg

Time: 15 minutes

Serving Size: 4

Ingredients:

- 4 oz rice noodles
- 45 oz firm tofu, cubed
- 1 cup bok choy
- 1 teaspoon sesame oil
- 1 cup carrots, thinly sliced
- ½ cup red bell peppers, chopped
- 2 medium celery sticks, sliced
- 2 spring onions, sliced
- ½ teaspoon ginger, grated
- ½ garlic clove, finely sliced
- 1 tablespoon peanuts, crushed
- 1 tablespoon light soy sauce
- 1 teaspoon sweet soy sauce

Directions:

1. Cook the rice noodles according to package instructions. Drain and set aside
2. Heat a large frying pan or wok over high heat. Add sesame oil. Add the tofu cubes and soy sauce. Saute until the tofu is golden brown.
3. Add carrots, bell peppers, celery, spring onion, garlic, ginger, and peanuts. Add a dash of water. Place a lid over the pan and simmer until the veggies have softened slightly.
4. Add the bok choy and continue cooking for 1 minute. Stir the pot occasionally so that the bottom does not burn.
5. Stir in the noodles and cook until the noodles have warmed.
6. Serve warm.

One Pot Keto Veggie Soup

Nutritional Information:

Total fat: 2.4g

Cholesterol: 1mg

Sodium: 59mg

Total carbohydrates: 33.7g

Dietary fiber: 8.7g

Protein: 11.9g

Calcium: 63mg

Potassium: 881mg

Iron: 4mg

Vitamin D: 0mcg

Time: 50 minutes

Serving Size: 10

Ingredients:

- 2 cups cauliflower florets
- 2 carrots, peeled and chopped
- 2 celery stalks, thinly sliced
- 1 red bell pepper, chopped
- 1 zucchini, chopped
- 2 tomatoes, diced
- ½ cup onion, chopped
- 4 garlic cloves, minced
- 2 cups cabbage, chopped
- 1 tablespoon olive oil
- 1 tablespoon tomato paste
- 1 15-oz can kidney beans, rinsed and drained
- 4 cups low-sodium vegetable broth
- ¾ teaspoon smoked paprika
- 2 teaspoons Italian seasoning
- Chopped parsley for serving
- Salt and pepper to taste

Directions:

1. Add olive oil to large pot and place over medium heat. Add onion and garlic. Season with salt and pepper. Saute until onions become translucent or for 5 minutes. Add tomato paste and cook for 1 minute.
2. Add all remaining ingredients except parsley. Stir to combine. Cover the pot and cook on high heat for 15 minutes.
3. Taste and add more salt and seasoning to preference. Allow to cook over low heat until liquid reduces by half.
4. Spoon into bowls, garnish with parsley, and drizzle with olive oil to serve.

Keto Zucchini Lasagna

Nutritional Information:

Total fat: 35.6g

Cholesterol: 2mg

Sodium: 321mg

Total carbohydrates: 20.3g

Dietary fiber: 7.1g

Protein: 6.7g

Calcium: 74mg

Potassium: 699mg

Iron: 3mg

Vitamin D: 0mcg

Time: 1 hour 15 minutes

Serving Size: 10

Ingredients:

- 3 large zucchini, thinly sliced with a mandolin
- 3 cups marinara sauce
- 3 cups macadamia nuts
- 2 tablespoons nutritional yeast
- 2 tablespoons lemon juice
- 2 tablespoons olive oil
- ½ cup fresh basil
- 2 teaspoons dried oregano
- ½ cup of water
- Salt and pepper to taste

Directions:

1. Preheat your oven to 375 degrees F.
2. Add macadamia nuts to a food processor and pulse until a fine meal consistency has been achieved. Scrape down sides of bowl if necessary.
3. Add nutritional yeast, basil, lemon juice, oregano, olive oil, salt, pepper, and water, and pulse to a pureed mixture.
4. Pour 1 cup of marinara sauce into a 9 x 13-inch baking dish. Top by lining with the thinly sliced zucchini. Add a layer of macadamia mixture on top.
5. Spread another layer of marinara sauce, top with zucchini, and add more macadamia filling. Continue until the top two layers are zucchini and then marinara sauce.
6. Cover baking dish with aluminum foil and bake for 45 minutes. Remove the aluminum foil and bake for another 15 minutes or until zucchini is easily pierced through with a knife.
7. Cool for 15 minutes before serving. Leftovers can be stored in an airtight container in the refrigerator for up to 3 days or in the freezer for up to 1 month.

Keto Red Pepper Curry

Nutritional Information:

Total fat: 8.4g

Cholesterol: 0mg

Sodium: 16mg

Total carbohydrates: 35.7g

Dietary fiber: 15.9g

Protein: 5.9g

Calcium: 66mg

Potassium: 1267mg

Iron: 2mg

Vitamin D: 0mcg

Time: 25 minutes

Serving Size: 4

Ingredients:

- 3 red bell peppers, chopped into large chunks
- 3 medium eggplants, chopped into large chunks
- 1 cup onion, diced
- 2 large tomatoes, diced
- 2 teaspoons of curry powder
- ⅛ teaspoon cumin
- ⅛ teaspoon coriander
- ⅛ teaspoon ground nutmeg
- ⅛ teaspoon cinnamon
- 1 teaspoon smoked paprika
- 2 garlic cloves, minced
- 1 tablespoon ginger, grated
- 2 tablespoons olive oil

Directions:

1. Add olive oil to large saucepan and place over medium heat. Add onions and saute until translucent.
2. Add eggplant, peppers, garlic, ginger, and all spices. Saute for 3 minutes.
3. Add tomatoes and bring to a boil. Reduce heat and simmer for 10 minutes or until vegetables are soft. Add a small amount of water if the sauce has become too thick. Plate and serve. Can be served over rice or with bread slices.

Easy Vegan Chili Soup

Nutritional Information:

Total fat: 25.3g

Cholesterol: 0mg

Sodium: 557mg

Total carbohydrates: 12.4g

Dietary fiber:3.4g

Protein: 11.4g

Calcium: 170mg

Potassium: 564mg

Iron: 4mg

Vitamin D: 49mcg

Time: 30 minutes

Serving Size: 4

Ingredients:

- 2 cups vegetable broth
- 1 ½ cup coconut milk
- 1 tablespoon coconut sugar
- 10 oz firm tofu, cubed
- ¼ cup red onion, chopped
- ½ cup red bell pepper, chopped
- 3 mushrooms, sliced
- 2 garlic cloves, finely chopped
- ½ tablespoon ginger, finely chopped
- ½ chili pepper, finely chopped
- 2 teaspoon lemon juice
- 1 tablespoon low sodium soy sauce
- ½ cup fresh cilantro, chopped

Directions:

1. Add all vegetables, vegetable broth, coconut milk and coconut sugar to a large pot.
2. Bring to a boil over medium heat and cook for 5 minutes.
3. Add tofu and cook for 5 more minutes
4. Remove pot from heat. Add soy sauce, lime juice, and cilantro. Stir and serve. Leftovers can be stored in an airtight container in the refrigerator for up to 5 days.

Mashed Cauliflower

Nutritional Information:

Total fat: 5.2g

Cholesterol: 0mg

Sodium: 918mg

Total carbohydrates: 15.5g

Dietary fiber: 5.7g

Protein: 7.9g

Calcium: 100mg

Potassium: 723mg

Iron: 1mg

Vitamin D: 0mcg

Time: 25 minutes

Serving Size: 4

Ingredients:

- 1 large head cauliflower, chopped into large chunks
- 1 cup vegetable broth
- 2 tablespoons vegan butter
- ¼ cup vegan parmesan
- 2 tablespoons unsweetened soy milk
- 4 garlic cloves, grated
- 1 teaspoon salt
- Black pepper
- Chopped parsley for topping

Directions:

1. Add cauliflower, vegetable broth, and garlic to a large pot. Boil over medium heat for 15 minutes.
2. Drain cauliflower/garlic mixture through a colander and transfer to a food processor. Add butter, salt, and vegan parmesan cheese. Process until a smooth consistency is achieved. This consistency should resemble mashed potatoes. Add soy milk if needed.
3. Serve by topping with black pepper, melted butter, and parsley.

Lentil Rice Dinner

Nutritional Information:

Total fat: 4.2g

Cholesterol: 0mg

Sodium: 585mg

Total carbohydrates: 17.6g

Dietary fiber: 4.7g

Protein: 5.9g

Calcium: 18mg

Potassium: 44mg

Iron: 1mg

Vitamin D: 0mcg

Time: 35 minutes

Serving Size: 6

Ingredients:

- 1 cup brown lentils
- 1 cup white basmati rice, rinsed
- 1 ½ tablespoon olive oil
- ¼ cup red onion, finely sliced
- 4 garlic cloves, chopped
- 2 teaspoon cumin
- 2 teaspoon ground ginger
- 1 ½ teaspoon salt
- 1 tablespoon fresh parsley, chopped
- 1 teaspoon allspice
- ½ teaspoon cinnamon
- Water

Directions:

1. Add water and lentils to a pot and bring to a boil over medium heat.
2. While lentils are cooking, heat olive oil in another large pot and saute onions until caramelized.
3. Add garlic and salt until fragrant or for about 2 minutes.
4. Add all spices, salt and 3 and 1/2 cups water. Stir to incorporate.
5. Drain lentils and add to pot with onions. Add rice. Stir. Bring to a simmer then cover pot and allow to cook over low heat for 20 minutes.
6. Fluff with a fork and divided among serving bowls. Drizzle with olive oil and toppings such as diced tomatoes, avocados or parsley.

Quinoa Lentil Chili

Nutritional Information:

Total fat: 3.2g

Cholesterol: 0mg

Sodium: 208mg

Total carbohydrates: 62.8g

Dietary fiber: 14g

Protein: 21.3g

Calcium: 98mg

Potassium: 1296mg

Iron: 6mg

Vitamin D: 0mcg

Time: 1 hour 15 minutes

Serving Size: 12

Ingredients:

- 1 ½ cup quinoa, rinsed and drained
- 1 cup brown lentils, rinsed
- 3 cups vegetable broth
- 1 15-oz can kidney beans, rinsed and drained
- 1 15-oz can black beans, rinsed and drained
- ¼ cup yellow onion chopped
- 1 red bell pepper, diced
- 2 large tomatoes, finely chopped
- ⅛ teaspoon cinnamon
- 3 teaspoons chili powder
- 1 teaspoon cumin
- ¼ teaspoon curry powder
- ½ cup cilantro finely chopped
- 1 teaspoon of olive oil
- Salt and pepper to taste

Directions:

1. Over medium heat, heat olive oil in a large pot. Add garlic and cook for 1 minute or until it becomes fragrant.
2. Add onion and bell peppers and cook for 5 minutes or until onion is translucent.
3. Add tomatoes, cinnamon, chili powder, cumin, curry powder, salt, and pepper.

Bring to a boil and lower heat. Allow to simmer for 8 minutes or until tomatoes start to break apart.

4. Add quinoa, lentils, and vegetable broth. Raise heat and bring to a boil. Reduce heat, cover pot and simmer for up to 40 minutes or until lentils are tender and quinoa expanded.

5. Add kidney beans, black beans, and cilantro. Stir and simmer for 2 more minutes. Serve warm.

Tofu Veggie Dinner

Nutritional Information:

Total fat: 19.7g

Cholesterol: 0mg

Sodium: 80mg

Total carbohydrates: 23.1g

Dietary fiber: 7.6g

Protein: 13.1g

Calcium: 306mg

Potassium: 789mg

Iron: 4mg

Vitamin D: 65mcg

Time: 35 minutes

Serving Size: 2

Ingredients:

- 8 oz tofu, cubed
- 2 mushrooms, sliced
- 2 cups cabbage, shredded
- 1 cup carrots
- 1 red bell pepper, sliced
- 1 cup green beans
- ½ cup yellow onions, sliced
- 2 tablespoons olive oil
- Salt and pepper to taste
- ¼ cup spicy garlic chili sauce (See recipe *Chapter 5: Sauces and Condiments: Spicy Garlic Chili Sauce*)

Directions:

1. Heat olive oil in a skillet over medium heat. Add salt and pepper to season oil. Stir. Add tofu and sear on all sides until the tofu becomes crispy and golden. Remove tofu and set aside.

2. Add mushrooms and onion to the same pan. Saute for 3 minutes. Add remaining vegetables and saute for 5 minutes or until vegetables are just tender but still vibrantly colored.
3. Add spicy garlic chili sauce. Cook for 2 more minutes. Add crisped tofu and cook until warmed.
4. Remove from heat and divide among serving bowls. Can be served over rice or zucchini noodles.

Whole Roasted Cauliflower

Nutritional Information:

Total fat: 7.3g

Cholesterol: 0mg

Sodium: 357mg

Total carbohydrates: 11.4g

Dietary fiber: 5.4g

Protein: 4.3g

Calcium: 53mg

Potassium: 655mg

Iron: 1mg

Vitamin D: 0mcg

Time: 1 hour 30 minutes

Serving Size: 4

Ingredients:

- 1 large whole cauliflower
- 1 cup water
- 2 tablespoons olive oil
- ½ teaspoon salt
- ¼ teaspoon black pepper
- ¼ teaspoon coriander
- ¼ teaspoon cumin
- Fresh parsley to garnish

Directions:

1. Preheat your oven to 425 degrees F.
2. Trim the cauliflower by cutting off the stem and trimming down the bottom so that it stands up straight.

3. Place in a baking pan. Drizzle with 1 tablespoon olive oil and sprinkle with salt, pepper, cumin, and coriander. Pour the water into the bottom of the pan
4. Lightly cover the pan with aluminum foil. Bake for 50 minutes.
5. Carefully remove the foil so that you do not burn yourself with resulting steam. Drizzle with the remaining olive oil and bake for 30 more minutes or until golden brown.
6. Remove from the oven and sprinkle with parsley. Cut the cauliflower into wedges like you would a cake and serve. Can be served with your favorite vinaigrette or other vegan friendly sauce.

Crispy Quinoa Cakes with Chickpea Hummus

Nutritional Information:
Total fat: 12.1g

Cholesterol: 0mg

Sodium: 377mg

Total carbohydrates: 31.1g

Dietary fiber: 3.9g

Protein: 7.7g

Calcium: 44mg

Potassium: 258mg

Iron: 3mg

Vitamin D: 0mcg

Time: 1 hour 20 minutes

Serving Size: 4
Ingredients:
- 1 cup quinoa, rinsed and drained
- 2 cups water
- 2 tablespoons olive oil
- 1 teaspoon cumin
- 1 teaspoon granulated garlic
- ½ teaspoon salt
- ½ teaspoon Italian seasoning
- Chickpea hummus for topping (See recipe *Chapter 5: Sauces and Condiments: Chickpea Hummus*)

Directions:

1. Add rinse quinoa, garlic powder, cumin, Italian seasoning, olive oil, and salt in a medium pot and place over high heat. Stir and bring to boil. Lower heat to low and simmer for 20 minutes or until all the water is gone.

2. Fluff quinoa with a fork and remove pot from heat. Allow to cool in the pot for about 15 minutes.
3. When the quinoa is cool enough to handle, shape into four balls with wet hands. Each ball should be the size of a tennis ball. Place the balls on a baking sheet and press them into one and a half inch thick cakes. Smooth any cracks on the edges and make them tidy.
4. Place in the refrigerator for 15 minutes or overnight. This can be prepared up to 4 days in advance.
5. Place a nonstick skillet over medium heat with olive oil and pansear quinoa cakes. Sear each side until golden brown.
6. Plate and serve with chickpea hummus.

Black Bean Soup

Nutritional Information:

Total fat: 2.3g

Cholesterol: 0mg

Sodium: 221mg

Total carbohydrates: 69.5g

Dietary fiber: 17.1g

Protein: 23.9g

Calcium: 145mg

Potassium: 1722mg

Iron: 6mg

Vitamin D: 0mcg

Time: 40 minutes

Serving Size: 12

Ingredients:

- 3 15-oz cans black beans, undrained
- 1 ½ cup tomato sauce
- ¾ cup vegetable broth
- 1 teaspoon of olive oil
- ½ cup yellow onion, chopped
- 3 garlic cloves, minced
- 1 tablespoon chili powder
- 1 teaspoon dried oregano
- Black pepper to taste

- 2 teaspoons cumin
- ⅛ teaspoon cayenne pepper

Directions:

1. Heat olive oil in a large pot over medium heat and add onions and garlic. Saute for 5 minutes or until onions are translucent.
2. Add all spices. Stir continuously for 30 seconds.
3. Add black beans and tomatoes sauce. The extra juice from the black beans will help the sauce thicken.
4. Bring to a boil then reduce heat to low. Simmer for 25 minutes. Serve warm.

Spicy Vegan Mac and Cheese Dinner

Nutritional Information:

Total fat: 17g

Cholesterol: 0mg

Sodium: 338mg

Total carbohydrates: 19.7g

Dietary fiber: 3.3g

Protein: 8.8g

Calcium: 74mg

Potassium: 362mg

Iron: 4mg

Vitamin D: 0mcg

Time: 1 hour 30 minutes

Serving Size: 8

Ingredients:

- 1 lb of gluten-free, dairy-free pasta
- 2 cups raw cashews
- 4 cups water
- ¼ cup nutritional yeast
- 1 1/4 cup unsweetened almond milk
- 3 garlic cloves, minced
- 1 large jalapeno, deseeded and chopped
- ½ teaspoon ground turmeric
- ½ teaspoon smoked paprika
- 1 teaspoon salt
- 1 teaspoon Dijon mustard
- ½ teaspoon onion powder

- Black pepper to taste

Directions:

1. Soak cashews in water for at least 2 hours.
2. Drain cashews. Add cashews along with garlic, nutritional yeast, almond milk, turmeric, paprika, onion powder, Dijon mustard, salt, and jalapenos to a blender. Blend until a smooth consistency is achieved. This will serve as your cheese mixture.
3. Cook pasta according to package instructions or until al dente. Drain and return to pot.
4. Stir in a costume mixture. Serve.

Black Bean Burgers with Garlic Tahini Sauce

Nutritional Information:
Total fat: 7.8g

Cholesterol: 0mg

Sodium: 301mg

Total carbohydrates: 49.7g

Dietary fiber: 12.6g

Protein: 17.6g

Calcium: 116mg

Potassium: 1131mg

Iron: 4mg

Vitamin D: 0mcg

Time: 40 minutes

Serving Size: 6

Ingredients:
- 1 15-oz can black beans, drained
- ¼ cup red onion, finely diced
- 3 garlic cloves, minced
- 1 large carrot, chopped
- 1 tablespoon flax meal
- 3 tablespoons water
- 1 teaspoon of olive oil
- ¼ cup gluten-free oat flour
- 1 teaspoon cumin
- 1 teaspoon chili powder
- ½ teaspoon salt

- ¼ teaspoon paprika
- ½ teaspoon garlic powder
- 4 tablespoon garlic tahini sauce

Directions:

1. In a small bowl, mix flax meal and water to form egg substitute. Allow to sit in the refrigerator for 5 minutes.
2. Heat olive oil in a large skillet over medium heat. Add carrots, garlic, and onions. Saute for 5 minutes or until onions are translucent. Transfer to a large bowl and set aside. Stir in all spices.
3. Add black beans to a food processor. Blend until you achieve a chunky consistency.
4. Add black beans to the veggie mixture. Stir in the egg substitute and oat flour.
5. Divide into 4 patties and place on a plate. Cover with plastic wrap. Refrigerate for 30 minutes.
6. After 40 minutes are up, place a large skillet over medium heat. Add patties and cook for 5 minutes on each side or until golden brown and heated through.
7. Serve on your favorite gluten-free, dairy-free burger buns with toppings such as avocados, tomatoes, and onions. Use garlic tahini sauce as your spread.

Black Bean Meatloaf

Nutritional Information:

Total fat: 4.6g

Cholesterol: 0mg

Sodium: 68mg

Total carbohydrates: 62.9g

Dietary fiber: 16.1g

Protein: 20.6g

Calcium: 134mg

Potassium: 1447mg

Iron: 6mg

Vitamin D: 0mcg

Time: 1 hour 15 minutes

Serving Size: 6

Ingredients:

- 2 15-oz cans of black beans, rinsed and drained
- ½ cup of gluten free oats

- ½ cup gluten-free oat flour
- ½ cup sweet corn
- 1 red bell pepper, finely chopped
- 1 carrot, chopped
- 3 garlic cloves, minced
- ¼ cup yellow onion, diced
- 1 jalapeno, deseeded and diced
- 3 tablespoon flax meal
- ½ cup water
- 2 teaspoon cumin
- 1 teaspoon dried oregano
- 1 tablespoon chili powder
- ¼ cup cilantro diced + 2 tablespoons
- Salt and pepper to taste
- ⅓ cup salsa verde
- ½ avocado, mashed

Directions:

1. Preheat your oven to 350 degrees F.
2. Prepare a baking pan by lining it with parchment paper.
3. In a small bowl, mix the flax meal and half a cup of water. Place in the refrigerator while you proceed with making the rest of the meatloaf.
4. In a large pan, heat some olive oil over medium heat. Once the oil is hot, add bell peppers, garlic, onion, carrots, and jalapeno peppers. Saute for 5 minutes or until onions are translucent. Transfer to a large bowl and stir in 1/4 cup cilantro and spices.
5. Add black beans to a blender and blend to a smooth consistency. Add pureed black beans to veggies. Also add cumin, oats, oat flour, salt, pepper, and flax meal egg. Stir to mix well.
6. Pour the mixture to the prepared loaf pan. Press and smooth top and sides so that the loaf bakes evenly. Bake for 40 minutes.
7. Remove from oven and allow to cool for 10 minutes.
8. Create salsa verde sauce by combining the remainder of diced cilantro, avocado, and salsa verde in a bowl. Smooth over the black bean loaf when it is time to serve. Can be stored in an airtight container in the freezer for up to 3 months.

Mushroom Wraps with Chipotle Sauce

Nutritional Information:

Total fat: 2g

Cholesterol: 1mg

Sodium: 163mg

Total carbohydrates: 20.3g

Dietary fiber: 42g

Protein: 4.3g

Calcium: 47mg

Potassium: 116mg

Iron: 1mg

Vitamin D: 0mcg

Time: 35 minutes

Serving Size: 5

Ingredients:

- 1 15-oz can refried black beans, warmed
- 5 tortillas, warmed
- 2 large portobello mushrooms, sliced into 1/2 inch thick wedges
- 1 bell pepper, sliced
- 1 small onion, cut into 1/2 inch thick rings
- 2 tablespoons Chipotle in adobo sauce
- 1 teaspoon of olive oil
- 1 garlic clove, minced
- ½ teaspoon cumin
- ½ teaspoon coriander
- Salt to taste

Directions:

1. Preheat your oven to 425 degrees F.
2. Place all prepared veggies on a greased baking sheet.
3. Mix all other ingredients, except refried beans and tortillas, in a small bowl to form chipotle marinade. Pour the marinade over the veggies and toss well to ensure that all sides are well coated. Sprinkle lightly with salt.
4. Roast for 20 minutes or until the mushrooms are fork tender.
5. When the tortillas are ready to assemble, generously spread refried beans over tortillas. Divided the mushroom mixture over the tortillas and wrap. Serve. Can be topped with fresh avocado slices or chopped cilantro.

Creamy Broccoli Pasta

Nutritional Information:

Total fat: 4.5g

Cholesterol: 0mg

Sodium: 537mg

Total carbohydrates: 29.4g

Dietary fiber: 6.2g

Protein: 10.8g

Calcium: 179mg

Potassium: 518mg

Iron: 3mg

Vitamin D: 0mcg

Time: 35 minutes

Serving Size: 4

Ingredients:

- 1 package gluten-free, dairy-free pasta
- 4 cups broccoli florets
- 2 tablespoons all-purpose gluten-free flour
- ½ cup vegetable broth
- 1 cup unsweetened almond milk
- ½ teaspoon salt
- Salt and pepper to taste
- ¾ cup vegan parmesan, grated
- 2 tablespoons nutritional yeast
- 1 tablespoon vegan butter
- 4 garlic cloves, minced

Directions:

1. Cook pasta and broccoli in a large pot, according to package instructions until the pasta is al dente. Drain pasta and broccoli and set aside.
2. In the same pot used to cook the broccoli and pasta, melt butter over medium heat. Add garlic and flour and stir until the flour has browned or for 1 minute.
3. Whisk in almond milk and broth until the mixture becomes smooth. Bring to a boil and reduce heat to low. Simmer for 8 minutes or until the sauce has thickened. Season with salt and pepper.
4. When the flour mixture has thickened, whisk in vegan parmesan cheese. Add more salt and pepper if necessary.
5. Stir in pasta and broccoli. Serve immediately. Can be garnished with parsley and extra parmesan.

Chapter 9: Dessert and Snack Recipes

Coconut Cacao Bites

Nutritional Information:

Total fat: 4.4g

Cholesterol: 0mg

Sodium: 5mg

Total carbohydrates: 10.5g

Dietary fiber: 1.8g

Protein: 0.9g

Calcium: 13mg

Potassium: 121mg

Iron: 1mg

Vitamin D: 0mcg

Time: 20 minutes

Serving Size: 10

Ingredients:

- ½ cup shredded coconut
- 2 teaspoon raw cacao
- ½ cup gluten free rolled oats
- 1 small carrot, chopped into large pieces
- 1 small ripe banana, peeled
- 3 dried figs
- 3 dates

Directions:

1. In a food processor, blender carrot, dried figs, and dates until minced. Set aside.
2. In a large bowl, add banana and rolled oats. Mashed the banana with a fork and ensure that it is work incorporated with the rolled oats. Add the carrot mixture and cacao to this bowl. Mix well to form a uniform mixture.
3. Shape into one inch round bites and set on a baking tray.
4. Pour the shredded coconut into a small bowl and roll each bite into the shredded coconut until it's fully coated. Replace on the baking sheet.
5. Serve. These make a great dessert but can also be used as an energizing snack for people who are on the go.

Keto Sugar-free Oatmeal Cookies

Nutritional Information:

Total fat: 21.g

Cholesterol: 0mg

Sodium: 29mg

Total carbohydrates: 7.3g

Dietary fiber: 0.9g

Protein: 1.7g

Calcium: 4mg

Potassium: 64mg

Iron: 1mg

Vitamin D: 0mcg

Time: 1 hour 20 minutes

Serving Size: 22

Ingredients:

- 1 cup gluten-free rolled oats
- ¾ cup almond flour

- 2 ripe bananas
- ¼ cup natural peanut butter
- 1 teaspoon vanilla extract
- ½ cups raisins
- ½ teaspoon ground cinnamon
- ¼ teaspoon salt

Directions:

1. Preheat your oven to 350 degrees F.
2. Prepare a baking sheet by lining it with parchment paper.
3. In a medium bowl, whisk the oats, almond flour, cinnamon and salt.
4. Mash bananas, peanut butter, and vanilla extract together in a large bowl until creamy, well combined mixture is formed.
5. Add the oats mixture and raisins to the banana. Stir with a wooden spoon until well combined.
6. Scoop tablespoons of dough into rough balls and place them on the prepared baking sheet. Press lightly with a fork to flatten slightly
7. Bake for 15 minutes or until light brown at the bottom and soft to touch
8. Allow the cookies to cool completely on a wire rack before serving. Can be stored in an airtight container at room temperature for up to 3 days.

Nutty Keto Crackers

Nutritional Information:

Total fat: 8.8g

Cholesterol: 0mg

Sodium: 122mg

Total carbohydrates: 7.9g

Dietary fiber: 6.6g

Protein: 5.2g

Calcium: 74mg

Potassium: 183mg

Iron: 5mg

Vitamin D: 0mcg

Time: 4 hours

Serving Size: 10

Ingredients:

- 3 tablespoons chia seeds
- 3 tablespoons sunflower seeds

- 3 tablespoons hemp seeds
- 1 cup flax seeds
- 3 tablespoons dried rosemary, finely chopped
- 1 cup water
- ½ teaspoon salt

Directions:

1. Preheat your oven to 200 degrees F.
2. Prepare 2 baking sheets by lining them with parchment paper.
3. Add the flax seeds, chia seeds, and water to a large bowl. Mix well to ensure that all the seeds are coated with water. Let sit for 25 minutes.
4. Add all the other ingredients to the seed mixture and mix well.
5. Spread the mixture thinly on one of the prepared baking sheets using the back of a spoon. Ensure that there are no holes in the layer. Divide the layer into 10 crackers by scoring with a knife.
6. Bake for an hour and a half. Remove the crackers from the over. Place the other baking sheet over the first and flip the layer onto the new baking sheet. Bake for another hour and a half.
7. Turn off the oven and let the crackers sit in the warm oven for 20 more minutes.
8. Remove from the oven and allow to cool completely.
9. Seperate the crackers and serve. Crackers can be stored in an airtight container for up to 7 days at room temperature.

Keto-Friendly Guacamole

Nutritional Information:

Total fat: 23.7g

Cholesterol: 0mg

Sodium: 12mg

Total carbohydrates: 15.2g

Dietary fiber: 9.4g

Protein: 3.2g

Calcium: 28mg

Potassium: 793mg

Iron: 1mg

Vitamin D: 0mcg

Time: 10 minutes

Serving Size: 5

Ingredients:

- 3 small ripe avocados

- ½ cup onion, finely diced
- 2 tablespoons fresh cilantro, chopped
- 2 large Roma tomatoes, diced
- 1 jalapeno pepper, deseeded and finely diced
- 2 garlic cloves, minced
- 1 teaspoon fresh lime juice
- Salt and pepper to taste

Directions:

1. Slice the avocados in half and remove the seeds and skin. Place the halves in a medium bowl.
2. Mash the avocado to the desired consistency with a fork.
3. Add all the other ingredients and mix well.
4. Let the guacamole sit for 5 minutes before serving to let the flavors marinade. Leftovers can be stored in an airtight container in the refrigerator for up to 2 days. Serve as a dip with your favorite vegan-friendly chips or tortillas.

Almond Coconut Keto Crackers

Nutritional Information:

Total fat: 3.2g

Cholesterol: 0mg

Sodium: 17mg

Total carbohydrates: 0.9g

Dietary fiber: 0.6g

Protein: 0.9g

Calcium: 2mg

Potassium: 9mg

Iron: 0mg

Vitamin D: 0mcg

Time: 30 minutes

Serving Size: 10

Ingredients:

- 1 cup almond flour
- 1 tablespoon coconut oil, melted
- 2 tablespoons sunflower seeds
- 1 tablespoon flax meal
- 2 tablespoons water
- Salt to taste

Directions:

1. Preheat your oven to 350 degrees F.
2. Prepare a baking sheet by lining it with parchment paper.
3. Add the almond flour, sunflower seeds, flax meal, and salt to a food processor. Pulse until the sunflower seeds are finely chopped.
4. Add the water and coconut oil into the food processor gradually.
5. Place the dough onto a working surface. Press flat and roll out into a ⅛ inch thick layer.
6. Cut into one inch squares with a knife. Sprinkle with salt.
7. Place the squares onto the prepared baking sheet and bake for 15 minutes or until the edges of the crackers are brown and crisp.
8. Transfer to a wire rack and allow to cool completely before serving. Can be stored in an airtight container at room temperature for up to 3 days.

Vegan Chocolate Chip Cookies

Nutritional Information:

Total fat: 4.5g

Cholesterol: 0mg

Sodium: 4mg

Total carbohydrates: 10.2g

Dietary fiber: 0.5g

Protein: 0.7g

Calcium: 22mg

Potassium: 66mg

Iron: 0mg

Vitamin D: 0mcg

Time: 30 minutes

Serving Size: 14

Ingredients:

- 1 cup almond flour
- 6 tablespoons maple syrup
- 1 teaspoon baking powder
- ¼ cup cornstarch
- 2 tablespoons coconut oil
- 1 teaspoon almond extract
- ¼ cup coconut milk
- ½ cup vegan chocolate chips

Directions:

1. Preheat your oven to 350 degrees F.
2. Prepare a baking sheet by lining it with parchment paper.
3. Add almond flour, baking powder, and cornstarch to a large bowl and mix well.
4. Add coconut oil, almond extract, and maple syrup to a microwave-safe bowl and melt the mixture in the microwave. Mix well.
5. Add the maple mixture and coconut milk to the dry ingredients and mix well. Stir in chocolate chips.
6. With slightly damp hands, form small balls of cookie dough. Place the balls onto the prepared baking sheet. Press balls down lightly.
7. Bake for 15 minutes or until the cookies are lightly browned.
8. Remove from the oven and allow to cool completely in the baking sheet. Can be stored in an airtight container at room temperature for up to 3 days. Can be stored in the refrigerator or freezer for longer.

Flourless Zucchini Brownies

Nutritional Information:

Total fat: 5.2g

Cholesterol: 0mg

Sodium: 3mg

Total carbohydrates: 5.9g

Dietary fiber: 0.5g

Protein: 0.4g

Calcium: 1mg

Potassium: 14mg

Iron: 0mg

Vitamin D: 0mcg

Time: 40 minutes

Serving Size: 18

Ingredients:

- 2 teaspoon vegan cocoa powder
- 1 ¼ cup vegan chocolate chips
- ¼ cup zucchini, grated, squeezed in a cheesecloth to remove all moisture
- ⅓ cup coconut oil
- ¼ cup coconut sugar
- 3 tablespoon cornstarch
- ½ cup applesauce

Directions:

1. Preheat your oven to 350 degrees F.
2. Prepare an 8x8 inch loaf pan with parchment paper. Grease.
3. Add coconut oil and chocolate chips to a small, microwave-safe bowl, and microwave for about 30 - 45 seconds to melt. Stir to a smooth consistency.
4. Transfer the chocolate mixture to a large bowl. Add the apple sauce, zucchini, and coconut sugar. Mix well.
5. Add cocoa powder and cornstarch, and whisk to incorporate well.
6. Pour batter into prepared loaf pan. Bake for 25 minutes or until an inserted toothpick comes out of the center clean. To make gooey brownies, underbake slightly.
7. Remove from the oven and allow the brownies to cool in the pan for 15 minutes. Transfer to a wire rack and cool completely. For gooey brownies, cool overnight in the refrigerator. It is best to store the brownies in the refrigerator for best texture. They can be stored in an airtight container in the freezer as well.

Apple Cinnamon Chips

Nutritional Information:

Total fat: 0g

Cholesterol: 0mg

Sodium: 0mg

Total carbohydrates: 2.3g

Dietary fiber: 0.5g

Protein: 0g

Calcium: 1mg

Potassium: 17mg

Iron: 0mg

Vitamin D: 0mcg

Time: 2 hour 20 minutes

Serving Size: 20

Ingredients:

- 2 Royal Gala apples
- ½ teaspoon ground cinnamon

Directions:

1. Preheat your oven to 220 degrees F.
2. Prepare a baking sheet with parchment paper.

3. Core the apple and then slice with a sharp knife or mandoline slicer.
4. Place the apple slices and cinnamon in a bowl and toss. Ensure that each apple slice is thoroughly coated with cinnamon.
5. Arrange the apple slices in a thin layer on the prepared baking sheet and bake for 1 hour.
6. Remove from the oven, flip the apple slices and bake for another hour.
7. Turn off the oven and leave the apple slices to cool completely in the oven.
8. Serve. Can be stored in an airtight container at room temperature for up to 7 days.

Raw Banana Pudding

Nutritional Information:

Total fat: 47.1g

Cholesterol: 0mg

Sodium: 21mg

Total carbohydrates: 48g

Dietary fiber: 11.2g

Protein: 21.4g

Calcium: 85mg

Potassium: 1117mg

Iron: 5mg

Vitamin D: 0mcg

Time: 5 minutes

Serving Size: 4

Ingredients:

- 2 frozen bananas
- 2 normal bananas
- 2 cups raw peanuts
- 4 dates
- ¾ cup almond milk
- Raspberries for topping, chopped

Directions:

1. Place all ingredients except for topping into a high-powered food processor. Blend until a smooth consistency is reached.
2. Transfer the mixture to a bowl and refrigerate for 2 or more hours.
3. Serve with raspberry topping.

Vegan Chocolate Ice-CReam

Nutritional Information:

Total fat: 18.1g

Cholesterol: 0mg

Sodium: 72mg

Total carbohydrates: 21.7g

Dietary fiber: 3.7g

Protein: 2.9g

Calcium: 34mg

Potassium: 332mg

Iron: 2mg

Vitamin D: 0mcg

Time: 6 hour 20 minutes

Serving Size: 10

Ingredients:

- 3 cups coconut milk, very cold
- ¾ cups vegan cocoa powder
- ⅔ cup maple syrup
- 2 teaspoon vanilla extract
- ¼ teaspoon salt

Directions:

1. Place a freezer-safe container in the freezer so that when the ice-cream is transferred to it, the mixture does not melt. This prevents the formation of ice crystals as the ice-cream freezes.
2. Add all the ingredients to a blender and blend to a smooth and creamy consistency.
3. If you have an ice-cream maker, transfer the mixture to it and use according to manufacturer's instructions. The ice-cream should freeze within 20 minutes. Transfer to the freezer container. Serve immediately or place in the freezer.
4. If you do not have an ice-cream maker, transfer the mixture to the freezer-safe container and freeze for about 6 hours or until the ice-cream is firm. Scoop and serve.

Cranberry Protein Bars

Nutritional Information:

Total fat: 8.2g

Cholesterol: 1mg

Sodium: 18mg

Total carbohydrates: 9.1g

Dietary fiber: 3.1g

Protein: 5.9g

Calcium: 102mg

Potassium: 151mg

Iron: 1mg

Vitamin D: 0mcg

Time: 1 hour

Serving Size: 8

Ingredients:

- ¼ cup dried cranberries
- ¾ cup raw almonds
- ¼ cup date, pitted
- ¼ cup pistachios, unsalted with shells removed
- 1 tablespoon of chia seeds
- 2 tablespoons applesauce
- 1 tablespoon coconut oil
- 1 scoop vanilla protein powder

Directions:

1. Add the almonds and pistachios to a food processor and pulse to coarse, sand-like texture.
2. Add dates and dried cranberries, and pulse for 30 seconds.
3. Add vanilla protein powder, chia seeds, applesauce, and coconut oil to the food processor. Pulse for 30 more seconds.
4. Transfer the mixture to a clean working surface. Place parchment paper over the mixture and roll into a ½ inch thickness.
5. Cut the mixture into 8 bars and transfer the working surface to the freezer. Freeze for 30 minutes.
6. Remove from the freezer and wrap the bars individually in plastic wrap to preserve shape and freshness. Can be stored in the refrigerator for 7 days or in the freezer for 2 months.

Mixed Berry Sorbet

Nutritional Information:

Total fat: 0.8g

Cholesterol: 0mg

Sodium: 6mg

Total carbohydrates: 24.4g

Dietary fiber: 5.2g

Protein: 1.4g

Calcium: 29mg

Potassium: 230mg

Iron: 1mg

Vitamin D: 0mcg

Time: 2 hour 20 minutes

Serving Size: 6

Ingredients:

- 6 cup mixed berries, frozen
- ¾ cup lemon juice
- 1 cup fresh basil
- 1 cup coconut sugar

Directions:

1. Add water and coconut sugar to a medium saucepan. Place over high heat and stir occasionally as the sugar dissolves.
2. Add basil once the sugar has dissolved.
3. Remove the pan from the heat, cover with a lid and let stand for 15 minutes
4. Strain the liquid into a medium bowl. Discard basil. Refrigerate the liquid until cold.
5. In a blender, puree the frozen mixed berries. Add liquid to a blender along with lemon juice to the blender and blend until mixture achieves a smooth consistency.
6. Transfer mixture to a metal 8 inch baking pan. Cover with plastic wrap and free for 2 hours or until the sorbet is thick enough to scoop.

Peanut Butter Chocolate Marble Cake

Nutritional Information:

Total fat: 24.4g

Cholesterol: 0mg

Sodium: 1597mg

Total carbohydrates: 8.2g

Dietary fiber: 3g

Protein: 4.1g

Calcium: 52mg

Potassium: 140mg

Iron: 1mg

Vitamin D: 0mcg

Time: 1 hour 10 minutes

Serving Size: 10

Ingredients:

- 1 ½ cup almond flour
- 1 teaspoon baking powder
- ¼ cup baking soda
- ¼ teaspoon salt
- 3 tablespoon natural creamy peanut butter
- 2 ½ tablespoon vegan cocoa powder
- 1 cup almond milk
- ⅔ cup coconut sugar
- 1 teaspoon vanilla extract
- ½ cup coconut oil, melted
- 1 tablespoon flax meal
- ⅓ cup vegan chocolate chips

Directions:

1. Preheat your oven to 350 degrees F.
2. Prepare a 9 x 5 loaf pan by lining it with parchment paper.
3. Add almond flour, baking powder, baking soda and salt to a large bowl. Whisk.
4. Add almond milk, coconut sugar, vanilla extract, coconut oil, and flax meal to another bowl and mix until the sugar is dissolved.
5. Pout the dry ingredients into the wet mixture and mix until just combined.

6. Transfer half the batter to a medium bowl and add cocoa powder. Mix until just combined. Fold in chocolate chips.
7. In a microwave-safe bowl, melt the peanut butter and add to the other half batter bowl. Mix until just combined.
8. Pour each bowl into opposite sides of prepared loaf pan. Using a spatula, swirl it into the mixtures to form a marble pattern.
9. Bake for 50 minutes to until a toothpick inserted into the center comes out clean.
10. Remove from the oven. Allow the cake to cool for 30 minutes then remove from the pan and transfer to a wire rack. Allow to cool completely then slice and serve.

Vegan Chocolate Pudding

Nutritional Information:

Total fat: 22.9g

Cholesterol: 0mg

Sodium: 57mg

Total carbohydrates: 31.3g

Dietary fiber: 5.2g

Protein: 4g

Calcium: 47mg

Potassium: 571mg

Iron: 4mg

Vitamin D: 0mcg

Time: 10 minutes

Serving Size: 4

Ingredients:

- ½ cup raw cacao powder
- 6 tablespoons maple syrup
- 2 teaspoon vanilla extract
- 1 ½ cup coconut cream
- Salt to taste

Directions:

1. Add coconut cream, cacao powder, and maple syrup to a small saucepan. Place over low heat and whisk until a smooth consistency is achieved. Continue to cook for 2 minutes or until mixture just begins to form small bubbles.
2. Remove from the heat and stir in vanilla extract and salt.
3. Pour mixture into individual containers and chill overnight to set.

Coconut Vanilla Macaroons

Nutritional Information:

Total fat: 4.1g

Cholesterol: 0mg

Sodium: 15mg

Total carbohydrates: 6.1g

Dietary fiber: 1.5g

Protein: 0.7g

Calcium: 24mg

Potassium: 62mg

Iron: 2mg

Vitamin D: 0mcg

Time: 30 minutes

Serving Size: 15

Ingredients:

- 1 teaspoon vanilla extract
- 2 cups unsweetened coconut, shredded
- 1 cup unsweetened almond milk
- 4 tablespoons maple syrup
- 1 tablespoon coconut flour
- 1 tablespoon almond flour

Directions:

1. Preheat your oven to 350 degrees F.
2. Prepare a baking sheet by lining it with parchment paper.
3. Add coconut milk and maple syrup to us a saucepan. Place over medium heat and heat up. Do not bring to a boil. Whisk constantly.
4. Add coconut flour and almond flour, and stir to ensure they are clump-free and evenly combined.
5. Increase to medium heat and bring this mixture to a boil for 3 minutes or until the mixture obtains a thick consistency.
6. Remove from heat and mix in shredded coconut and vanilla extract.
7. Place spoonfuls of the mixture onto the baking sheet.
8. Bake for 15 minutes or until the macaroons are golden brown.
9. Cool and serve.

Chapter 10: Smoothies and Other Beverage Recipes

Smoothies are great as on-the-go breakfast meals since you can pack veggies and fruits into one drink to get all the nutrition you need. They are great as snacks because they taste delicious. They usually take less than 5 minutes to prepare!

Banana-Berry Blast Cauliflower Smoothie

Nutritional Information:

Total fat: 2.2g

Cholesterol: 0mg

Sodium: 121mg

Total carbohydrates: 38.7g

Dietary fiber: 6.1g

Protein: 3.5g

Calcium: 320mg

Potassium: 717mg

Iron: 1mg

Vitamin D: 1mcg

Time: 5 minutes

Serving Size: 3

Ingredients:

- 2 cups cauliflower florets
- 1 cup frozen blueberries
- 1 cup frozen banana slices
- 2 cups sweetened almond milk

Directions:

1. Place the cauliflower florets in a blender and blend until a rice-like consistency is reached.
2. Add the rest of the ingredients and blend until a smooth consistency is reached.
3. Serve immediately.

Cleansing Green Tea Smoothie

Nutritional Information:

Total fat: 12.6g

Cholesterol: 0mg

Sodium: 189mg

Total carbohydrates: 40.9g

Dietary fiber: 14.8g

Protein: 8g

Calcium: 488mg

Potassium: 756mg

Iron: 3mg

Vitamin D: 1mcg

Time: 5 minutes

Serving Size: 1

Ingredients:

- 1 cup unsweetened almond milk
- ½ cup ice
- 1 medium banana, sliced
- ½ teaspoon matcha green tea powder
- 1 tablespoon of chia seeds
- 1 tablespoon stevia powder

Directions:

1. Add all ingredients to a blender and blend until a smooth consistency is achieved.
2. Allow the smoothie to sit for 5 minutes so that the chia seeds can thicken. Serve.

Blueberry Chia Smoothie

Nutritional Information:

Total fat: 12.6g

Cholesterol: 0mg

Sodium: 186mg

Total carbohydrates: 41g

Dietary fiber: 15.2g

Protein: 6.7g

Calcium: 489mg

Potassium: 435mg

Iron: 4mg

Vitamin D: 1mcg

Time: 5 minutes

Serving Size: 1

Ingredients:

- ½ cup frozen blueberries
- ¼ cup frozen raspberries
- 1 tablespoon of chia seeds
- 1 cup unsweetened almond milk
- ½ teaspoon vanilla extract

Directions:

1. Add all ingredients to a blender and blend until a smooth consistency is achieved.
2. Allow the smoothie to sit for 5 minutes so that the chia seeds can thicken. Serve.

Strawberry Oats Smoothie

Nutritional Information:

Total fat: 29.8g

Cholesterol: 0mg

Sodium: 21mg

Total carbohydrates: 32g

Dietary fiber: 6.4g

Protein: 5.5g

Calcium: 37mg

Potassium: 602mg

Iron: 3mg

Vitamin D: 0mcg

Time: 5 minutes

Serving Size: 2

Ingredients:

- 8 fresh strawberries
- ½ cup ice
- 1 cup almond milk
- ½ cup gluten-free rolled oats
- 1 banana
- ½ teaspoon vanilla extract

Directions:

1. Add all ingredients to a blender and blend until a smooth consistency is achieved. Serve immediately.

Peanut Butter Strawberry Smoothie

Nutritional Information:

Total fat: 26g

Cholesterol: 0mg

Sodium: 98mg

Total carbohydrates: 30.6g

Dietary fiber: 6.8g

Protein: 13.3g

Calcium: 163mg

Potassium: 338mg

Iron: 2mg

Vitamin D: 1mcg

Time: 5 minutes

Serving Size: 2

Ingredients:

- ⅓ cup unsalted, natural peanut butter
- 1 cup frozen strawberries
- 1 large banana, sliced and frozen
- 1 cup unsweetened almond milk

Directions:

1. Add the banana slices to a blender and blend until the banana obtains a crumbly texture.
2. Add almond milk and blend until smooth and creamy consistency is achieved. Scrape down the sides of the blender if necessary.
3. Add strawberries and blend well.
4. Add peanut butter and blend for 1 minute.
5. Serve immediately.

Coconut Avocado Smoothie

Nutritional Information:

Total fat: 77.3g

Cholesterol: 0mg

Sodium: 67mg

Total carbohydrates: 46.1g

Dietary fiber: 15.3g

Protein: 9.4g

Calcium: 85mg

Potassium: 1648mg

Iron: 6mg

Vitamin D: 0mcg

Time: 5 minutes

Serving Size: 1

Ingredients:

- ½ medium avocado
- 1 cup unsweetened coconut milk

- 1 small banana
- 1 cup spinach

Directions:

1. Add all ingredients to a blender and blend until a smooth consistency is achieved. Serve immediately.

Breakfast Oatmeal Smoothie

Nutritional Information:

Total fat: 6.8g

Cholesterol: 0mg

Sodium: 1212mg

Total carbohydrates: 35.4g

Dietary fiber: 5.1g

Protein: 6.9g

Calcium: 100mg

Potassium: 274mg

Iron: 3mg

Vitamin D: 0mcg

Time: 5 minutes

Serving Size: 2

Ingredients:

- 1 cup gluten-free rolled oats
- 1 banana
- ½ cup unsweetened almond milk
- 1 tablespoon natural peanut butter
- ½ tablespoon pure maple syrup
- ½ teaspoon vanilla extract
- ½ teaspoon ground cinnamon
- ⅛ tps salt
- ½ cup ice

Directions:

1. Place the oats in the blender first. Pulse a few times until the oats become finely ground.

2. Add the banana, almond milk, peanut butter, maple syrup, vanilla, cinnamon, and salt to the blender. Blend until smooth and creamy consistency is achieved. Scrape down the sides of the blender if necessary. Add the ice last and blend for a few more seconds.
3. Serve immediately.

Green Apple Avocado Smoothie

Nutritional Information:

Total fat: 22.2g

Cholesterol: 0mg

Sodium: 149mg

Total carbohydrates: 60.9g

Dietary fiber: 15.5g

Protein: 5.4g

Calcium: 232mg

Potassium: 1387mg

Iron: 4mg

Vitamin D: 1mcg

Time: 5 minutes

Serving Size: 2

Ingredients:

- 4 cups fresh spinach
- 2 medium green apples, cored and quartered
- 1 medium avocado, peeled and pitted
- 1 cup unsweetened almond milk
- 1 frozen banana, sliced
- ½ teaspoon ginger
- 2 teaspoon maple syrup
- ½ cup ice

Directions:

1. Add all ingredients to a blender and blend until a smooth consistency is achieved. Serve immediately.

Detoxifying Orange Smoothie

Nutritional Information:

Total fat: 57.7g

Cholesterol: 0mg

Sodium: 60mg

Total carbohydrates: 39.7g

Dietary fiber: 11.3g

Protein: 8.4g

Calcium: 149mg

Potassium: 1205mg

Iron: 5mg

Vitamin D: 0mcg

Time: 5 minutes

Serving Size: 1

Ingredients:

- 1 orange, peeled
- ⅓ cup strawberries
- 1 cup raw spinach
- 1 cup almond milk

Directions:

1. Add all ingredients to a blender and blend until a smooth consistency is achieved. Serve immediately.

Apple Pie Smoothie

Nutritional Information:

Total fat: 6.1g

Cholesterol: 0mg

Sodium: 106mg

Total carbohydrates: 25.4g

Dietary fiber: 9.6g

Protein: 3.8g

Calcium: 337mg

Potassium: 374mg

Iron: 3mg

Vitamin D: 1mcg

Time: 5 minutes

Serving Size: 2

Ingredients:

- 1 large green apple, peeled and cored
- ¼ cup raspberries
- ¼ teaspoon cinnamon
- ⅛ teaspoon nutmeg
- 1 cup spinach
- 1 tablespoon of chia seeds
- 1 teaspoon vanilla extract
- 1 cup unsweetened almond milk

Directions:

1. Add all ingredients to a blender and blend until a smooth consistency is achieved. Serve immediately.

Exotic Kale Smoothie

Nutritional Information:

Total fat: 3.2g

Cholesterol: 0mg

Sodium: 35mg

Total carbohydrates: 59.1g

Dietary fiber: 10.5g

Protein: 7.1g

Calcium: 200mg

Potassium: 1149mg

Iron: 4mg

Vitamin D: 0mcg

Time: 5 minutes

Serving Size: 1

Ingredients:

- 1 cup mango, cubed
- 1 orange, peeled
- 1 cup cucumber, chopped
- 1 tablespoon flax seeds
- 1 cup kale, chopped

Directions:

1. Add all ingredients to a blender and blend until a smooth consistency is achieved. Serve immediately.

Ginger Tea

Nutritional Information:

Total fat: 2.6g

Cholesterol: 0mg

Sodium: 37mg

Total carbohydrates: 44g

Dietary fiber: 5.4g

Protein: 3.9g

Calcium: 85mg

Potassium: 628mg

Iron: 5mg

Vitamin D: 0mcg

Time: 35 minutes

Serving Size: 1

Ingredients:

- ½ cup fresh ginger, sliced
- 3 cups water
- 1 tablespoon maple syrup

Directions:

1. Place the ground ginger and water in small saucepan. Bring to a boil over high heat. Reduce heat to medium and simmer for about 25 minutes.
2. Strain ginger slices. Can be discarded or reserved for another use. Stir in maple syrup and serve hot. Tea can be refrigerated and reheated if necessary.

Vegan Chai Latte

Nutritional Information:

Total fat: 1.8g

Cholesterol: 0mg

Sodium: 98mg

Total carbohydrates: 5.5g

Dietary fiber: 0.5g

Protein: 0.5g

Calcium: 162mg

Potassium: 114mg

Iron: 0mg

Vitamin D: 1mcg

Time: 25 minutes

Serving Size: 2

Ingredients:

- 1 tablespoon black tea
- 2 tablespoons chai spice blend
- 2 cups water
- 1 cup unsweetened almond milk
- 2 teaspoon maple syrup

Directions:

1. Add black tea, chai spices, and water to a medium saucepan. Bring to a boil over high heat. Reduce the heat to low and simmer for 15 minutes.
2. Remove the pan from the heat and add the almond milk and maple syrup. Stir and allow to sit for 3 minutes.
3. Pour into 2 mugs using a fine mesh strainer. Add more maple syrup if desired. Serve warm.

Pumpkin Spice Latte

Nutritional Information:

Total fat: 29g

Cholesterol: 0mg

Sodium: 22mg

Total carbohydrates: 18.2g

Dietary fiber: 4g

Protein: 3.3g

Calcium: 39mg

Potassium: 426mg

Iron: 3mg

Vitamin D: 0mcg

Time: 10 minutes

Serving Size: 2

Ingredients:

- ⅓ cup pumpkin puree
- 1 cup unsweetened almond milk
- ¼ teaspoon vanilla extract
- 1 tablespoon maple syrup
- ½ teaspoon coconut sugar
- ½ teaspoon nutmeg
- ¼ teaspoon cloves

Directions:

1. Add all the ingredients to a medium pot and mix well. Bring to a boil over medium heat then let simmer for 6 minutes on low heat. Stir constantly to ensure that the pot does not overflow.
2. Remove from the heat and let cool. Serve warm.

Carrot Ginger Juice

Nutritional Information:

Total fat: 0.4g

Cholesterol: 0mg

Sodium: 224mg

Total carbohydrates: 33.2g

Dietary fiber: 8.4

Protein: 3.7g

Calcium: 130mg

Potassium: 1161mg

Iron: 2mg

Vitamin D: 0mcg

Time: 5 minutes

Serving Size: 1

Ingredients:

- 4 large carrots
- 1 piece ginger, thumb-sized
- 1 cup spinach

Directions:

1. Using a juicer, juice the carrots and ginger. Once a smooth consistency has been reached, add the spinach and juice for 30 more seconds.
2. Pour into a glass and serve.

Cucumber Kale Lemonade

Nutritional Information:

Total fat: 0.6g

Cholesterol: 0mg

Sodium: 36mg

Total carbohydrates: 16.3g

Dietary fiber: 2.8g

Protein: 1.7g

Calcium: 56mg

Potassium: 373mg

Iron: 1mg

Vitamin D: 0mcg

Time: 1 hour 5 minutes

Serving Size: 3

Ingredients:

- ½ cup lemon juice
- 3 cups water
- 2 stalks celery, chopped
- 1 cup kale, chopped
- 2 cups cucumber, chopped
- 1 apple, cored and chopped

Directions:

1. Add all the ingredients to a blender and blend to achieve a uniform consistency.
2. Refrigerate for 1 hour then serve.

Mint Grapefruit Juice

Nutritional Information:

Total fat: 0.3g

Cholesterol: 0mg

Sodium: 2mg

Total carbohydrates: 19.7g

Dietary fiber: 3g

Protein: 1.4g

Calcium: 26mg

Potassium: 331mg

Iron: 1mg

Vitamin D: 0mcg

Time: 5 minutes

Serving Size: 4

Ingredients:

- 2 cups grapefruit juice
- 1 large cucumber
- 1 large apple
- 5 mint leaves

Directions:

1. Add all the ingredients to a juicer and blend until a smooth, uniform consistency is achieved.
2. Can be served as is or over ice.

Orange Strawberry Infused Water

Nutritional Information:

Total fat: 0.3g

Cholesterol: 0mg

Sodium: 15mg

Total carbohydrates: 8.9g

Dietary fiber: 3.2g

Protein: 1.4g

Calcium: 78mg

Potassium: 228mg

Iron: 3mg

Vitamin D: 0mcg

Time: 2 hours 5 minutes

Serving Size: 4

Ingredients:

- 6 strawberries, sliced
- 1 orange, sliced
- 4 cups water
- 10 mint leaves

Directions:

1. Place all the ingredients into a glass jar, stir, and refrigerate for at least 2 hours. Overnight works best because the longer this sits, the more flavorful the water becomes.
2. Serve with or without the fruit still going in the liquid.

Blackberry Sage Infused Water

Nutritional Information:

Total fat: 0.2g

Cholesterol: 0mg

Sodium: 8mg

Total carbohydrates: 3.8g

Dietary fiber: 2.1g

Protein: 0.6g

Calcium: 26mg

Potassium: 66mg

Iron: 0mg

Vitamin D: 0mcg

Time: 5 minutes

Serving Size: 4

Ingredients:

- 1 cup blackberries, chopped
- 10 sage leaves
- 4 cups water
- 1 cup ice

Directions:

1. Add the blackberries and sage to the bottom of a glass jar. Cover with the ice and water. Stir.
2. Serve.

Conclusion

So there you have it, your complete guide and cookbook to a plant-based, vegan diet and lifestyle. I hope that you feel more confident and comforted in knowing that your life does not have to be controlled by the use of animal-based products any longer. You do not have to use them, wear them, have them in your home (unless they are your beloved furry best friend) or eat them. I hope that this book has given you a newfound awareness to the simple lifestyle and diet changes that you can make to eliminate animal products from your life so that you can live happier and healthier.

Using animal-based products not only contributes negatively to the environment, climate, and world hunger issues, but it also takes a toll on your body. You do not have to live this way and now that you have seen just how delicious and mouth-watering vegan meals can be, and how easy the transition to a plan-based lifestyle can be, I hope that you take the steps necessary to make the switch today. Do not be confused or disheartened by the misinformation that exists about veganism. Now that you know better, you can take the steps necessary for changing your life and your diet.

Having gained this wealth of wisdom, it is time to put it into practice. It does not have to be hard or overly complicated. Take it one step and one recipe at a time and go at a pace that is comfortable for you. Experiment with the recipes and come up with some of your own. Half the fun of the vegan lifestyle is experimenting with your cooking skills.

Once again, thank you for downloading this book. My wish is that you take the tools provided in this book to take control of your life and your eating habits, not only because animals will be treated less cruelly and remain unharmed, but as a way for you to improve your general health and wellness holistically as well.

Vegan Keto

The Complete 100% Plant-Based Whole Foods Ketogenic Diet. Tasty Low Carb Recipes Cookbook to Nourish Your Mind and Promote Weight Loss Naturally. (21-Day Time Saving Meal Plan Included)

Introduction

Veganism is a vegetarian diet that excludes the use of products derived from animals including but not limited to their meat, dairy products, and eggs. Veganism is a popular diet, and this is due in part to its many health-related benefits, which include:

- Reducing the risk of developing cardiovascular diseases such as heart disease, stroke and high blood pressure. Veganism promotes the consumption of fruits, vegetables, whole grains, nuts and legumes, all of which provide valuable nutrition that improves cardiovascular function and therefore, lowers the risk of developing cardiovascular diseases.
- Providing valuable nutrition that is often deficit in normal eating routines. We live in a fast-paced world and often our diet, and therefore overall health, suffer as a result. Veganism allows you to be more conscious of what you eat and to obtain higher amounts of nutrients like fiber, potassium, magnesium, vitamin A, vitamin C, vitamin D and antioxidants that are often missing in "convenient" products that are on store shelves and available at fast-food restaurants.
- Providing protection against certain cancers. The same products on store shelves and in fast-food restaurants that claim to be convenient are often detrimental to your health in the long run as they introduce unsafe products to the diet. Poor diet practices often lead to cancer development. Therefore, the healthier consumption of food products on the vegan diet significantly lowers the risk of developing

certain cancers, namely breast, prostate and colon cancer.

- Decreasing inflammation throughout the body. Raw foods are often consumed on a vegan diet. In fact, there is a type of veganism whereby the practitioner consumes only raw food products. Raw foods are rich in antioxidants and probiotics which helps decrease chronic inflammation, which is an overreaction of the immune system. This can also decrease the symptoms of rheumatoid arthritis which include swelling, joint pain and morning sickness.

These are only a few of the many health benefits gained by practicing veganism. Others include improved kidney function, lowered blood sugar levels, and decreased risk of developing type 2 diabetes. The benefits of practicing veganism are not just dietary or health-related though. There are many lifestyle benefits as well.

There is a saying that goes, "If you stand for nothing then you will fall for anything." There is a lot that is wrong in this world and many of these injustices are perpetrated in the name of helping humanity and advancing our way of life. One of the greatest injustices that has going on throughout the ages is the killing, torture, and harm of animals to sustain human life. Animals should not have to suffer so that we can eat or be protected from the elements when there are alternative sources for food, clothing, shelter and more that are naturally given. Animals should not suffer so that we can purchase clothing, wear makeup, or use sanitary products. Animals should not be treated cruelly or die simply because we want to live a certain lifestyle. Especially if living that lifestyle can be attained by much safer, greener, and animal cruelty-free means.

In the same regard, deforestation should not be rampant, the use of global resources should not be strained and the protection of the environment should be paramount. However, that is not the way it is. Instead, deforestation is a growing problem, the strain on global resources is becoming heavier, and the environment continues to suffer. This happens all in the name of farming and the upkeep of livestock and other animals.

Going vegan can completely change the world and the way it operates. Going vegan does not just describe a diet. It describes a lifestyle. It goes way past what we choose to eat and extends to how we live. Being a vegan means that you completely stop supporting practices that exploit animals for profit or gain. Just as human beings have the right to live freely and happily, these rights should be extended to our animal counterparts. They are an essential part of the circle of life and killing or harming them will ultimately harm humanity and the Earth itself.

This book is about showing you what it means to be vegan as well as how you can lose weight naturally and quickly from a popular diet that seems to go against everything a vegan lifestyle entails. This diet is called the ketogenic diet. The ketogenic diet is a high-fat diet that promotes the reduction of carbohydrates so that the body can use energy in a more efficient and cleaner way. Even though this is a high-fat diet, it is very effective at helping the practitioner lose weight safely and naturally.

Unfortunately, the "gurus" of the ketogenic diet often promote the consumption of animals and their byproducts to achieve the benefits that this diet offers. The good news is that you as a vegan can still hold your ideals for practicing a vegan lifestyle while reaping the benefits of the ketogenic diet. This book was created to show you how you can do this without ever harming or consuming animals and their byproducts.

What you will learn in this book

- The difference between the ketogenic diet and the vegan diet
- What is the ketogenic vegan diet
- The benefits of practicing the keto vegan diet
- What it means to live a keto vegan lifestyle
- The steps you can take before starting such a lifestyle
- How you can lose weight naturally with the keto vegan diet
- The foods to eat and to avoid on the ketogenic vegan diet
- A 21-day meal plan
- How to prepare and store food on the keto vegan diet
- How to grocery shop to suit your keto vegan lifestyle, including a comprehensive shopping list
- Recipes for breakfast, lunch, dinner, smoothies, desserts and more

In addition to being a comprehensive guidebook for the transition into a keto vegan lifestyle, this book provides tasty recipes that have a powerful effect on your body as it relates to weight loss and improving overall health. Eating healthy does not translate into boring, tasteless food. You can lose weight, improve your cardiovascular health, improve your kidney function and the host of many other health-related benefits of veganism while still treating your taste buds to something good and delicious with every single meal. In the upcoming pages, you will find over 100 recipes for breakfast, lunch, dinner, dessert, snacks and more that will delight your taste buds, help you lose weight, improve your mental function, help elevate your mood and more!

Thank you for downloading this book. My hope is that you gain extreme value with every word that you read so that you can live a healthier and happier life while upholding ideals that will benefit not only the planet and animals but future generations as well.

Chapter 1: Introduction to Keto Veganism

With a surface glance, the ketogenic diet, a diet which thrives off of receiving higher amounts of fat and protein from mainly animal-based products and the vegan diet, which is one that strictly forbids the use of any animal-based products, seem to have nothing in common. But things are hardly ever as they seem from first glance. Take a deeper look and you will see how combining these two diets can completely change your life and improve your health holistically.

What is the Ketogenic Diet?

The human body needs fuel to perform. This fuel often comes in the form of carbohydrates. The simplest form of carbohydrate is called sugar. The cycle of getting energy from sugar starts with the consumption of food that contains sugar. This causes a spike in insulin levels and the liver turns sugar into fat. As the sugar enters the bloodstream, it causes blood pressure to rise. In addition, the consumption of sugar has an effect similar to heroin on the brain. It makes the consumer feel happy because the brain produces high levels of the hormone called dopamine in response to its presence.

As a result, the person experiences high levels of energy, elevated mood, and a feeling similar to a drug user's high. This effect does not last long. Insulin levels begin to rapidly fall and so the person feels very tired as their energy levels decrease. Their mood also changes as dopamine levels begin to fall.

In response, the body demands more sugar which starts a chronic cycle of addiction and dependency on sugar. Sugar is eight times more addictive than cocaine and having a sweet tooth may be more dangerous than you realize. Most people do not even realize that they are addicted to sugar but there are signs that clearly indicate a sugar addiction and they include:

- Craving comfort food in response to both high and low times in your life.
- Craving sweet foods and beverages.
- Rewarding accomplishments with sugary food.
- Experiencing physical withdrawal symptoms when going without sugary foods for even a short amount of time.
- Trying to stay away from sugary foods unsuccessfully
- Binge eating sugary foods.

The Consequences of Sugar Addiction

Sugar has many negative effects on the body. They include:

- Causing the growth of bacteria in the mouth which can lead to bad breath and cavities.
- Increasing the risk of developing cardiovascular diseases. This is caused by the extra insulin that excessive sugar intake produces. This extra insulin causes the walls of blood vessels to grow faster than normal and become rigid. The resulting tautness of the blood vessels, narrow space available for blood to travel. This places extra stress on the heart, which can lead to cardiovascular diseases such as heart attack and stroke.
- Increasing the risk of developing type 2 diabetes. Insulin is produced by the pancreas, which works overtime when excessive sugar is introduced into the body. This can lead to the development of type 2 diabetes.
- Increasing the risk of kidney damage. The kidneys filter blood sugar and the extra work resulting from the excessive intake of sugar can cause damage.
- Causing erectile dysfunction in men. The function of the cardiovascular system becomes impaired due to excessive insulin levels. This causes interruptions in the blood supplied to the groin, which causes impaired sexual function.
- Causing inflammation, which can cause joint pain and increase the risk of developing rheumatoid arthritis. Inflammation also causes the skin to age faster because it breaks down proteins in the skin and causes the creation of harmful molecules called Advanced Glycation End-products (AGEs). These molecules cause the skin to lose its elasticity and therefore, to form wrinkles.

These are only a few of the negative effects that excessive intake of sugar can cause. These negative consequences extend to sugar's contribution to excessive weight gain and obesity.

Obesity and its Health Implications

Obesity is a disease that occurs when a person carries excessive body weight or body fat which has adverse effects on their health.

Unfortunately, this is a far-reaching disease. More than 90 million Americans were affected by obesity between the years 2015 and 2016 in the US. It was estimated that 1 in 5 adults were morbidly obese in the United States in 2017. These are truly staggering figures because no one is born obese or has to become obese! Obesity is often a consequence of lifestyle and diet choices, both of which are normally within a person's control.

Obesity is determined by the use of body mass index also known as BMI. BMI is an assessment of whether or not a person carries the appropriate amount of weight for their age and height. A BMI of 30 and over means that a person is obese. A BMI between 25 and 29.9 indicates that a person is carrying excess weight but is not yet obese. A BMI between 18.5 and 24.9 indicates that a person carries a healthy weight. A BMI that is below 18.5 means that a person is underweight and needs to gain weight.

The implications of obesity are far-reaching. This disease does not occur in isolation. It increases the risk of developing many other health complications such as:

- Cardiovascular disease. This occurs because obesity places a strain on the cardiovascular system. It also causes a rise in blood pressure and cholesterol levels.
- Type 2 diabetes. Excessive weight gain has an adverse effect on the production of insulin and blood sugar levels, which can increase the risk of developing insulin resistance and therefore, type 2 diabetes.
- Sleep apnea. Sleep apnea occurs when a person stops breathing for a few seconds intermittently. Obesity increases the likelihood of developing this condition, which can lead to death.
- Certain cancers. Fat deposits are often seen as a foreign entity by the body and as such, the immune system attacks the body in an effort to get rid of them. This causes the deformation of cells and tissues and produces an environment conducive to the development of cancer cells. As a result, certain cancers such as ovarian, colon, breast, rectum, liver, pancreas, prostate and kidney have been linked to obesity.
- Osteoarthritis. Excessive weight gain places stress on the joints, which increases inflammation and therefore, the risk of developing this condition.
- Digestive issues. A person who is overweight is more likely to develop digestive issues such as problems with liver function, gallbladder disease, and heartburn to name a few.

These are only a few of the negative health implications that are linked to obesity. Luckily, these diseases and obesity can be prevented and reversed by changing your diet and not relying on carbohydrates as your body's primary source of energy and fuel. The ketogenic diet provides the body with an alternative source of energy that does not have these negative effects.

The ketogenic diet is a low-carb, high-fat and moderate protein diet that places the body in a metabolic state called ketosis. The ketogenic diet is one that entails a daily meal plan that consists of between 5 and 10% carbohydrates, 20 and 25% protein and 70 and 75% fat. On this diet, the average person will consume less than 50 grams of carbohydrates for the day. This forces the person's body to rely on an alternative source of energy rather than carbohydrates. This alternate source is body fat.

The Science Behind Ketosis and How it Aids in Weight Loss Management

The reason that the ketogenic diet is so efficient at not only causing weight loss but improving overall health is that it replaces carbohydrate intake with healthy fat intake. This shifts the body away from metabolizing carbohydrates and towards metabolizing fat in an effort to gain energy. Simply put, when you practice the ketogenic diet, your body no longer uses standard sugar to gain energy but instead burns body fat, which can lead to weight loss in addition to many more significant health benefits.

The ketogenic diet has been around for over 100 years and was initially developed in an effort to fight epilepsy. However, its many other health benefits and its efficiency at causing weight loss cannot be denied.

This diet causes weight loss through a process known as ketosis. Ketosis is a metabolic state that only occurs when foods that are rich in carbohydrates are restricted. This restriction forces the body to look for alternative fuel sources and it turns to fat for that source. Ketosis can occur naturally such as when a person is fasting, during pregnancy or during starvation. If you have ever skipped a meal or two or partook in strenuous exercise then you have likely undergone this process unknowingly. Practicing the ketogenic diet is a less extreme way of forcing the body to seek out alternative sources of energy.

The process is so named because the fat molecules transformed into an energy source are called ketones. Ketones are fat-derived energy molecules that are generated in the liver and flows through the bloodstream. When the term 'ketones' or 'ketone bodies' is used, it typically refers to three main types. The first two are called acetoacetate and beta-hydroxybutyrate. They are more abundant that the third type, which is called, acetone.

Ketones are always present in the blood, but their presence increases dramatically when there are conditions that force the body away from metabolizing carbohydrates. They are used by the major organs such as the brain, heart, and kidney. Ketosis and therefore, ketones are particularly important to the brain because the brain has no other way of deriving energy apart from the metabolism of carbohydrates and fats.

How Ketosis Occurs

Before the process of ketosis is activated, gluconeogenesis occurs. Gluconeogenesis is the process whereby used non-carbohydrate components like amino acids, which are the units from which proteins are made, produce energy. This process occurs when sugar intake is limited and glycogen, which is your body's storage of sugar is being used. As glycogen becomes depleted, gluconeogenesis increases and jumpstarts the fat burning process even though ketone production does not yet occur at this point.

The next stage occurs when glycogen is completed depleted. Gluconeogenesis completely takes over and ketones begin to be produced in low quantities. This is called the gluconeogenic phase.

As the body does not get supplied with sufficient carbohydrates, ketosis occurs. This is characterized by a decrease in the use of non-carbohydrate components like amino acids to create energy and a complete shift to prioritizing the production of ketones.

Ketones are formed in the liver as fat cells get broken down in a process called ketogenesis. The first ketone that is produced is acetoacetate. Acetoacetate is then converted to beta-hydroxybutyrate, or BHB for short, and acetone. As your body adapts to gaining energy from ketosis, BHB becomes the most common ketone. When you full adapted to ketosis, ketones provide up to 50% of the body's base energy while catering to up to 70% of the brain's energy needs.

How Ketosis Causes Weight Loss

It might be difficult to understand how a diet can recommend the consumption of fat to lose weight while traditional diets preach the exact opposite. This might seem like madness to an outside observer. However, taking a closer look shows that the ketogenic diet promotes the burning of fat to form ketones, which leads to natural weight loss.

Also, because of the foods that are recommended for consumption are high in healthy fat and protein, the practitioner is left feeling fuller and more satisfied after every meal. This leads to not overeating and therefore, better weight reduction and metabolic health.

It also creates a reduction in appetite as well so that the person does not overeat by indiscriminately reaching for snacks during the day. Unfortunately, the most convenient snacks that are available happen to be those loaded in carbohydrates. Even if the person has healthy snack options but indulges is sweets too often, the results are often linked to weight gain. On the ketogenic diet, appetite is curbed to lessen the likelihood of reaching for unhealthy snacks or for snacking too much.

One of the most common problem areas that people experience when losing weight is the belly area. Belly fat consists of visceral fat, which is a type of fat that encases internal organs around the abdominal area. The build-up of this type of fat has been linked to the development of type 2 diabetes and heart disease. The ketogenic diet makes it possible to eliminate visceral fat because visceral fat production has been closely linked to the consumption of carbohydrates and refined sugars. Both of these are discouraged on the ketogenic diet which leads to a reduction of the development of this type of fat and therefore, weight loss in the abdominal area as well as all over the body.

Other Benefits of Ketosis

Ketosis is not just about fat burning. It has many serious and positive implications for your health and wellness. They include:

- The stimulation of mitochondrial production. Mitochondria are the part of body cells that generate the chemical energy needed to facilitate the cell's biochemical reactions. New mitochondria are synthesized in cells that used ketones as a fuel. This is especially prominent in brain cells. The formation of more mitochondria helps improve energy production and the overall health of cells.
- Ketones function similarly to an antioxidant. An antioxidant is a substance that removes potentially damaging oxidizing agents from forming in the body. Oxidation is a chemical process that occurs in cells and can produce free radicals, which are chemicals that damage cells. Vitamin C and E are popular antioxidants. Ketones produce less reactive oxygen and therefore, less free radicals than sugar and thus protects cells from damage.
- The protection and regeneration of nervous system cells. Ketosis aids in regenerating damaged nerve cells as well as preserving the function of aging nerve cells.
- Aids in preventing certain cancers. Most cancer cells cannot use ketones as fuel and therefore, die because they have nothing to facilitate their growth. This aids the immune system in removing them from the body.
- Aids in improving brain function. There have been promising studies on how the ketogenic diet and ketosis improve the brain function in people with autism, epilepsy, Alzheimer's disease, and Parkinson's disease, This can be attributed to the fact that the brain uses energy derived from ketones more effectively than it does with energy obtained from sugar. Ketosis also has an inhibitory effect on nerve cells, which makes the brain less excitable and therefore, more efficient in its function.
- Triggers the process of autophagy. Autophagy means "self-eating". It is the process whereby the body cleans out damaged cells and toxins in addition to regenerating new, healthier cells. Damaged cells and toxins accumulate over time if this process does not work efficiently. This causes several negative effects such as inducing dementia, increasing the risk of developing certain cancers and accelerating aging. Consuming more fat on the ketogenic diet activates autophagy because your cells

become more efficient at cleaning out old cells and regenerating new ones once it stops relying on carbohydrates to provide energy.

How The Keto Ketogenic Diet and Vegan Diets Differ

Both the ketogenic and vegan diets are great for their aid in weight loss management. However, individually, they take different approaches to doing so. The ketogenic diet, also known as the keto diet, emphasizes the consumption of fat and moderate protein. The most abundant sources of these are animal products like chicken, beef and fish, and animal-based products such as dairy products.

The vegan diet is completely different. It promotes the reduction of weight through plant-based eating and eliminates all food that comes from animal sources. The vegan diet is one that is rich in vegetables, fruits, and whole grains. Most vegans extend their diet into a lifestyle and do not use any products that involve the abuse, harm, or misuse of animals and their products.

However, these two diets can be paired as quite the winning team for weight loss and improve overall health.

What is the Keto Vegan Diet?

While veganism is one of the healthiest diets because it promotes the consumption of naturally given animal-based products, the ketogenic diet is more effective for weight loss. Unfortunately, the ketogenic diet is not as environmentally-safe as the vegan diet. The keto vegan diet takes what is great about both of these diets and combines them into one diet that allows the practitioner to still eat healthy, clean and environmentally-safe while losing weight quickly and efficiently.

The keto vegan diet, also called the ketogenic vegan diet, is a high-fat, moderate protein and low carbohydrate diet that entails eating vegetable-based products only. This diet allows the practitioner to reap all the benefits of the ketogenic diet while still decreasing animal abuse and death, decreasing the carbon footprint and improving overall health.

This diet is so effective at allowing vegans to lose weight quickly and efficiently because it limits carbohydrate consumption to less than 50 grams per day. This is done through the consumption of low carb vegetables like cauliflower and broccoli and vegan-friendly protein sources like tofu, seeds, and nuts.

Unfortunately, many vegan-friendly favorites are filled with carbohydrates that defy the purpose of practicing the ketogenic diet. Some of these vegan-friendly favorites that are prohibited on the ketogenic diet include:

- Fruits such as bananas and apples.
- Natural sweeteners such as maple syrup and agave.
- Starchy vegetables such as potatoes and yams.
- Grains such as wheat, rice, and corn.
- Legumes like black beans and lentils.

All of these products are strictly prohibited on the ketogenic diet because they kick your body out of ketosis in order to metabolize the carbohydrates.

I will provide a comprehensive list of foods that are to be avoided and those to be consumed on the keto vegan diet, later on in this book. However, I will concentrate on how you can get enough fat to facilitate ketosis on the keto vegan diet in this section. Plant-based oils are a common replacement for animal fats in the keto vegan diet. They are commonly used in cooking, baking, making dressing, desserts, and a lot more. Here is a list of a few of these oils and how you can use them to make tasty dishes.

Olive oil. Olive oil is one of the healthiest oils that humans can consume because it is rich in monounsaturated fatty acids. It is great for stir-frying, sautéing, making dressings, sauces and condiments, baking and more. It can be used in both sweet and savory dishes. The benefits of this oil are far-reaching and extend past aiding in weight loss. It is also rich in antioxidants, has anti-inflammatory properties, helps improve cardiovascular health, and aids in reducing the development of type 2 diabetes.

Avocado oil. Avocado oil is rich in healthy monounsaturated fats and has a very high smoke point which is great for cooking, baking, and deep-frying. In addition to facilitating ketosis, this oil helps reduce cholesterol to improve heart health, enhances the absorption of fat-soluble nutrients, is rich in an antioxidant that helps improve eye health, and helps reduce the symptoms of arthritis.

Coconut oil. This oil is abundant in several types of fatty acids which is great for providing a fuel source for ketosis to occur. It is great for baking and cooking, for making desserts and as a primary ingredient in fat bombs. Recipes for fat bombs can be found in the dessert chapter. Coconut oil helps lower blood sugar levels, decreases the risk of developing type 2 diabetes, boosts good cholesterol, improves liver health and aids in digestion.

MCT oil. MCT stands for medium-chain triglycerides, which is a saturated fatty acid that skips the digestive process and goes straight to the liver where it is converted to ketones in the ketosis process. MCT oil is derived from coconut oil and palm oil and is a great addition to sauces, condiments, smoothies, fat bombs, salad dressings, and even hot drinks like coffee and tea. It is a potent energy booster.

Red palm oil. This can also be used as a vitamin supplement because it is a great source of both vitamin A and E. It enhances the flavor of several dishes because it has a mild buttery texture and carrot-like flavor. It is good to note that you should purchase red palm oil which is RSPO certified or a certified sustainable palm oil product as some of these products are made in environmentally unsafe ways.

Vegans are not limited to consuming plant-based oils to get the necessary intake of fat to facilitate ketosis. Avocados, nuts, seeds, and vegan dairy alternatives are also great sources of fat in addition to being packed with vitamins, minerals, and antioxidants.

Obtaining the necessary protein is also a concern on the keto vegan diet as animal products, which are the most common source of proteins is prohibited. Here are a few vegan-friendly protein sources that are safe to consume on the keto vegan diet:

- Tofu. Tofu is made from soybeans and is an excellent source of calcium and protein. It is a common substitute for meat, poultry, and fish because it can assume a texture that is similar and is great for absorbing flavor as it sucks up flavors from a marinade like a sponge.
- Tempeh. This is a fermented form of soy. It is firmer than tofu and has a grainy texture. It makes a great substitute for fish and ground beef.
- Seitan. This is a less common meat substitute that is made from wheat gluten, soy sauce, ginger, garlic, and seaweed. It is a great source of iron and protein. However, it must be noted that this protein substitute contains gluten and needs to be avoided if you have a sensitivity to gluten.
- Nuts and seeds. Examples of these include pumpkin seeds, pistachios, almonds, and flax seeds. They are naturally packed with protein. However, you should be careful with their consumption because they do contain some carb content. While peanuts are technically a legume, they are a low carb and high protein source and can be consumed in moderate quantities on the keto vegan diet.
- Protein powders. Protein powders are a great way of infusing your diet with protein. They are especially great additions to smoothies. Protein powders that are safe to be consumed on the keto vegan diet should be 100% plant-based protein and organic in nature. Some examples are soybean protein powder, mixed protein powder, or pea protein powder.

Vegan Alternatives to Eggs and Dairy

While the consumption of eggs and dairy are allowed on vegetarian diets, it is strictly prohibited on the vegan diet. Luckily, you can still get the nutrition that these two products provide with dairy replacements such as:

- Coconut cream for heavy cream
- Vegan butter or coconut oil for butter
- Vegan cheese, or nutritional yeast, for dairy-based cheeses
- Vegan soft cheese for cream cheese
- Vegan eggs and flax eggs for the use of eggs
- Nut-based yogurt such as cashew yogurt to replace yogurt and sour cream

Benefits of Keto Vegan Diet

We have discussed the major benefit of effective weight loss on the keto vegan diet. We have also discussed its contribution to lowering the risk of developing cardiovascular diseases and type 2 diabetes. Now, let's take a moment to go more in-depth in the other benefits of practicing this diet. Those benefits include:

- Having more energy throughout the day. On a carb-heavy diet, your body is constantly converting carbohydrates into sugar which elevates your blood sugar levels. While this results in an initial surge of energy, it soon becomes depleted and leaves you feeling less energetic and hungrier at fast intervals. This results in the chronic cycle of craving sugar and carbohydrates to get that energy back. Ketosis works differently from the metabolism of carbohydrates. Energy is maintained at consistent levels without spikes or drops. Also, there are no cravings for carbs on this diet, which leads to fewer feelings of hunger.
- Reducing the possibility of metabolic syndrome. Metabolic syndrome is a group of risk factors that increase your risk of developing heart disease and other related health problems such as type 2 diabetes and stroke. These risk factors include increased blood pressure, abdominal obesity, high blood sugar, high triglyceride (a type of fat) levels, and low HDL (good) cholesterol levels. You will be diagnosed with metabolic syndrome if you suffer 3 or more out of 5 of these risk factors. Practicing the keto vegan diet lowers your chances of developing these risk factors because it changes the way your body processes fat. Instead of being stored, fat is being used efficiently in the fat-converting process of ketosis.
- Improving sleep quality. Ketosis allows you to maintain steady energy levels throughout the day which makes it easier to fall asleep and stay asleep at night. Practicing the keto vegan diet also aids in the production of a chemical in the brain called adenosine, which aids in the regulation of the sleep cycle. This means that you are better able to fall asleep and wake up at the same time consistently every day. This helps with feeling more refreshed when awake and achieving Stage 4 REM sleep, which is the most restful and rejuvenating phase of sleep.
- Aids in making skin healthier and clearer. The consumption of carbohydrates results in inflammation which is one of the most common reasons that acne flare-ups occur. This occurs because insulin levels in the blood spike due to higher blood sugar levels. This results in higher oil production of oil in the skin, which leads to the clogging of follicles and breakouts. Consuming sugars and other carbohydrates also cause the skin to age faster because insulin causes the production of chemicals that erode the skin's elasticity, which causes wrinkles. On the other hand, consuming good fats prevents inflammation and does not induce the production of insulin. This results in fewer breakouts of pimples, blackheads, whiteheads, and other acne symptoms. The skin is also able to better maintain its elasticity. It also helps to soothe dry skin.
- Aids in the maintenance of a healthy digestive system. A healthy digestive system relies on the maintenance of a balanced environment where good bacteria can

thrive, and nutrients are absorbed faster and more effectively. Certain bacteria in the digestive system help provide your body with vitamins such as vitamins K and B12, which are essential in regulating your body's store of minerals like calcium. The metabolism of fat in the process of ketosis aids in maintaining a diverse and healthy environment for good bacteria to grow in the digestive system. On the other hand, the metabolism of carbohydrates can result in an imbalance of good and bad bacteria in the digestive system, which can have negative health implications.

- Aids in improving eyesight. Because the keto vegan diet is rich in good fats, it helps retinal cells in the eye maintain good health. This diet also prevents cell degeneration in that area. The symptoms of common eye problems such as cataracts and glaucoma have been shown to be reduced in persons who practice keto veganism.

- Improves mental health. Using fat as an energy source is far more efficient for the brain. Therefore, practicing keto veganism helps improve your focus and concentration as well as improve your critical thinking skills. Keto veganism also helps to clear up a protein called beta-amyloid. These proteins tend to stick together, which prevents fast and efficient flow of signals in the brain. This results in slowed thinking and reactions. By clearing this protein up, the keto vegan diet facilitates the faster and more efficient flow of signals in the brain as well as lowered risk of developing neurodegenerative diseases like Alzheimer's disease. It also helps reduce the symptoms of epilepsy. Epilepsy is a neurological disorder perpetuated by sudden recurring episodes of loss of consciousness, convulsions and sensory disturbances. These symptoms arise due to abnormal electrical activity the brains. The ketogenic diet is now famous for its weight loss benefits but it was actually initially created in the 1920s as a therapy to treat the symptoms of epilepsy. It aids by encouraging a mental environment that facilitates more normal electrical activity in the brain.

The keto vegan diet offers a wide array of health benefits because it combines high fat intake with low carb intake to boost nutrient absorption, to facilitate cleaner, faster internal processes and to improve the operation of mental facilities. You can experience all of these benefits and more by becoming a keto vegan practitioner today.

How to Get Started with the Keto Vegan Diet

There are two ways you can get started with a keto vegan diet. The first way is by simply jumping right in and cutting out all carbohydrates from your diet. This method can be quite shocking as the transition is very steep. However, the practitioner usually sees results in a quicker time frame and is less likely to deal with sugar withdrawal symptoms for a long period of time.

The second way involves slowly implementing keto vegan practices. This involves slowly reducing your carbohydrate consumption by progressively eating low amounts of carbs every day. The second way is less jarring to beginner practitioners and allows for a learning curve that is not so steep. While it can be easier for newbie keto vegan practitioners to follow the second method, it takes longer to see noticeable results.

The method that you choose to start the keto vegan diet is entirely up to you and depends on your goals and lifestyle. You can start by practicing one method, and then the other to see what works best for you.

No matter how you get started here are a few tips that are useful:

- Clear the non-keto vegan foods out of your cupboards and refrigerator and fill them up with keto-vegan friendly food so that you have an easier time sticking to this diet.
- Keep things simple at the beginning. Simply up your fat and protein intake and ensure that you are consuming less than 50 grams of carbohydrates every day without worrying too much about the comparative proportions of each. Adjust to the diet then worry about these later.
- Consult a licensed health care practitioner before you begin the keto vegan diet. Ensure that you do not have any preexisting medical conditions that might need addressing before you begin this diet.

Side Effects of the Keto Vegan Diet

Transitioning into a keto vegan lifestyle can be quite an adjustment and this has physical implications. It is not uncommon for new practitioners of the keto vegan diet to experience a condition known as the keto flu. Keto flu symptoms can include:

- Muscle cramps
- Low energy and weakness
- Dizziness
- Sleep disturbances
- Fatigue
- Poor concentration
- Diarrhea
- Constipation
- Nausea
- Headaches
- Irritability

The keto flu is typically experienced by people who jump right into this diet and follow all the rules off the bat. People who allow themselves to ease into this diet and lifestyle are less likely to experience the keto flu as the body is trained to slowly start burning more and more fat as carbohydrates are slowly removed from the diet.

The keto flu is typically caused by the alteration in water and mineral balances that the ketogenic vegan diet causes. You can restore this balance, and thereby curb the side effects of the keto flu, by adding more salt to your diet and taking mineral supplements such as sodium, potassium, and magnesium. These supplements are especially great at easing headaches, insomnia and muscle aches.

Additional supplements and substances that can aid in fighting the side effects of the keto flu include:

- Exogenous ketones. These are simply ketones that are synthesized outside your body. Taking the supplement increases blood ketone levels and therefore, helps fight keto flu.
- MCT oil. As mentioned earlier, this oil skips the digestive process and goes directly to the liver to be converted into ketones. This allows less of an adjustment period for your body to develop higher levels of ketones and thus, fights the symptoms of the keto flu. You can simply drink this oil as is or add it to your smoothies and other dishes
- Caffeine. Low energy is a common symptom of the keto flu and caffeine helps fight this symptom by boosting energy. Caffeine also increases athletic performance, increases fat loss, and reduces the risk of developing type 2 diabetes. You can increase the supply of caffeine in your diet by consuming unsweetened coffee and tea.

Other strategies that can be implemented to fight keto flu include staying hydrated, eating fiber-rich foods, engaging in light activity, and getting adequate rest.

Luckily, the symptoms of the keto flu typically only last for a few days and the practitioner can continue with his or her life without any negative consequence.

Exercising on the Keto Vegan Diet

Exercise and dieting go hand-in-hand if a person wants to live a healthy lifestyle and to lose weight in a safe and sustainable way. Experiencing the keto flu at the initial stages of starting this diet may make it difficult to partake in a normal exercise routine but long-term, practicing the keto vegan diet can actually improve your athletic performance, especially in endurance sports.

In the first few weeks of practicing the ketogenic vegan diet, it is recommended that you start with light exercises as your body begins to adjust to this fat-adapted way of eating. Such exercises include light hiking, walking, cycling, and yoga. It is also recommended that you stick to relatively flat surfaces as dizziness is a common symptom of the keto flu. No matter what exercise you choose to partake in or what stage in your ketogenic diet you are in be sure to be aware of your water intake so that you do not become dehydrated. You should also increase your mineral and electrolyte consumption accordingly to your level of exercise.

Chapter 2: What to Eat on Keto Vegan Diet

Foods That Should be Avoided on the Keto Vegan Diet

- Meat and poultry such as pork, beef, turkey, and chicken.
- Seafood like fish, shrimp, clams, scallops and mussels.
- Dairy products like milk, butter, and yogurt.
- Eggs including egg whites and egg yolks.
- Animal-based products like whey protein and honey.
- Fruits. Small amounts of some berries like raspberries and strawberries are allowed.
- Grains and starches like cereal, bread, baked goods, rice, pasta, and grains.
- Sugary drinks like sweet tea, soda, juice, fruit-based smoothies, sports drinks, and chocolate milk.
- Sugar-free drinks like diet soda. These are often high in sugar alcohols and are highly processed.
- Sweeteners like brown sugar, white sugar, agave, and maple syrup.
- Starchy root vegetables such as potatoes, sweet potatoes, winter squash, and beets.
- Beans and legumes like black beans, chickpeas, and kidney beans.

- Alcohol such as beer, sweetened cocktails, and wine. These do not need to be cut from the diet entirely, but they need to be severely limited.
- Common sauces and condiments like barbecue sauce, sweetened salad dressings, marinades, and ketchup. They often contain sugar and unhealthy fats.
- Highly processed foods. Packaged foods must be limited on the keto vegan diet.

Foods That You Can Eat on the Keto Vegan Diet

- Nuts and seeds such as chia seeds, pumpkin seeds, almonds, flax seeds, walnuts, sesame seeds, pistachios, Brazil nuts, and macadamia nuts.
- Nut and seed kinds of butter like peanut butter, almond butter, sunflower butter, cashew butter.
- Avocados. In addition to providing great fat content to this diet, avocados have large amounts of vitamins and minerals like potassium, which can help combat the keto flu.
- Coconut products like unsweetened coconut, coconut cream, full-fat coconut milk
- Healthy oils such as extra virgin olive oil, avocado oil and coconut oil.
- Vegetables with low carbohydrate content like onions, tomatoes, and peppers.
- Cruciferous vegetables such as broccoli, kale, zucchini, and cauliflower.
- Berries. Most fruits have a high sugar content and are thus excluded from this diet, but some berries are the exception. Berries blueberries, blackberries, raspberries and strawberries are low in carbohydrates and sugar.
- Condiments such as herbs, garlic, nutritional yeast, vinegar, pepper and salt.
- Dark chocolate. The dark chocolate must be constituted of at least 70% cocoa.
- Sweeteners like stevia, erythritol, and xylitol, which must be used in moderation.
- Vegan full-fat "dairy" like Coconut yogurt, vegan butter, cashew cheese and vegan cream cheese.
- Vegan protein sources such as tofu and tempeh.

Common Mistakes People Make on the Keto Vegan Diet and How to Avoid Them

Mistake #1 - Being unprepared to deal with keto flu

Many people do not realize that their bodies need some time to adjust to not just a diet but a lifestyle. Therefore, they are typically unprepared to deal with the symptoms of starting a keto vegan diet. Moving from metabolizing carbohydrates to metabolizing fats is a big shift for the body. While the symptoms of the keto flu are not life-threatening on their own, they can be uncomfortable to deal with. Therefore, do not allow the keto flu to catch you unawares. Keep your schedule light when you first begin this journey. Ensure that you are in a position to get adequate rest to compensate for low energy and tiredness. Keep plenty of fluid on hand and up your intake of electrolytes.

Mistake #2 - Increasing fat intake too quickly

Consuming more healthy fat is essential for ketosis to occur on the keto vegan diet. However, adding too much to your diet too soon can be detrimental to your health because it can cause digestive issues to arise. To avoid this, gradually increase your fat intake over time.

Mistake #3 – Consuming too much protein and not enough fat

The keto vegan diet is a moderate protein diet and thus consuming too much protein should be avoided because it interferes with the process of ketosis. Consuming too much protein can occur because we often reach for high protein sources like nuts when hunger strikes between meals. To ensure that you consume a moderate amount of protein throughout the day, carefully plan your meals and snacks to ensure that your diet remains high in fats, moderate in proteins and low in carbohydrates.

Mistake #4 – Consuming the wrong types of fat

There are different types of fat and some are healthier to consume than others. On the keto vegan diet, it is recommended that you consume monounsaturated and saturated fats because they are the type of fats that are readily used up in ketosis. These types of fats are found in oils like olive, canola, and avocado. On the other hand, polyunsaturated fats should only be consumed in limited quantities because they cause unhealthy weight gain, which can counteract the great benefits of practicing the keto vegan diet.

Mistake #5 – Not consuming enough salt

When the body uses ketones to obtain energy, the rate at which the kidneys secrete sodium (salt) increases. This decrease in salt levels can be detrimental to health. Therefore, to compensate for this, the practitioner of the keto vegan diet needs to up their salt intake. Doing this also helps combat the symptoms of keto flu.

Mistake #6 – Still eating overly processed foods

The quality of food you consume on the keto vegan diet matters just as much as consuming higher amounts of fat. Avoid processed foods even if they are low in carbohydrates because they can introduce other harmful substances to your body. This includes energy bars and diet sodas. Concentrate on consuming nutrient-rich, fresh foods as well as supplementing your diet with supplements like MCT oil.

Mistake #7 – Forgetting to indulge in other forms of self-care

The keto vegan diet helps in improving overall health, but you cannot limit your self-care to this diet. Self-care involves practicing routines that promote conditions that improve health. Practice other means of self-care like getting quality sleep, exercising, taking out quality 'me' time, and managing your stress levels. The combination of these self-care routines, in addition to practicing the keto vegan diet, helps develop overall well-being.

Mistake #8 – Becoming nutrient deficient

It is not uncommon for people who practice the keto vegan diet to have nutrient deficiencies because they do not ensure they have a balanced diet. Ensure that this does not happen to you by adding supplements like sodium, potassium, and magnesium to your diet.

Mistake #9 – Comparing yourself to other people

Everyone's body works differently. Some people see faster results on the keto vegan diet than others. You should not be discouraged if this happens to you. Also, you should not be overly focused on the numbers of the scale. This is a journey that you should enjoy. Therefore, you need to avoid comparing your progress to that of other people. Focus on the improvements you see and find encouragement to keep on going based on that progress.

Chapter 3: Meal Plan, Preparation and Storage

21-Day Keto Vegan Meal Plan

Day 1

Breakfast: Cashew Coconut Breakfast Bars

Lunch: Cucumber Tomato Salad

Dinner: Cauliflower Steaks

Snack 1: Lemon Squares

Snack 2: Raspberry Avocado Smoothie

Day 2

Breakfast: Cauliflower Berry Breakfast Bowl

Lunch: Oven Baked Spicy Cauliflower Wings

Dinner: Veggie Walnut Soup

Snack 1: Peanut Butter Energy Bars

Snack 2: Handful of Berries

Day 3

Breakfast: Breakfast Cereal with Almond Milk

Lunch: Spicy Cucumber Salad

Dinner: Roasted Red Pepper Soup

Snack 1: Raw Strawberry Crumble

Snack 2: Sliced cucumber topped with Cauliflower Hummus

Day 4

Breakfast: Breakfast Bagels with Pecan Butter

Lunch: Grilled Tofu Skewers

Dinner: Zucchini Spinach Ravioli

Snack 1: Cashew Yogurt topped with Chopped Almonds

Snack 2: Coconut Protein Crackers

Day 5

Breakfast: Cranberry Breakfast Bar

Lunch: Creamy Tomato Soup

Dinner: Keto Vegan Shepherd's Pie

Snack 1: Celery Sticks topped with Pecan Butter

Snack 2: Almond Cookies

Day 6

Breakfast: Pumpkin Spice Pancakes

Lunch: Avocado Zucchini Noodles

Dinner: Green Soup

Snack 1: Sliced Bell Peppers and Guacamole

Snack 2: Candied Toasted Cashew Nuts

Day 7

Breakfast: Lemon Pancakes

Lunch: Creamy Pumpkin Soup

Dinner: Portobello Mushroom Tacos with Guacamole

Snack 1: Coconut Fat Cups

Snack 2: Spiced Kale Chips

Day 8

Breakfast: Keto Vegan Vanilla French Toast

Lunch: Lime Coconut Cauliflower Rice

Dinner: Roasted Mushroom Burgers

Snack 1: Almond Coconut Fat Cups

Snack 2: Baked Zucchini Chips

Day 9

Breakfast: Cashew Yogurt Bowl

Lunch: Sautéed Jackfruit Cauliflower Bowl

Dinner: Roasted Radishes

Snack 1: Peanut Butter Cups

Snack 2: Handful of Raw Pumpkin Seeds

Day 10

Breakfast: Cinnamon Coconut Porridge

Lunch: Tuna Imitation Salad

Dinner: Roasted Pepper Zoodles

Snack 1: Coconut cream with Berries

Snack 2: Pitted Olives

Day 11

Breakfast: Zucchini Breakfast Bar

Lunch: Lettuce Salad Bowl

Dinner: Creamy Curry Zucchini Noodles

Snack 1: Keto Vegan Granola Mix

Snack 2: Toasted Coconut Chips

Day 12

Breakfast: Overnight Coconut Pumpkin Porridge

Lunch: Keto Vegan Empanada

Dinner: Creamy Spinach Shirataki

Snack 1: Macadamia Nut Bar

Snack 2: Celery Sticks and Almond Butter

Day 13

Breakfast: Cheesy Scrambled Tofu

Lunch: Avocado Fries

Dinner: Tempeh Broccoli Stir Fry Dinner

Snack 1: Cashew Coconut Bar

Snack 2: Handful of Raw Brazil Nuts

Day 14

Breakfast: Chocolate Waffles

Lunch: Sautéed Squash Kale Bowl

Dinner: Sautéed Brussel Sprouts Dish

Snack 1: Handful of Raw Macadamia Nuts

Snack 2: Coconut Milk Dairy-Free Yogurt

Day 15

Breakfast: Macadamia Nut Bar

Lunch: Avocado Cauliflower Salad

Dinner: Cauliflower Pizza Crust with Veggie Toppings

Snack 1: Flax Seed Crackers

Snack 2: Handful of Dried Coconut

Day 16

Breakfast: Spaghetti Squash Hashbrowns

Lunch: Avocado Cauliflower Salad

Dinner: Tofu Tomato Stir Fry

Snack 1: Apple Cider Donut

Snack 2: Blueberry Protein Smoothie

Day 17

Breakfast: Blueberry Scones

Lunch: Zucchini Veggie Wraps

Dinner: Walnut Zucchini Chili

Snack 1: Avocado Slices

Snack 2: Mint Cauliflower Smoothie

Day 18

Breakfast: Chocolate Zucchini Pancakes

Lunch: Cauliflower Cabbage Tortillas

Dinner: Roasted Veggies on Broccoli Rice

Snack 1: Seaweed Snacks

Snack 2: Handful of Cherry Tomatoes

Day 19

Breakfast: Avocado Breakfast Bowl

Lunch: Zucchini Green Bean Salad

Dinner: Falafel with Tahini Sauce

Snack 1: Vanilla Coconut Smoothie

Snack 2: Handful of Almonds

Day 20

Breakfast: 4 Seed Keto Vegan Bread with Strawberry Jam

Lunch: Cauliflower Pizza Bites

Dinner: Keto Vegan Thai Curry

Snack 1: Chocolate Avocado Smoothie

Snack 2: Handful of Peanuts

Day 21

Breakfast: Protein-Packed Blueberry Smoothie

Lunch: Tofu and Veggie Stir Fry

Dinner: Pesto Zucchini Noodles with Cherry Tomatoes

Snack 1: Avocado Fries

Snack 2: Handful of Cashew nuts

Keto Vegan Shopping List

One of the best things about preparing your own meals is having complete control of what goes into the dishes and therefore, what goes into your body. Good quality ingredients can make or break a dish. You need to get the best ingredients to not only keep your body within ketosis limits but to also make yourself feel good as well as look great. Luckily, I have made this easy for you. To help kick-start your keto vegan diet in the right way, I have compiled a shopping list that will take the hassle and headache out of figuring what to get at the grocery store.

Peruse the list below and simply eliminate items that are already in your kitchen cabinet and shop based on what you plan to prepare for that week or month. This will save you time, money, and energy.

Fruits (fresh, dried and frozen)

Avocados, berries (consumed in moderation), coconut, cranberries, lemon, lime, olives, tomatoes

Nuts and seeds

Almonds, Brazil nuts, cashew nuts (consumed in moderation), chia seeds, flax seeds, hazelnuts, hemp seeds, macadamia nuts, pecans, peanuts, pine nuts (consumed in moderation), pistachios (consumed in moderation), pumpkin seeds, sunflower seeds, walnuts

Nut and seed butters

Almond butter, coconut butter (also called the coconut manna), hazelnut butter, macadamia nut butter, peanut butter, pecan butter, sunflower seed butter, tahini, walnut butter

Vegetables

Artichoke hearts, arugula, asparagus, bell peppers, beets (consumed in moderation), bok choy, broccoli, Brussel sprouts (consumed in moderation), butternut squash, cabbage, carrots (consumed in moderation) cauliflower, celery, collards, cucumber, daikon radishes, eggplant, fennel, garlic, kale, lettuce, mushrooms, mustard greens, okra, onion (consumed in moderation), pumpkin, shallots, spinach, spaghetti squash, sprouts, turnips, zucchini

Dairy Alternatives

Cashew cheese, vegan butter, vegan cheeses, vegan cream cheese, vegan mayo

Sweeteners

Erythritol, liquid and powdered stevia, monk fruit sweetener

Spices

Bay leaf, black pepper, cayenne pepper, cinnamon, clove, coriander, cumin, curry powder, garlic powder, nutmeg, onion powder, paprika, salt, thyme, turmeric

Oils and Fats

Almond oil, avocado oil, cacao butter, coconut oil, flaxseed oil, hazelnut oil, macadamia nut oil, MCT oil, olive oil, walnut oil

Other Ingredients

Almond extract, almond flour, apple cider vinegar, baking powder, baking soda, balsamic vinegar, coconut aminos, coconut flour, coconut milk (canned and full fat), dairy-free yogurt such as cashew yogurt, dark chocolate (70% and up), jackfruit, kelp noodles, nutritional yeast, psyllium husk, seaweed snacks, seitan, shirataki noodles, soy sauce, tamari, tempeh, tofu, vanilla extract, white vinegar

Preparing and Storing Food on the Keto Vegan Diet

Food poisoning is a big concern no matter what diet you practice. Therefore, here are a few tips for ensuring that you not only prepare food that is safe and healthy to eat but you also store food in a way that extends this health and safety.

- Ensure that your hands are washed thoroughly before handling food. This prevents the transfer of bacteria and helps prevent sickness. Also, ensure that the work surface and equipment that you use to prepare and store food are cleaned before and after use.

- Keep food out of the food temperature danger zone. This zone is between 40 and 140 degrees Fahrenheit. Bacteria grows rapidly in this zone. Therefore, it is important to keep food out of this temperature zone.
- Take special care with high-risk foods. Food-poisoning bacteria thrive better on certain foods such as lasagna, curries, vegan dairy substitutes, prepared salads, sandwiches, mousse, and others. Therefore, special care needs to be taken to keep them out of the temperature danger zone.
- Ensure that your refrigerator and freezer is set to the correct temperature. In keeping with the food temperature zone, your refrigerator should be set to 40 degrees Fahrenheit or below. Your freezer should be 5 degrees Fahrenheit or lower.
- Transport frozen and chilled goods in the right way. After grocery shopping, place your chilled and frozen goods in an insulated cooler bag to keep them cold while moving them from the grocery store to your home. Keep them separated from warm and hot goods and place them in the refrigerator and freezer on immediate arrival at home.
- Store cooked food safely. Never place warm or hot food in the refrigerator or freezer as this increases the internal temperature of the appliance and potentially places not only that food item in the food temperature danger zone but all others in there as well. Allow food to cool completely first. Store food in the refrigerator or freezer by placing them in airtight containers or bags. It is also important that you store cooked food away from raw food to avoid the transfer of bacteria.
- When cooking food, ensure that all food is thoroughly cooked to kill any harmful bacteria.

Chapter 4: Sauces and Condiments Recipes

Sauces and condiments are great for adding flavor and variation to any dish. They are great for dipping fruits and vegetables, tossing salads, spreading on sandwiches and burgers, topping soups and more. Unfortunately, many traditional sauces and condiments contain high carb ingredients like sugar and/or animal-based products like eggs.

You are not confined to dishes that lack flavor on the ketogenic vegan diet, luckily. This section of the book provides recipes for sauces and condiments that will infuse your meals with flavor and variety, and they do so with ingredients that are both vegan and ketogenic friendly.

Keto Salsa Verde

Nutritional Information:

Total fat: 25.3g

Cholesterol: 0mg

Sodium: 475mg

Total carbohydrates: 0.8g

Dietary fiber: 0.3g

Protein: 0.2g

Calcium: 8mg

Potassium: 27mg

Iron:0mg

Vitamin D: 0mcg

Time: 5 minutes

Serving Size: 5

Ingredients:

- 4 tbsp fresh cilantro, finely chopped
- ¼ cup fresh parsley, finely chopped
- 2 garlic cloves, grated
- 2 tsp lemon juice
- ¾ cup of olive oil
- 2 tbsp small capers
- 1 tsp of salt
- ½ tsp black pepper

Directions:

1. Add all ingredients to a large mixing bowl. Can be mixed with by hand or with an immersion blender. Mix until desired consistency is achieved.
2. Can be served over burgers, sandwiches, salads and more. Can be stored in the refrigerator for up to 5 days or for longer in the freezer.

Chimichurri

Nutritional Information:

Total fat: 25.3g

Cholesterol: 0mg

Sodium: 3mg

Total carbohydrates: 1.6g

Dietary fiber: 0.3g

Protein: 0.3g

Calcium: 8mg

Potassium: 47mg

Iron: 0mg

Vitamin D: 0mcg

Time: 5 minutes

Serving Size: 8

Ingredients:

- ½ yellow bell pepper, deseeded and finely chopped
- 1 green chili pepper, deseeded and finely chopped
- Juice and zest of 1 lemon
- 1 cup olive oil
- ½ cup parsley, chopped
- 2 garlic cloves, grated
- Salt and pepper to taste

Directions:

1. Add all ingredients to a large mixing bowl. Can be mixed with by hand or with an immersion blender. Mix until desired consistency is achieved.
2. Can be served over burgers, sandwiches, salads and more. Can be stored in the refrigerator for up to 5 days or for longer in the freezer.

Keto Vegan Raw Cashew Cheese Sauce

Nutritional Information:

Total fat: 15.5g

Cholesterol: 0mg

Sodium: 34mg

Total carbohydrates: 9.23g

Dietary fiber: 1.6g

Protein: 5.1g

Calcium: 14mg

Potassium: 217mg

Iron: 2mg

Vitamin D: 0mcg

Time: 5 minutes

Serving Size: 6

Ingredients:

- 1 cup raw cashews, soaked in water for at least 3 hours prior to making recipe
- 2 tbsp olive oil
- 2 tbsp nutritional yeast
- ¼ tsp garlic powder
- 2 tbsp fresh lemon juice
- ½ cup water
- Salt to taste

Directions:

1. To prepare cashews prior to making the sauce, boil 2 cups of water turn off heat and add cashews. This can be allowed to soak overnight. Rinse and strained cashews. Discard water.
2. Add all ingredients to a food processor and blend until a smooth consistency is achieved. Can be used to make pizzas, over roasted veggies, in lasagna, as a dip and more.

Spicy Avocado Mayonnaise

Nutritional Information:

Total fat: 9.8g

Cholesterol: 0mg

Sodium: 23mg

Total carbohydrates: 4.6g

Dietary fiber: 3.4g

Protein: 1g

Calcium: 7mg

Potassium: 252mg

Iron: 0mg

Vitamin D: 0mcg

Time: 10 minutes

Serving Size: 8

Ingredients:

- 2 ripe avocados, pitted and peeled
- ¼ jalapeno pepper, minced
- 2 tbsp lemon juice
- ½ tsp onion powder
- 2 tbsp fresh cilantro, chopped
- Salt to taste

Directions:

1. Add all ingredients to a food processor and blender until a smooth creamy consistency is achieved. The jalapeno peppers can be foregone if you prefer a cooler mayo. Can be enjoyed in sandwiches, on toast, as a topping, in veggie wraps and in salads

Green Coconut Butter

Nutritional Information:

Total fat: 5.2g

Cholesterol: 0mg

Sodium: 3mg

Total carbohydrates: 1.7g

Dietary fiber: 1.2g

Protein: 0.7g

Calcium: 0mg

Potassium: 3mg

Iron: 0mg

Vitamin D: 0mcg

Time: 10 minutes

Serving Size: 18

Ingredients:

- 2 cups unsweetened shredded coconut
- 2 tsp matcha powder
- 1 tbsp coconut oil

Directions:

1. Add shredded coconut to a food processor and blend for 5 minutes or until a smooth but runny consistency is achieved.
2. Add matcha powder and olive oil. Blend for 1 more minute.
3. Can be stored in an airtight container at room temperature for up to 2 weeks. Makes a delicious fruit dip and can be added to smoothies, on pancakes and on toast.

Spiced Almond Butter

Nutritional Information:

Total fat: 9.5g

Cholesterol: 0mg

Sodium: 117mg

Total carbohydrates: 4.1g

Dietary fiber: 2.4g

Protein: 4g

Calcium: 52mg

Potassium: 140mg

Iron: 1mg

Vitamin D: 0mcg

Time: 10 minutes

Serving Size: 10

Ingredients:

- 2 cups raw almond
- ⅛ tsp allspice
- ⅛ tsp cinnamon
- ⅛ tsp cardamom
- ⅛ tsp ground ginger
- ⅛ tsp ground cloves
- ½ tsp salt

Directions:

1. Place all ingredients in a food processor and blend until a smooth consistency is achieved. Makes a delicious fruit and veggie dip and can be added to smoothies, on toast, on pancakes and waffles.

Keto Strawberry Jam

Nutritional Information:

Total fat: 0g

Cholesterol: 0mg

Sodium: 0mg

Total carbohydrates: 1g

Dietary fiber: 0.2g

Protein: 0.1g

Calcium: 1mg

Potassium: 14mg

Iron: 0mg

Vitamin D: 0mcg

Time: 25 minutes

Serving Size: 18

Ingredients:

- 1 cup fresh strawberries, chopped
- 1 tbsp lemon juice
- 4 tsp xylitol
- 1 tbsp water

Directions:

1. Add all ingredients to a small saucepan and place over medium heat. Stir to combine and cook for about 15 minutes. Stir occasionally.
2. After 15 minutes are up, mash-up strawberries with a potato masher or fork.
3. Pour into a heat-safe container such as a mason jar.
4. Allow to cool then cover with a lid and refrigerate. Can be stored in the refrigerator for up to 3 days. Goes great with toast and sweet sandwiches.

Chocolate Coconut Butter

Nutritional Information:

Total fat: 17.4g

Cholesterol: 0mg

Sodium: 17mg

Total carbohydrates: 0.9g

Dietary fiber: 0.6g

Protein: 0.3g

Calcium: 0mg

Potassium: 0mg

Iron: 0mg

Vitamin D: 0mcg

Time: 25 minutes

Serving Size: 20

Ingredients:

- ½ lb. unsweetened shredded coconut
- 3 tbsp cocoa butter
- ⅛ tsp salt

Directions:

1. Preheat your oven to 350 degrees F.

2. Place shredded coconut on a greased baking sheet. Spread out into a thin, even layer.
3. Bake for up to 15 minutes or until the coconut flakes are golden brown. Stir the coconut shreds every 3 minutes and watch them closely because they burn very easily and quickly.
4. Allow the coconut flakes to cool for 15 minutes.
5. Add coconut flakes to a food processor and blend until smooth and creamy yet runny in consistency.
6. Adding cocoa butter and salt and blend to incorporate well.
7. Pour into an airtight jar and seal lid. The consistency will thicken up as the butter cools. The oil may separate and float to the top of the container as the butter cools. Simply reheat a portion in the microwave just before using. Can be stored for up to a whole year at room temperature!

Orange Dill Butter

Nutritional Information:

Total fat: 1.5g

Cholesterol: 0mg

Sodium: 199mg

Total carbohydrates: 1g

Dietary fiber: 0.3g

Protein: 0.1g

Calcium: 11mg

Potassium: 19mg

Iron: 0mg

Vitamin D: 0mcg

Time: 15 minutes

Serving Size: 12

Ingredients:

- ½ cup vegan butter
- 2 tbsp fresh dill, finely chopped
- 2 tbsp orange zest
- 1 tsp salt

Directions:

1. Add 4 cups of water to a small pot and bring to a boil over high heat. Reduce heat to low and allow water to simmer.

2. Add vegan butter to a glass mason jar and screw on lid loosely.
3. Place mason jar in the boiling water. Ensure that the jar does not get submerged or over turn.
4. Allow the butter to melt and add remaining ingredients.
5. Remove the mason jar from the pot and allow to cool until the mixture becomes partially solidified.
6. Can be used alongside your favorite veggies to infuse them with flavor and fat. Can be stored in the refrigerator for up to 2 weeks.

Keto Caramel Sauce

Nutritional Information:

Total fat: 9.8g

Cholesterol: 0mg

Sodium: 29mg

Total carbohydrates: 4.6g

Dietary fiber: 0.7g

Protein: 1.7g

Calcium: 6mg

Potassium: 90mg

Iron: 1mg

Vitamin D: 0mcg

Time: 35 minutes

Serving Size: 8

Ingredients:

- ½ cup raw cashews
- ½ cup coconut cream, melted
- 10 drops liquid stevia
- 2 tbsp vegan butter
- 3 tsp vanilla extract
- A pinch of salt

Directions:

1. Preheat your oven to 325 degrees F
2. Place nuts on a greased baking tray and toast for 20 minutes or until lightly golden and crunchy.

3. Allow the nuts to cool slightly then add to a food processor and blend to a slightly lumpy consistency.
4. Add remaining ingredients and blend until a smooth and creamy consistency is achieved. Do not over blend or the coconut cream will become separated from the rest of the ingredients.
5. Can be stored in a glass, airtight container in the refrigerator if not being served immediately. To reheat the caramel to make it more flowable, add to a saucepan and gently warm on low heat. Can be served with your favorite keto vegan treats such as ice-cream.

Pecan Butter

Nutritional Information:

Total fat: 25g

Cholesterol: 0mg

Sodium: 0mg

Total carbohydrates: 5g

Dietary fiber: 3.8g

Protein: 3.8g

Calcium: 25mg

Potassium: 145mg

Iron: 1mg

Vitamin D: 0mcg

Time: 10 minutes

Serving Size: 8

Ingredients:

- 3 cups pecans, soaked well at least 3 hours, rinsed, strained and dried

Directions:

1. Add the pecans to a food processor and blend until a smooth and creamy consistency is achieved. Scrape down the sides of the bowl when necessary.
2. Transfer to a mason jar and store in the refrigerator. Can be stored in the refrigerator for several months. Makes a great spread on toast and sandwiches and a great fruit and veggie dip.

Keto Vegan Ranch Dressing

Nutritional Information:

Total fat: 11.9g

Cholesterol: 0mg

Sodium: 50mg

Total carbohydrates: 4.8g

Dietary fiber: 1.3g

Protein: 1.7g

Calcium: 79mg

Potassium: 223mg

Iron: 3mg

Vitamin D: 0mcg

Time: 5 minutes

Serving Size: 10

Ingredients:

- 1 cup vegan mayo
- 1 ½ cup coconut milk
- 2 scallions
- 2 garlic cloves, peeled
- 1 cup fresh dill
- 1 tsp garlic powder
- Salt and pepper to taste

Directions:

1. Add scallion, fresh dill and garlic cloves to a food processor and pulse until finely chopped.
2. Add the rest of the ingredients and blend until a smooth, creamy consistency is achieved. Makes a great creamy salad dressing. Store in the refrigerator.

Cauliflower Hummus

Nutritional Information:

Total fat: 2.7g

Cholesterol: 0mg

Sodium: 12mg

Total carbohydrates: 2.7g

Dietary fiber: 1.2g

Protein: 1.3g

Calcium: 11mg

Potassium: 138mg

Iron: 1mg

Vitamin D: 0mcg

Time: 20 minutes

Serving Size: 7

Ingredients:

- 1 large head cauliflower
- 1 tbsp almond butter
- 1 garlic clove, finely chopped
- 1 tbsp lemon juice
- 2 tsp olive oil
- ¼ tsp cumin
- Salt and pepper to taste

Directions:

1. Cut cauliflower into florets and place in a large microwave-safe bowl. Microwave for 10 minutes on high heat or until completely cooked through.
2. Transfer cauliflower florets to a food processor. Add the rest of the ingredients. Blend until smooth, creamy consistency is reached. Can be stored in the refrigerator in an airtight container for up to 5 days. Makes a great dip for fruits and veggies.

Cauliflower Cream

Nutritional Information:

Total fat: 0g

Cholesterol: 0mg

Sodium: 0mg

Total carbohydrates: 2.1g

Dietary fiber: 1g

Protein: 0.8g

Calcium: 9mg

Potassium: 121mg

Iron: 0mg

Vitamin D: 0mcg

Time: 10 minutes

Serving Size: 10

Ingredients:

- 4 cups cauliflower florets
- ½ cup of water
- ¼ tsp salt

Directions:

1. Add cauliflower, salt and water to a medium pan and place over high heat. Bring to a boil then reduce heat to low and allow to simmer for 12 minutes.
2. Allow the cauliflower mixture to cool for 10 minutes then transfer to a blender and blend until a smooth and creamy consistency is achieved. Can be used immediately or stored in the refrigerator in an airtight container for up to 2 days. Makes a great addition to soups casserole and even sweet treats like brownies.

Eggplant Dip

Nutritional Information:

Total fat: 6.1g

Cholesterol: 0mg

Sodium: 3mg

Total carbohydrates: 5.9g

Dietary fiber: 3.5g

Protein: 1.3g

Calcium: 27mg

Potassium: 222mg

Iron: 1mg

Vitamin D: 0mcg

Time: 40 minutes

Serving Size: 10

Ingredients:

- 2 large eggplants, cut lengthwise
- ½ tsp ground cumin
- ¼ cup olive oil
- 1 tbsp lemon juice
- 2 tbsp toasted sesame seeds
- Salt and pepper to taste

Directions:

1. Preheat your oven to 400 degrees F.
2. Prepare a baking sheet by lining it with parchment paper.
3. Sprinkle salt along the surface of the eggplants and place salt side up on baking sheet.
4. Bake for 30 minutes or until the eggplant is soft.
5. Allow eggplant to cool then peel the skin off and cut into cubes. Transfer to a blender.
6. Add cumin, olive oil, lemon juice and pepper and blend until a smooth and creamy consistency is achieved.
7. Transfer to a serving bowl and sprinkle with toasted sesame seeds. Makes a great dip for vegetables and a topping for sandwiches and burgers.

Chapter 5: Breakfast Recipes

Breakfast is often referred to as the most important meal of the day. This is with good reason because a nutrition-packed breakfast can give you that initial boost to optimize your physical and mental facilities so that you perform efficiently and productivity from the jump. Keto vegan breakfasts provide high fat and protein values while remaining low in carbs so that your body achieves and maintains ketosis. Therefore, not only are you performing at your best, but you gain all the benefits of veganism while managing your weight.

Cauliflower Berry Breakfast Bowl

Nutritional Information:

Total fat: 8g

Cholesterol: 0mg

Sodium: 40mg

Total carbohydrates: 13.8g

Dietary fiber: 7.1g

Protein: 4.3g

Calcium: 155mg

Potassium: 220mg

Iron: 3mg

Vitamin D: 0mcg

Time: 15 minutes

Serving Size: 6

Ingredients:

- ½ cup cauliflower, frozen
- ¼ cup zucchini, frozen
- 1 cup fresh spinach
- ½ cup frozen raspberries
- 1 cup unsweetened almond milk
- 2 tbsp almond butter
- 3 tbsp chia seeds
- 1 tsp ground cinnamon

Directions:

1. Add all ingredients to a blender. Place the frozen ingredients closest to the blades. Blend until smooth and creamy consistency is achieved and all the ingredients are well incorporated.
2. Divide the mixture between serving bowls. Can be topped with fresh raspberries and serve.

No - Fuss Breakfast Cereal

Nutritional Information:

Total fat: 18.7g

Cholesterol: 0mg

Sodium: 23mg

Total carbohydrates: 8g

Dietary fiber: 4.4g

Protein: 4.7g

Calcium: 62mg

Potassium: 124mg

Iron: 2mg

Vitamin D: 0mcg

Time: 35 minutes

Serving Size: 8

Ingredients:

- 1 cup unsweetened coconut flakes
- ½ cup raw pumpkin seeds
- ½ cup sunflower seeds
- ¼ cup chia seeds
- 1 tbsp toasted sesame seeds
- ¼ cup coconut oil
- 1 1/2 tsp vanilla extract
- A pinch of salt
- Coconut milk and fresh berries, like blackberries or blueberries for serving

Directions:

1. Preheat your oven to 300 degrees F.
2. Prepare a baking sheet by lining it with parchment paper.
3. In a large mixing bowl, add coconut flakes, pumpkin seeds, sunflower seeds, chia seeds, sesame seeds and salt. Mix well.
4. Add coconut oil and vanilla extract. Mix again.
5. Spread mixture onto prepared baking sheet in an even layer.
6. Bake for 20 minutes or until cereal golden brown. Stir halfway through.
7. Remove cereal from oven and allow cereal to cool to preference. Serve with coconut milk and berries.

Easy Breakfast Bagels

Nutritional Information:

Total fat: 13.7g

Cholesterol: 0mg

Sodium: 95mg

Total carbohydrates: 29.8g

Dietary fiber: 23.2g

Protein: 5.1g

Calcium: 125mg

Potassium: 247mg

Iron: 5mg

Vitamin D: 0mcg

Time: 1 hour

Serving Size: 12

Ingredients:

- 1 cup ground flax seed
- 1 cup tahini
- ½ cup psyllium husks
- 2 cup water
- 2 tsp baking powder
- A pinch of salt

Directions:

1. Preheat your oven to 375 degrees F.
2. Prepare a baking sheet by lining it with parchment paper.
3. Add flax seeds, psyllium husk, baking powder and salt to a bowl. Whisk to combine.
4. In a small bowl, whisk together water and tahini. Pour into dry ingredients and fold in. Knead to form the dough.
5. Create 12 circles about 4" in diameter, and 1/4" thick.
6. Place circles on prepared baking sheet, spaced equally apart. Cut a small circle from the middle of each circle.
7. Bake for around 40 minutes or until golden brown.
8. Remove from oven and allow to cool.
9. Cut in half and top as desired. Serve.

Cranberry Breakfast Bars

Nutritional Information:

Total fat: 15.7g

Cholesterol: 0mg

Sodium: 5mg

Total carbohydrates: 6.3g

Dietary fiber: 3.4g

Protein: 2.3g

Calcium: 49mg

Potassium: 151mg

Iron: 1mg

Vitamin D: 0mcg

Time: 55 minutes

Serving Size: 10

Ingredients:

- ⅓ cup dried cranberries
- 1 cup pecans
- 1 cup water
- ¼ cup coconut butter, softened
- 2 tbsp granulated erythritol
- 1 tbsp ground flax seed
- 2 tsp allspice blend
- 1 ½ tsp baking powder
- 1 tsp vanilla extract

Directions:

1. Preheat your oven to 350 degrees F.
2. Prepare an 8x8 brownie pan by lining it with parchment paper.
3. Add all ingredients to a blender and blend until slightly lumpy consistency is achieved.
4. Pour mixture into prepared brownie pan. Use a spatula to smooth the top.
5. Bake for 45 minutes or until a toothpick comes out clean when inserted into the center.
6. Remove the pan from the oven and allow to cool completely before removing and slicing into individual bars. If you do not allow the bars to cool completely then they will fall apart. Serve.

Pumpkin Spice Pancakes

Nutritional Information:

Total fat: 6.1g

Cholesterol: 0mg

Sodium: 3mg

Total carbohydrates: 5.9g

Dietary fiber: 3.5g

Protein: 1.3g

Calcium: 27mg

Potassium: 222mg

Iron: 1mg

Vitamin D: 0mcg

Time: 25 minutes

Serving Size: 6

Ingredients:

- ¼ cup pumpkin puree
- ⅓ cup almond milk
- ⅓ cup coconut flour
- ⅓ cup water
- ⅓ cup almond flour
- ¼ tsp baking soda
- 1 tbsp vanilla protein powder
- ⅛ tsp ground cinnamon
- ⅛ tsp ground ginger
- 1 tsp stevia powder

Directions:

1. Add coconut flour, almond flours, baking soda, cinnamon, ginger, stevia and protein powder to a mixing bowl. Mix well.
2. Add almond milk, water and pumpkin puree to a blender and blend to a smooth consistency. Pour into dry ingredients and combine until no lumps are visible.
3. Grease a nonstick skillet and place on medium heat. Add 1/4 cup of batter to heated skillet at a time. Cook for 1 minute or until the bottom edges turn golden brown. Flip and cook for 1 more minute. Repeat until all batter is used up.
4. Remove, plate and serve with toppings such as fresh berries or berry jam.

Lemon Pancakes

Nutritional Information:

Total fat: 18.5g

Cholesterol: 0mg

Sodium: 52mg

Total carbohydrates: 16.6g

Dietary fiber: 11.2g

Protein: 2.7g

Calcium: 29mg

Potassium: 80mg

Iron: 1mg

Vitamin D: 0mcg

Time: 1 hour

Serving Size: 6

Ingredients:

- ½ tsp vanilla extract
- 1 tbsp lemon juice
- 2 tbsp coconut butter, melted
- 1 tbsp granulated erythritol
- 5 tbsp almond milk
- ¼ cup coconut flour
- ½ tsp baking powder
- 1 tbsp psyllium husk
- A pinch of salt

Directions:

1. In a medium mixing bowl, whisk together coconut flour, baking powder, salt and psyllium.
2. In a large mixing bowl, whisk together remaining ingredients then stir into dry mixture. Combine thoroughly and ensure that there are no lumps.
3. Allow the mixture to sit for 5 minutes or until a stiff dough forms. You should be able to mold this dough with your hands. If not, stir in additional coconut flour.
4. Divide the dough into 5 equal portions to form 5 balls.
5. Heat a nonstick skillet over medium heat. Grease with coconut oil.
6. Flatten dough and add to pan. Cook for 5 minutes on each side or until golden brown and cooked through.
7. Allow to cool for a few minutes and serve.

Keto Vegan Vanilla French Toast

Nutritional Information:

Total fat: 8.3g

Cholesterol: 0mg

Sodium: 11mg

Total carbohydrates: 23.5g

Dietary fiber: 2.6g

Protein: 3.9g

Calcium: 12mg

Potassium: 166mg

Iron: 1mg

Vitamin D: 0mcg

Time: 20 minutes

Serving Size: 5

Ingredients:

- 5 slices fresh coconut bread (or any other keto vegan friendly sandwich bread)
- ¼ tsp ground cinnamon
- ¼ cup vanilla protein powder
- ½ cup almond milk
- A pinch of ground nutmeg

Directions:

1. Whisk together almond milk, protein powder, nutmeg and cinnamon in a shallow but wide dish that the bread can fit into. Ensure that there are no lumps in the mix.
2. Heat a nonstick skillet over medium heat and grease with coconut oil.
3. Soak each piece of bread in the vanilla protein powder mixture for 5 seconds on each side.
4. Place the soaked pieces of bread in the skillet and cook for 5 minutes so that the bottom turns golden brown. Flip and cook for another 5 minutes or until the other side is golden brown.
5. Plate and serve.

Cashew Yogurt Bowl

Nutritional Information:

Total fat: 11.4g

Cholesterol: 0mg

Sodium: 18mg

Total carbohydrates: 15.6g

Dietary fiber: 7.5g

Protein: 6.6g

Calcium: 180mg

Potassium: 170mg

Iron: 3mg

Vitamin D: 0mcg

Time: 5 minutes

Serving Size: 2

Ingredients:

- ¾ cup vegan cashew yogurt
- 1 tbsp flaxseed
- 1 tbsp chia seeds
- 1 tbsp hemp seed
- ¼ cup frozen blueberries

Directions:

1. Add the cashew yogurt to the bottom of the serving bowl.
2. Top with the remaining ingredients, going around steadily in a circle until all the ingredients are used up. Serve.

Cinnamon Coconut Porridge

Nutritional Information:

Total fat: 31.5g

Cholesterol: 0mg

Sodium: 8mg

Total carbohydrates: 9.8g

Dietary fiber: 9g

Protein: 21.7g

Calcium: 49mg

Potassium: 95mg

Iron: 11mg

Vitamin D: 0mcg

Time: 5 minutes

Serving Size: 1

Ingredients:

- 2 tbsp shredded coconut
- 1 tbsp ground flax seeds
- 2 tbsp hemp hearts
- ⅛ tsp cinnamon
- ⅛ tsp stevia powder
- ½ cup of boiling water
- Fresh mixed berries to top

Directions:

1. Add all ingredients except for fresh mixed berries and water to a serving bowl and stir to combine.
2. Add boiling water. Stir.
3. Allow the porridge to sit until it reaches a suitable eating temperature. The porridge will thicken as it cools down. Top with fresh mixed berries and serve.

Zucchini Breakfast Bars

Nutritional Information:

Total fat: 17g

Cholesterol: 0mg

Sodium: 35mg

Total carbohydrates: 10g

Dietary fiber: 6.3g

Protein: 7.1g

Calcium: 56mg

Potassium: 77mg

Iron: 3mg

Vitamin D: 0mcg

Time: 45 minutes

Serving Size: 6

Ingredients:

- 1 cup zucchini grated
- ¼ cup coconut butter, softened
- 2 tsp cinnamon
- 1 tbsp chia seeds
- ½ cup hemp hearts
- 2 tbsp granulated erythritol
- A pinch of salt

Directions:

1. Preheat your oven to 375 degrees F.
2. Prepare a 9 x 13 loaf pan by lining it with parchment paper.
3. To a large mixing bowl, add coconut butter, zucchini and erythritol. Combine thoroughly

4. Add the rest of the ingredients and stir to thoroughly incorporate. Allow the mixture to sit for 5 minutes so that the chia seeds thicken the batter.
5. Pour mixture into prepared pan and smooth top with a spatula.
6. Bake for 35 minutes or until the bars are golden brown and firm to the touch.
7. Allow to cool for at least 30 minutes before removing from the. Slice into individual bars and serve.

Overnight Coconut Pumpkin Porridge

Nutritional Information:

Total fat: 46g

Cholesterol: 0mg

Sodium: 313mg

Total carbohydrates: 16.9g

Dietary fiber: 9.8g

Protein: 11.4g

Calcium: 134mg

Potassium: 515mg

Iron: 6mg

Vitamin D: 0mcg

Time: 10 minutes

Serving Size: 2

Ingredients:

- 2 tsp of shredded coconut
- ½ cup coconut cream at room temperature
- 8 drops liquid stevia
- 2 tsp powdered stevia
- ½ cup almond milk
- 1 tsp hemp hearts
- 2 tbsp raw pumpkin seeds
- 1 tsp chia seeds
- ¼ tsp salt
- 1 tsp ground cinnamon
- 8 walnuts, halved

Directions:

1. In a small bowl, combine pumpkin seeds, chia seeds, hemp hearts, salt and half of cinnamon.

2. In another small bowl, whisk together almond milk and coconut cream. Pour this mixture into the seed mixture and stir to combine. Cover the resulting mixture and chill overnight.
3. When it is time to serve, heat the porridge in the microwave for 1 minute or in a saucepan over medium heat for 4 minutes or until warmed through.
4. Add remaining cinnamon, liquid stevia and powdered cinnamon stevia to mixture and mix. If the porridge is too thick, add more almond milk until desired consistency is reached.
5. Top with walnuts and shredded coconut and serve.

Cheesy Scrambled Tofu

Nutritional Information:

Total fat: 18.8g

Cholesterol: 0mg

Sodium: 418mg

Total carbohydrates: 9.6g

Dietary fiber: 3.3g

Protein: 10.9g

Calcium: 215mg

Potassium: 373mg

Iron: 3mg

Vitamin D: 0mcg

Time: 15 minutes

Serving Size: 4

Ingredients:

- 14 oz firm tofu
- 1 ½ tbsp nutritional yeast
- 3 oz vegan cheddar cheese
- 1 medium tomato, diced
- 1 cup spinach
- ½ tsp salt
- ½ tsp turmeric
- ½ tsp garlic powder
- 3 tbsp olive oil
- 2 tbsp yellow onion, diced

Directions:

1. Wrap the block of tofu in a clean cloth towel and gently squeeze to remove excess moisture. Set aside.
2. Place a nonstick skillet over medium heat. Add 1/3 of the olive oil and add onions. Sauté until the onions become translucent.
3. Add the block of tofu to the skillet and crumble using a fork or potato masher. Do this until the tofu resembles scrambled eggs.
4. Add the remaining oil, nutritional yeast, garlic powder, turmeric and salt and stir.
5. Cover the pot and continue to cook, stirring occasionally, until most of the moisture in the pot has evaporated.
6. Add spinach, tomato and vegan cheese. Cook for 1 more minute or until the spinach has wilted and the cheese is melted. Serve hot. Can be stored in the refrigerator for up to three days in an airtight container.

Chocolate Waffles

Nutritional Information:

Total fat: 58.3g

Cholesterol: 0mg

Sodium: 93mg

Total carbohydrates: 22.4g

Dietary fiber: 15.9g

Protein: 1.3g

Calcium: 32mg

Potassium: 168mg

Iron: 1mg

Vitamin D: 0mcg

Time: 25 minutes

Serving Size: 4

Ingredients:

- 3 tbsp cocoa powder
- ½ cup coconut flour
- ¼ cup coconut oil, softened
- 1 cup coconut milk at room temperature
- ½ teaspoon baking powder
- 3 tbsp granulated erythritol
- 2 tbsp psyllium husk
- A pinch of salt

Directions:

1. Preheat your waffle iron according to manufacturer's instructions.
2. Add cocoa powder, coconut flour, granulated erythritol, baking powder, salt and psyllium to a medium bowl. Stir to combine.
3. Add coconut oil to the dry mixture and stir until a stiff dough forms.
4. Add coconut milk in increments. Stir to fully incorporate before next addition. Once the milk has been added completely, let the mixture sit for 3 minutes so that it sets.
5. Divide the dough into 4 equal portions and make waffles according to waffle iron instructions. Allow to cool for a few minutes before serving.

Macadamia Nut Bars

Nutritional Information:

Total fat: 19.7g

Cholesterol: 0mg

Sodium: 4mg

Total carbohydrates: 3.6g

Dietary fiber: 2.3g

Protein: 1.6g

Calcium: 7mg

Potassium: 38mg

Iron: 1mg

Vitamin D: 0mcg

Time: 5 minutes

Serving Size: 8

Ingredients:

- 1/2 cup macadamia nuts
- 6 tbsp unsweetened shredded coconut
- 10 drops liquid stevia
- ¼ cup coconut oil
- ½ cup almond butter

Directions:

1. Prepare a 9x9 baking sheet by lining it with parchment paper.
2. Add macadamia nuts to a food processor and process until a fine meal consistency is achieved.
3. Combine shredded coconut, coconut oil and almond butter in a large mixing bowl.

4. Add macadamia nuts and the stevia drops.
5. Mix batter thoroughly.
6. Paul into the prepared baking sheet and refrigerate overnight. Slice into individual bars and serve.

Spaghetti Squash Hashbrowns

Nutritional Information:

Total fat: 7.2g

Cholesterol: 0mg

Sodium: 7mg

Total carbohydrates: 5.2g

Dietary fiber: 2.4g

Protein:0.9g

Calcium: 12mg

Potassium: 208mg

Iron: 0mg

Vitamin D: 0mcg

Time: 35 minutes

Serving Size: 10

Ingredients:

- 1 spaghetti squash
- 3 tbsp avocado oil
- ⅛ teaspoon sage, diced
- Salt and pepper to taste

Directions:

1. Wash and dry the spaghetti squash then cut into two halves. Using a knife, pierce the spaghetti squash several times.
2. Place in a shallow microwave-safe dish and add 1 inch of water. Microwave in 2 minute intervals for up to 8 minutes or until the squash becomes soft enough to pierce easily with a knife.
3. Allow the squash to become cool enough to handle then scoop out the seeds and stringy pieces. Shred with fork and place spaghetti strands in a bowl.
4. Add salt, pepper and sage to spaghetti squash. Mix well.

5. Form into 10 compact balls with your hand then press down into 1/2 inch thick hash brown patties. Use a paper towel to squeeze out any excess moisture from patties.
6. Place a nonstick skillet over medium heat and add avocado oil. When the oil is hot, add as many patties as the pan can carry to fry. Cook for 5 minutes or until underside is golden brown and the Patty is heated all the way through. Flip and cook for another 5 minutes or until the next side is golden brown as well.
7. Repeat with any remaining patties.
8. Allow to cool for a few minutes and serve with your favorite keto vegan friendly sauce or dip.

Blueberry Scones

Nutritional Information:

Total fat: 3g

Cholesterol: 0mg

Sodium: 30mg

Total carbohydrates: 2.4g

Dietary fiber: 0.9g

Protein: 1.2g

Calcium: 19mg

Potassium: 58mg

Iron: 0mg

Vitamin D: 0mcg

Time: 40 minutes

Serving Size: 6

Ingredients:

- ¼ cup fresh blueberries
- 1 cup almond flour
- ½ tsp baking powder
- ⅛ tsp powdered stevia
- ½ tbsp ground flax seed
- 1 ½ tbsp water
- 1 tbsp almond milk
- A pinch of salt

Directions:

1. Preheat your oven to 375 degrees F.

2. Prepare a baking sheet by lining it with parchment paper.
3. Create an egg substitute by mixing flaxseed and water in a small bowl. Set aside for 5 minutes.
4. In a large bowl, sift together almond flour, stevia, baking powder and salt.
5. Add blueberries to dry mixture. Mix to coat with dry mixture.
6. Combine egg substitute and almond milk in a small bowl. Pour into dry mixture and stir until fully incorporated. A soft dough should be created.
7. Shape 6 scones with 1/2 inch thickness and place on prepared baking sheet.
8. Bake for 20 minutes or until golden brown.
9. Remove and allow to cool for at least 10 minutes before serving.

Chocolate Zucchini Pancakes

Nutritional Information:

Total fat: 13.3g

Cholesterol: 0mg

Sodium: 11mg

Total carbohydrates: 11.3g

Dietary fiber: 5.2g

Protein: 5.2g

Calcium: 39mg

Potassium: 167mg

Iron: 2mg

Vitamin D: 0mcg

Time: 20 minutes

Serving Size: 4

Ingredients:

- 2 tbsp dark chocolate chips
- ¼ cup zucchini, shredded
- ½ cup almond flour
- 2 tbsp coconut flour
- 2 tbsp granulated erythritol
- ½ tsp baking powder
- 3 tbsp flaxseed
- ½ cup water
- 1 tsp of cinnamon
- ¼ cup almond milk

Directions:

1. Make egg substitute by combining flaxseed and water. Set aside for 5 minutes.
2. Add flax egg along with all of the ingredients except for chocolate chips to a blender. Blend until just combined or to a thick, pourable mixture.

3. Allow batter to sit for 10 minutes. Just before cooking, stir in chocolate chips.
4. Place a nonstick skillet oiled with a small bit of avocado or olive oil over medium heat. Pour small portions of batter into the heated pan. Cook for 3 minutes or until edges are golden brown. Flip and cook for another 3 minutes.
5. Repeat with any remaining. Serve warm.

Avocado Breakfast Bowl

Nutritional Information:

Total fat: 17.4g

Cholesterol: 2mg

Sodium: 28mg

Total carbohydrates: 11.4g

Dietary fiber: 5.6g

Protein: 6.5g

Calcium: 110mg

Potassium: 550mg

Iron: 2mg

Vitamin D: 0mcg

Time: 5 minutes

Serving Size: 3

Ingredients:

- 1 avocado, peeled and deseeded
- ¼ cup fresh spinach
- ¼ cup fresh mint
- 1 cup full fat coconut milk
- ¼ cup water
- 1 medium cucumber, peeled and chopped
- ½ scoop vanilla protein powder
- 2 tbsp apple cider vinegar
- 2 tbsp fresh lemon juice
- ½ cup ice cubes

Directions:

1. Add all ingredients except for the mixed berries to a blender and blend until a thick, smooth and creamy consistency is achieved.
2. Divide the mixture between serving bowls and top with fresh mixed berries or other toppings such as toasted coconut flakes, sesame seeds or pumpkin seeds. Serve immediately.

4 Seed Keto Vegan Bread

Nutritional Information:
Total fat: 10.9g

Cholesterol: 0mg

Sodium: 132mg

Total carbohydrates: 5.4g

Dietary fiber: 3.3g

Protein: 4.5g

Calcium: 28mg

Potassium: 148mg

Iron: 3mg

Vitamin D: 0mcg

Time: 1 hour 20 minutes

Serving Size: 18
Ingredients:
- ½ cup chia seeds
- ½ cup flax seeds
- 1 cup raw sunflower seeds
- 1 ½ cup raw pumpkin seeds
- ½ cup whole psyllium husk
- 1 tsp salt
- A pinch of powdered stevia
- 3 tbsp sunflower oil
- 1 ½ cup of warm water

Directions:
1. Preheat your oven to 350 degrees F.
2. Prepare a 1-pound loaf pan and a baking sheet by lining them with parchment paper.
3. Add pumpkin seeds to a food processor and process until finely chopped to a medium coarse flour consistency.
4. Transfer pumpkin seed flour to a medium mixing bowl. Add chia seeds, flax seeds, sunflower seeds, stevia and psyllium husks. Stir to mix.
5. Stir in warm water and olive oil to form a uniform batter.
6. Transfer batter into prepared loaf pan. Press into a uniform loaf with your hands.
7. Bake for 45 minutes.
8. Remove the loaf pan from the oven and remove loaf. Place the loaf onto the prepared baking sheet so that the top is down and return it to the oven to bake for 15 more minutes or until tapping the top produces a hollow sound.

9. Remove from the oven and cool completely before slicing. Serve. Can be topped with your favorite keto vegan jam, avocado slices, nut butter and more when served. Can be stored in the refrigerator in an airtight container up to 7 days. Can be stored in the freezer for longer.

Cashew Coconut Breakfast Bars

Nutritional Information:

Total fat: 8.8g

Cholesterol: 0mg

Sodium: 3mg

Total carbohydrates: 5.7g

Dietary fiber: 3.5g

Protein: 1.8g

Calcium: 30mg

Potassium: 104mg

Iron: 1mg

Vitamin D: 0mcg

Time: 10 minutes

Serving Size: 25

Ingredients:

- 2 cups raw cashews
- 2 tbsp unsweetened shredded coconut
- 1 cup raw almonds
- 1 cup almond butter
- ¼ cup chia seeds
- Full fat coconut milk

Directions:

1. Prepare an 8x8 freezer-safe dish with parchment paper.
2. Add cashews and almonds to a food processors and process to form a crumbly texture.
3. Add almond butter and chia seeds and blend to form a sticky batter. If the batter is too thick, add coconut milk gradually until desired texture is achieved.
4. Pour cashew mixture into prepared freezer-safe dish and smooth into an even layer. Sprinkle with coconut flakes and place in freezer for at least 2 hours. Slice and serve. Keep frozen to store.

Chapter 6: Lunch Recipes

It is a common occurrence for people to skip lunch. This can be for a variety of reasons such as rushing to class, being buried in paperwork, trying to meet a deadline or having tons of errands to do that day. We often believe that we can gain time throughout the day by skipping this vital meal but that is not the case. Taking a lunch break actually helps you accomplish more because it allows your brain to switch off and regroup so that it can perform better.

Skipping lunch is a bad habit because it has detrimental effects on your overall health. Eating lunch is what gives you energy to keep plowing on through the day so that you cut through your to-do list. It helps you stay focused to perform at your best.

In addition, skipping lunch tends to lead to overeating at dinner time to compensate for the missed meal. This can lead to unhealthy weight gain.

Also, eating lunch helps improve the workings of your digestive system as it helps prevent bloating, acid reflux and indigestion.

Not only is eating lunch important for your physical, mental and emotional health, but it also helps you socialize more as it forces you to take a step back from your commitments and sit with other people so that you can have small talk or deeper conversations. Socialization is very important to healthy human development.

Below you can find a list of time-saving, good-for-your gut, tasty recipes that you can prepare in advance so that you have a healthy lunchtime meal rather than reaching for unhealthy convenience dishes. Preparing your own lunch helps you save time and money.

Quick and Easy Cucumber Tomato Salad

Nutritional Information:

Total fat: 16.5g

Cholesterol: 0mg

Sodium: 9mg

Total carbohydrates: 13.3g

Dietary fiber: 6.8g

Protein: 2.9g

Calcium: 30mg

Potassium: 662mg

Iron: 1mg

Vitamin D: 0mcg

Time: 15 minutes

Serving Size: 4

Ingredients:

- 1 large cucumber, skinned and chopped
- 1 ½ cup cherry tomatoes, quartered
- 2 ripe avocados, pitted, peeled and chopped into large chunks
- 1 green bell pepper, chopped
- 2 tbsp fresh cilantro chopped
- ½ tbsp avocado oil
- 1 tbsp red wine vinegar
- 1 tbsp almond
- Salt and pepper to taste

Directions:

1. Add all veggies to a large mixing bowl.
2. Whisk together almond oil, red wine vinegar, lemon juice, cilantro, salt and pepper to make vinaigrette.
3. Pour into veggies and toss to coat. Divide the salad among serving bowls and serve.

Oven Baked Spicy Cauliflower Wings

Nutritional Information:

Total fat: 1.1g

Cholesterol: 0mg

Sodium: 284mg

Total carbohydrates: 4.9g

Dietary fiber: 2.3g

Protein: 2g

Calcium: 19mg

Potassium: 264mg

Iron: 0mg

Vitamin D: 0mcg

Time: 45 minutes

Serving Size: 5

Ingredients:

- 4 cups cauliflower florets
- 3 tbsp hot sauce
- 1 tbsp almond flour
- 1 tbsp avocado oil
- Salt to taste

Directions:

1. Preheat your oven to 350 degrees F.
2. Prepare a baking sheet by lining it with parchment paper.
3. Mix all the ingredients in a medium mixing bowl and toss to thoroughly cut the cauliflower florets.
4. Place the cauliflower in a single layer on the prepared baking sheet.
5. Bake for 40 minutes or until the cauliflower is crisp at the edges. Turn the cauliflower halfway through the baking process. Serve warm with extra hot sauce if desired. Hot sauce can be removed from the recipe if you would like a milder flavor.

Spicy Cucumber Salad

Nutritional Information:

Total fat: 9.5g

Cholesterol: 0mg

Sodium: 404mg

Total carbohydrates: 5.7g

Dietary fiber: 1g

Protein: 1.6g

Calcium: 31mg

Potassium: 205mg

Iron: 1mg

Vitamin D: 0mcg

Time: 40 minutes

Serving Size: 3

Ingredients:

- 1 large cucumber, sliced
- 2 scallions, finely sliced
- 2 tbsp sesame oil
- ½ tsp toasted sesame seeds
- 1 tbsp rice vinegar
- 2 tbsp of low sodium soy sauce
- ½ tsp red pepper flakes, crushed
- Salt and pepper to taste

Directions:

1. In a small bowl, combine sesame oil, sesame seeds, rice vinegar, soy sauce, red pepper flakes, salt and pepper to create salad dressing.
2. Add cucumber and scallions to a mixing bowl and toss with salad dressing.
3. Refrigerate for at least 30 minutes to let the flavors marinade. Serve chilled.

Grilled Tofu Skewers

Nutritional Information:

Total fat: 3.8g

Cholesterol: 0mg

Sodium: 211mg

Total carbohydrates: 9.4g

Dietary fiber: 2.4g

Protein: 3.3g

Calcium: 61mg

Potassium: 385mg

Iron: 1mg

Vitamin D: 0mcg

Time: 35 minutes

Serving Size: 6

Ingredients:

- 1 block firm tofu
- 1 red bell pepper, cut into squares
- 1 yellow bell pepper, cut into squares
- 1 red onion, cut into squares
- 2 small zucchini, sliced
- 2 cups cherry tomatoes
- 2 tbsp low sodium soy sauce
- 2 tsp sesame seeds
- 3 tsp olive oil
- Salt and pepper to taste

Directions:

1. Press the tofu to extract any liquid for about half an hour and cut into cubes. Marinade in the soy sauce for 15 minutes.
2. While the tofu marinades, prepare veggies. Ensure that they are cut into the same size to ensure even cooking.
3. Assemble skewers by sticking vegetables and tofu cubes on bamboo sticks alternately until all the vegetables have been used.
4. Heat a grill or pan until sizzling hot. Grease with olive oil and place skewers on. Cook for a few minutes on each side until the vegetables are soft but not mushy, the peppers begin to char, and the tofu becomes golden brown. Season with salt

and pepper, brush with olive oil and sprinkle with sesame seeds at the end of the cooking process.

5. Remove from grill or pan and serve hot with your favorite vegan keto friendly condiment.

Creamy Tomato Soup

Nutritional Information:

Total fat: 0.3g

Cholesterol: 0mg

Sodium: 10mg

Total carbohydrates: 5.6g

Dietary fiber: 1.8g

Protein: 1.3g

Calcium: 22mg

Potassium: 323mg

Iron: 1mg

Vitamin D: 0mcg

Time: 35 minutes

Serving Size: 10

Ingredients:

- 3 15-oz cans diced tomatoes with juice
- 3 ½ cup water
- 3 scallions, chopped
- 1 garlic clove, minced
- 1 tsp dried oregano
- 6 basil leaves
- ½ tsp smoked paprika
- Salt and pepper to taste

Directions:

1. Add all ingredients to a large pot and stir. Place over high heat and bring to a boil.
2. Reduce heat to medium low and simmer for 20 minutes or until the sauce thickens.
3. Can be served as is or an immersion blender can be used to achieve a smoother consistency. Separate into serving bowls and serve.

Avocado Zucchini Noodles

Nutritional Information:

Total fat: 31.7g

Cholesterol: 0mg

Sodium: 26mg

Total carbohydrates: 16.8g

Dietary fiber: 9.2g

Protein: 6.5g

Calcium: 53mg

Potassium: 997mg

Iron: 2mg

Vitamin D: 0mcg

Time: 15 minutes

Serving Size: 2

Ingredients:

- 1 medium zucchini
- 1 small avocado
- 1 cup cherry tomatoes, sliced
- ⅓ cup water
- 1 cup basil
- 2 tbsp lemon juice
- 4 tbsp pine nuts

Directions:

1. To make the zucchini noodles, use a spiralizer or peeler.
2. Add all the other ingredients except the cherry tomato to a blender and blend until a smooth creamy consistency is attained.
3. Transfer mixture to a large mixing bowl. Add zucchini noodles and tomatoes. Mix to combine. Serve. Can be stored in an airtight container in the refrigerator for up to 2 days.

Creamy Pumpkin Soup

Nutritional Information:

Total fat: 15.5g

Cholesterol: 0mg

Sodium: 1281mg

Total carbohydrates: 12.2g

Dietary fiber: 6.2g

Protein: 2.4g

Calcium: 27mg

Potassium: 244mg

Iron: 2mg

Vitamin D: 0mcg

Time: 20 minutes

Serving Size: 5

Ingredients:

- 1 15-oz can pumpkin puree
- ½ cup unsweetened coconut milk
- 2 tsp unsweetened Thai red curry paste
- ½ tsp salt
- ½ tsp onion powder
- ½ tsp garlic powder
- Water, if needed

Directions:

1. Add all ingredients to a medium pot and place over high heat. Bring to a boil while stirring constantly. Add water if needed to reach the desired consistency.
2. Reduce heat to low, cover the pot and allow to simmer for 10 minutes, stirring at 3 minutes intervals. Serve.

Lime Coconut Cauliflower Rice

Nutritional Information:

Total fat: 12.1g

Cholesterol: 0mg

Sodium: 97mg

Total carbohydrates: 8.6g

Dietary fiber: 4.3g

Protein: 8.8g

Calcium: 13mg

Potassium: 164mg

Iron: 2mg

Vitamin D: 0mcg

Time: 15 minutes

Serving Size: 2

Ingredients:

- 1 cup cauliflower florets
- 1 tbsp lime juice
- ½ cup full fat coconut milk
- ¼ cup hulled hemp seeds
- A pinch of salt

Directions:

1. To make a cauliflower rice, add cauliflower to food processor and pulse until a rice-like consistency is achieved.
2. Add riced cauliflower to a Dutch oven placed over medium heat. Stir in remaining ingredients except for lime juice.
3. Cover and cook for 10 minutes or until the liquid has evaporated from hemp seeds and the cauliflower rice is tender.
4. Remove from heat and allow to cool slightly and stir in lime juice. Serve.

Sautéed Jackfruit Cauliflower Bowl

Nutritional Information:

Total fat: 15.4g

Cholesterol: 0mg

Sodium: 172mg

Total carbohydrates: 13.6g

Dietary fiber: 6.6g

Protein: 5.3g

Calcium: 37mg

Potassium: 375mg

Iron: 1mg

Vitamin D: 0mcg

Time: 20 minutes

Serving Size: 4

Ingredients:

- 1 can jackfruit in water, drained and chopped
- 3 cups cauliflower rice
- 1 cup kale
- 1 tbsp chili powder
- 1 tbsp olive oil
- 1 tsp garlic powder
- 1 tsp onion powder
- Avocado slices for serving

Directions:

1. Add olive oil to a nonstick skillet and place over medium heat. Once it is heated and all the other ingredients except for the avocado.
2. Sauté until the cauliflower rice is tender. Stir often to incorporate the spices.
3. Plate and serve with avocado slices.

Tuna Imitation Salad

Nutritional Information:

Total fat: 15.8g

Cholesterol: 0mg

Sodium: 306mg

Total carbohydrates: 8.9g

Dietary fiber: 2.9g

Protein: 20.3g

Calcium: 383mg

Potassium: 54mg

Iron: 4mg

Vitamin D: 0mcg

Time:10 minutes

Serving Size: 4

Ingredients:

- 1 block extra firm tofu, drained, pressed to remove any extra moisture and crumbled
- ¼ cup celery, finely chopped
- ¼ cup carrots, finely chopped
- 1 tsp onion powder
- 1 tsp garlic powder
- 1 tsp lemon juice
- ½ cup vegan mayonnaise
- Salt and pepper to taste

Directions:

1. Add all ingredients to a large mixing bowl and mix to combine well.
2. Chill for 15 minutes before serving. Can be served with celery sticks or other fresh cut veggies as well as used to make a sandwich. Can be stored in the refrigerator in an airtight container for up to 4 days.

Lettuce Salad Bowls

Nutritional Information:

Total fat: 17.9g

Cholesterol: 0mg

Sodium: 21mg

Total carbohydrates: 7.9g

Dietary fiber: 4.9g

Protein: 3.6g

Calcium: 72mg

Potassium: 72mg

Iron: 2mg

Vitamin D: 0mcg

Time: 10 minutes

Serving Size: 4

Ingredients:

- 1 avocado, halved, pitted and chopped
- 4 lettuce leaves
- ¼ cup purple cabbage, chopped
- 4 tbsp tahini

- Salt and pepper to taste

Directions:

1. Combine tahini and purple cabbage in a bowl. Ensure that purple cabbage is well coated.
2. To arrange salad bowls, add cabbage mixture to the center of each lettuce bowl. Top with the rest of the ingredients. Sprinkle will salt and pepper to season. Serve.

Keto Vegan Empanadas

Nutritional Information:

Total fat: 6g

Cholesterol: 0mg

Sodium: 100mg

Total carbohydrates: 15.5g

Dietary fiber: 10.7g

Protein: 2.8g

Calcium: 34mg

Potassium: 38mg

Iron: 0mg

Vitamin D: 0mcg

Time: 45 minutes

Serving Size: 8

Ingredients:

- ½ cup coconut flour
- ½ cup almond flour
- ¼ cup cold vegan butter, cubed
- ½ tsp olive oil
- ½ cup tofu, pressed, drained of any excess liquid and finely crumbled
- 1 tsp of soy sauce
- ¼ cup water
- ½ tsp paprika
- ¼ tsp ground cumin
- ¼ tsp oregano
- 2 tbsp tomato sauce
- 2 tbsp of psyllium husk
- A pinch of salt

Directions:

1. Add coconut flour, almond flour, salt vegan butter and psyllium husk to a food processor and process to form a crumbly dough. You can also do this by using your hands.
2. Add water and knead to form a wet dough. Divide the dough and form small 8 balls. Place these balls in the refrigerator to rest for up to 10 minutes.
3. To create filling, add olive oil to a small skillet and place over medium heat. Once oil is heated, add crumbled tofu. Sauté until tofu is warmed then add soy sauce, water and other spices. Stir. Bring to a boil and simmer for 5 minutes or until all the liquid has been.
4. Stir in tomato sauce and allow mixture to cool.
5. Preheat your oven to 350 degrees F.
6. Prepare a baking sheet by lining it with parchment paper.
7. Remove the dough from the refrigerator and roll out into 2 millimeter thick circles. You can also use a tortilla press to do this.
8. Place a spoonful of filling in the center of each piece of dough.
9. Fold the dough over and shape empanada. If any tears form, just smooth over gently with your fingers. Place empanada on prepared baking sheet.
10. Repeat with the rest of the dough balls.
11. Baked empanadas for 12 minutes.
12. Allow to cool slightly before serving. Can be served warm or cold. Can be served alongside a salad.

Avocado Fries

Nutritional Information:

Total fat: 15.7g

Cholesterol: 1mg

Sodium: 5mg

Total carbohydrates: 6.3g

Dietary fiber: 4.1g

Protein: 3g

Calcium: 32mg

Potassium: 297mg

Iron: 1mg

Vitamin D: 0mcg

Time: 30 minutes

Serving Size: 5

Ingredients:

- 1 large not overly ripe avocado
- 1 tsp Italian seasoning
- ¼ cup almond milk
- ½ cup almond meal

Directions:

1. Preheat your oven to 450 degrees F.
2. Prepare a baking sheet by spraying it with nonstick spray.
3. Half avocado lengthwise and pit. Peel off skin and cut into wedges of preferred size.
4. Mix the rest of the ingredients in a shallow bowl wide enough to fit avocado slices. This should form a thick batter.
5. Dip avocado slices in batter and coat thoroughly.
6. Place avocado fries on prepared baking sheet and bake for up to 20 minutes or until lightly golden.
7. Allow to cool for a few minutes then serve immediately. Can be served with your favorite keto vegan dipping sauce.

Sautéed Squash Kale Bowl

Nutritional Information:

Total fat: 18.1g

Cholesterol: 0mg

Sodium: 412mg

Total carbohydrates: 11.9g

Dietary fiber: 3.4g

Protein: 3.8g

Calcium: 69mg

Potassium: 379mg

Iron: 1mg

Vitamin D: 0mcg

Time: 30 minutes

Serving Size: 6

Ingredients:

- 2 cups butternut squash, cubed
- 2 cups kale, stems discarded, and leaves chopped
- ½ cup pecans, toasted

- 1 tsp ginger, grated
- 1 tsp garlic, grated
- 4 tbsp low-sodium tamari
- 2 tbsp olive oil

Directions:

1. Add olive oil to a nonstick skillet and place over medium heat. Once the oil is heated, add butternut squash. Toss to coat with oil. Cover pan and cook for 5 minutes.
2. Add garlic, ginger and tamari. Stir. Cook for 10 more minutes.
3. Add kale, cover pan and cook for 5 more minutes or until the kale leaves have wilted.
4. Remove pan from heat and toss in toasted pecans. Serve.

Avocado Cauliflower Salad

Nutritional Information:

Total fat: 23.1g

Cholesterol: 33mg

Sodium: 214mg

Total carbohydrates: 6.2g

Dietary fiber: 1.7g

Protein: 6.5g

Calcium:46mg

Potassium: 318mg

Iron: 1mg

Vitamin D: 0mcg

Time: 25 minutes

Serving Size: 3

Ingredients:

- 2 cups cauliflower florets
- 1/2 cup tempeh, cooked and diced
- 5 tablespoons spicy avocado mayonnaise (See recipe *Chapter 4: Sauces and Condiments: Spicy Avocado Mayonnaise*)
- 1/2 tsp fresh parsley, chopped
- Salt and pepper to taste

Directions:

1. Steam cauliflower by placing a steamer basket over a large pot with at least 2 cups of water in it. Bring water to a boil then add cauliflower florets to steamer basket. Steam cauliflower for about 8 minutes or until tender.
2. Remove cauliflower florets from heat and allow to cool down for a few minutes.
3. Add tempeh to a large skillet and crisp for about 5 minutes. Remove from heat and allow to cool completely.
4. Add all ingredients to a large bowl except for parsley and mix well to form creamy salad. Top with parsley and serve warm or chilled.

Mushroom Cauliflower Soup

Nutritional Information:

Total fat: 2.7g

Cholesterol: 0mg

Sodium: 113mg

Total carbohydrates: 10.6g

Dietary fiber: 3.5g

Protein: 2.5g

Calcium: 181mg

Potassium: 389mg

Iron: 1mg

Vitamin D: 1mcg

Time: 45 minutes

Serving Size: 3

Ingredients:

- 2 cups cauliflower florets
- 1 ½ cup white onions, diced
- 1 ½ cup unsweetened almond milk
- 1 tsp onion powder
- 1/2 tsp olive oil
- ⅓ cup mushrooms, sliced
- 2 tbsp yellow onion, diced
- Salt and pepper to taste

Directions:

1. Add cauliflower, almond milk, onion powder, salt and pepper to a saucepan and place over medium heat. Bring to a boil. Reduce heat to low and simmer for 8 minutes or until cauliflower is tender.

2. Puree mixture with an immersion blender or by adding to a food processor or blender.
3. Place another pan over high heat. Add olive oil, mushrooms and onion and sauté until onions are translucent and begin to brown slightly. This will take about 10 minutes.
4. Add pureed cauliflower mixture to sautéed mushrooms. Bring mixture to a boil, cover and simmer for 10 minutes or until sauce is thick. Serve immediately.

Zucchini Veggie Wraps

Nutritional Information:
Total fat: 6.2g

Cholesterol: 0mg

Sodium:229mg

Total carbohydrates: 5.2g

Dietary fiber: 1.8g

Protein: 2.2g

Calcium: 41mg

Potassium: 197mg

Iron: 1mg

Vitamin D: 0mcg

Time: 20 minutes

Serving Size: 10

Ingredients:
- 2 medium zucchini, thinly sliced lengthwise
- 1 yellow bell pepper, deseeded and sliced
- 1 red bell pepper, deseeded and sliced
- 6 green lettuce leaves, torn into pieces the same size as the zucchini slices
- 1 cup basil
- 1 cup spinach
- 1 garlic clove
- 2 tbsp almond butter
- 3 tbsp olive oil
- Salt and pepper to taste

Directions:
1. To create pesto dressing, add basil, spinach, garlic, almond butter, olive oil and salt to a food processor and process until a uniform consistency is achieved.
2. To assemble wraps, lay zucchini slices down first and layer with the dressing mixture.

3. Add the rest of the vegetables. Roll the zucchini and stick with a toothpick in the center. Top with salt and pepper to taste. Serve.

Cauliflower Cabbage Wraps

Nutritional Information:

Total fat: 6.5g

Cholesterol: 0mg

Sodium: 74mg

Total carbohydrates: 8.6g

Dietary fiber: 4.4g

Protein: 3.2g

Calcium: 66mg

Potassium: 333mg

Iron: 2mg

Vitamin D: 0mcg

Time: 45 minutes

Serving Size: 6

Ingredients:

- 6 green lettuce leaves
- 4 cups cauliflower florets
- 1 cup red cabbage, thinly sliced
- ½ small avocado, peeled and pitted
- 1 tbsp lime juice
- ½ tsp chili powder
- ⅓ cup cilantro, chopped
- 1 14-oz can green chilies
- ½ cup cashew butter
- 1 tbsp olive oil
- Salt and pepper to taste

Directions:

1. Preheat your oven to 400 degrees F.
2. Toss cauliflower florets with olive oil, salt and pepper and spread across a baking sheet. Roast for 30 minutes.
3. Add cashew butter, green chilies, lime juice, cilantro and chili powder in a blender and process to a smooth consistency.

4. Once the cauliflower is done roasting, toss with cashew chili sauce.
5. Mash avocado with lime juice until a creamy consistency is achieved.
6. Toss avocado mixture with red cabbage and season with salt and pepper.
7. Layer each lettuce leave with a scoop of the avocado mixture and a scoop of the cashew cauliflower mixture. Can be served with additional toppings such as hot sauce or additional cilantro.

Zucchini Green Bean Salad

Nutritional Information:

Total fat: 3.7g

Cholesterol: 1mg

Sodium: 4mg

Total carbohydrates: 8.4g

Dietary fiber: 3.2g

Protein: 2.3g

Calcium: 38mg

Potassium: 437mg

Iron: 1mg

Vitamin D: 0mcg

Time: 40 minutes

Serving Size: 9

Ingredients:

- 2 large zucchini, sliced
- 4 cups green beans, trimmed
- 2 tbsp olive oil
- 2 tsp Italian seasoning
- 4 medium tomatoes, chopped
- ½ cup fresh basil, sliced
- ½ cup balsamic vinegar
- 2 tbsp dried cranberries
- Salt and pepper to taste

Directions:

1. Preheat your grill on high heat.
2. Place green beans and zucchini in a large bowl. Whisk Italian seasoning, olive oil, salt and pepper in a small bowl. Conserve half of olive oil for dressing. Add Italian

seasoning mixture to zucchini and green beans and toss so that veggies are evenly coated.
3. Place the zucchini and green beans on the grill and cook for 10 minutes or until charred. Stir occasionally.
4. To make dressing, add balsamic vinegar, cranberries, remaining olive oil, salt and pepper to a food processor and process until well mixed.
5. Add grilled veggies to a large bowl. Add chopped tomatoes. Toss with prepared balsamic vinegar dressing. Serve.

Quick and Easy Cauliflower Pizza Bites

Nutritional Information:

Total fat: 0.6g

Cholesterol: 0mg

Sodium: 31mg

Total carbohydrates: 2.5g

Dietary fiber: 1g

Protein: 0.8g

Calcium: 10mg

Potassium: 95mg

Iron: 0mg

Vitamin D: 0mcg

Time: 35 minutes

Serving Size: 12

Ingredients:

- 3 cups cauliflower florets
- ¾ cups vegan cheese, shredded
- 1 tbsp of flaxseed
- 3 tbsp water
- 3 tbsp marinara sauce
- ½ tsp garlic powder
- ½ tsp onion powder
- Salt and pepper to taste

Directions:

1. Preheat your oven to 400 degrees F.
2. Prepare a 12 mini muffin tin pan by lining with parchment paper strips.

3. Add cauliflower to food processor and process until a rice like consistency is achieved.
4. Transfer cauliflower rice to microwave-safe bowl. Microwave for 5 minutes.
5. Allow cauliflower to cool for a few minutes then place in a cheesecloth and squeeze tightly to remove any excess moisture.
6. Add cauliflower to a large mixing bowl. Add all the other ingredients to the mixing bowl and mix. Reserve 1/4 cup of vegan cheese.
7. Scoop out tablespoonfuls of cauliflower mixture and place in cups of muffin tin pan.
8. Press the mixture down tightly and bake for 15 minutes.
9. Remove the pizza bites from the oven and top with remaining vegan cheese then broil for 1 minute.
10. Allow the cauliflower pizza bites to cool down for 15 minutes then remove from pan by pulling on the parchment paper edges. Can be served with marinara sauce.

Chapter 7: Dinner Recipes

Breakfast gives you nutrition to kick-start the day and lunch is the great opportunity to refuel and refocus to keep that same energy throughout the rest of the day. This begs the question of why dinner is important. The first reason is that this meal provides fuel for the body so that you do not wake up in the middle of the night hungry. This interruption can disrupt your sleep patterns, make you gain inadequate amounts of sleep, and cause you to feel drained the next day.

Eating dinner is also the perfect opportunity to spend time with your family and friends which helps with social bonding.

There is a common misperception that skipping dinner results in weight loss but, more often than not, the opposite is true. Not eating dinner can actually make it more difficult to lose weight because the body goes into survival mode when it is starved and stores more fat.

It is essential that you partake in this meal so here are a few tips to ensure that you get the best out of your dinner:

- Eat slowly and relax so that your body can properly digest the nutrition that you are providing. Eating slowly also helps in weight loss management since it takes the body about 20 minutes to register that it is full. Eating slowly allows you to not overeat.

- Eat early in the evening so that your body has an adequate amount of time to digest a meal before bedtime. This helps reduce the risk of developing obesity and weight loss problems, helps lower the risk of developing cancer, helps improve heart health, improves energy and mood levels, improves digestive health and helps you sleep better.
- Do not partake in foods that are high in carbohydrates as they increase blood sugar and make it difficult to fall asleep and stay asleep during the night.

After realizing how important the last meal of the day is, I am sure that you are eager to get started in trying out the recipes outlined below.

Cauliflower Steaks

Nutritional Information:

Total fat: 3g

Cholesterol: 0mg

Sodium: 283mg

Total carbohydrates: 9.4g

Dietary fiber: 4.3g

Protein: 3.4g

Calcium: 39mg

Potassium: 517mg

Iron: 1mg

Vitamin D: 0mcg

Time: 45 minutes

Serving Size: 5

Ingredients:

- 1 large head cauliflower
- 1 tbsp olive oil
- ½ tsp curry powder
- 1 garlic clove, grated
- 1 tbsp lime juice
- ½ teaspoon salt

Directions:

1. Thoroughly washed the cauliflower and allow to dry. Trim of the leaves and the bottom stem off the cauliflower. Leave the core intact and cut through the center

of the cauliflower to ensure that the florets remain intact. Cut one inch slices and place in a large mixing bowl.

2. In a small bowl, create the marinade by combining the rest of the ingredients. Pour over cauliflower steaks, mix and allow to sit for 1 hour.
3. Preheat your oven to 400 degrees F.
4. Prepare a baking sheet by lining it with parchment paper.
5. Place marinated cauliflower steaks on the prepared baking sheet and bake for 20 minutes or until cauliflower is crisp at the edges. Serve with a side of roasted veggies.

Veggie Walnut Soup

Nutritional Information:

Total fat: 17.1g

Cholesterol: 0mg

Sodium: 34mg

Total carbohydrates: 11.7g

Dietary fiber: 4.1g

Protein: 6.8g

Calcium: 56mg

Potassium: 640mg

Iron: 2mg

Vitamin D: 0mcg

Time: 45 minutes

Serving Size: 8

Ingredients:

- 5 celery stalks, finely diced
- 2 green bell peppers, finely diced
- 2 medium zucchini, diced
- 8 oz cremini mushrooms
- 1 cup raw walnuts, minced
- 2 garlic cloves, minced
- 2 tbsp olive oil
- 1 tsp ground cinnamon
- 2 tsp chili powder
- 4 tsp ground cumin
- 1 tsp smoked paprika

- 1 tbsp tomato paste
- ½ cup coconut milk
- 3 cups water
- 1 tbsp unsweetened cocoa powder
- 2 cup tomatoes, diced
- Salt and pepper to taste

Directions:

1. Over medium heat, heat olive oil in a large pot. Add celery and sauté for 4 minutes.
2. Add cumin, paprika, chili powder, cinnamon and garlic and sauté until mixture becomes fragrant or about 2 minutes.
3. Add mushrooms, zucchini, and bell peppers and sauté for 5 more minutes.
4. Add tomato paste, tomatoes, coconut milk, water, walnuts and cocoa powder. Reduce heat to low and simmer for 25 minutes or until the sauce thickens and vegetables are so soft.
5. Season with salt and pepper and serve.

Roasted Red Pepper Soup

Nutritional Information:

Total fat: 17.1g

Cholesterol: 0mg

Sodium: 552mg

Total carbohydrates: 9.6g

Dietary fiber: 4g

Protein: 3.4g

Calcium: 41mg

Potassium: 482mg

Iron: 1mg

Vitamin D: 0mcg

Time: 30 minutes

Serving Size: 5

Ingredients:

- ½ cup roasted red peppers, chopped
- 5 cups cauliflower florets
- 4 cups water
- ½ tsp apple cider vinegar

- 1 cup coconut milk
- 2 tbsp coconut oil
- 1 scallion, finely chopped
- 1 tsp salt
- 1 tsp smoked paprika
- A pinch of red pepper flakes, crushed
- A pinch of fresh thyme

Directions:

1. Add coconut oil to a heavy-bottomed pan and place over medium heat. Add scallions and sauté for 3 minutes.
2. Add roasted red peppers and all spices and sauté for 3 minutes.
3. Add cauliflower water and vinegar. Bring to a simmer, cover pot and allow to cook for 15 minutes or until the cauliflower is soft and breaking apart easily.
4. Use an immersion blender to blend to a smooth consistency.
5. Add coconut milk and cook until warm. Serve.

Zucchini Spinach Ravioli

Nutritional Information:

Total fat: 23.7g

Cholesterol: 0mg

Sodium: 461mg

Total carbohydrates: 12.8g

Dietary fiber: 3.8g

Protein: 11.1g

Calcium: 51mg

Potassium: 499mg

Iron: 3mg

Vitamin D: 0mcg

Time: 1 hour

Serving Size: 7

Ingredients:

- 4 medium zucchini, sliced with mandolin
- 1 cup fresh spinach
- 1 cup raw cashews
- 1 cup walnuts

- 1 cup water
- 1 cup fresh basil
- 1 ½ tsp salt
- ½ tsp ground black pepper
- ¼ cup pine nuts
- 4 garlic cloves
- ¼ cup hemp hearts
- Cashew Cheese Sauce (See Recipes *Chapter 4: Sauces and Condiments: Keto Vegan Raw Cashew Cheese Sauce*)

Directions:

1. Preheat your oven to 350 degrees F.
2. Prepare a baking sheet by lining it with parchment paper.
3. Place zucchini slices on paper towels and sprinkle with salt to draw out excess moisture. Allow to sit.
4. Create "Parmesan" by placing pine nuts, hemp hearts and salt in a food processor and pulse to a crumbly texture. Set aside
5. Place spinach, cashews, walnuts, garlic, salt, pepper, water and basil in a food processor and pulse to a ricotta-like texture.
6. Wipe off any remaining moisture from zucchini slices and taking 4 at a time, make an X shape. Place a spoonful of ricotta mixture and place in the center where the zucchini slices meet.
7. Fold the tips of the zucchini over to make a ravioli pocket. Place in the prepared baking sheet and repeat until all the zucchini slices have been used up. Make enough ravioli for a serving of 4 each.
8. Sprinkle with Parmesan mixture.
9. Bake for 30 minutes or until zucchini is fully cooked.
10. Allow to sit for 15 minutes before serving. Top with cashew cheese sauce and serve.

Keto Vegan Shepherd's Pie

Nutritional Information:

Total fat: 7.4g

Cholesterol: 0mg

Sodium: 47mg

Total carbohydrates: 14.5g

Dietary fiber: 3.9g

Protein: 7.1g

Calcium: 68mg

Potassium: 455mg

Iron: 3mg

Vitamin D: 41mcg

Time: 1 hour 10 minutes

Serving Size: 8

Ingredients:

- 6 cups cauliflower florets
- 1 yellow onion, diced
- 2 medium carrots, peeled and diced
- 3 garlic cloves, chopped
- 1 celery stalk, diced
- 5 dried wild mushrooms
- 3 cups cremini mushrooms, diced
- ¼ cup water
- 1 cup vegetable stock
- 4 tbsp olive oil
- 1 tbsp thyme leaves, roughly chopped
- 1 tbsp tomato paste
- 3 tbsp nutritional yeast
- A pinch ground nutmeg

Directions:

1. Reconstitute wild mushrooms by soaking in 1/4 cup boiling water for 30 minutes.
2. Preheat your oven to 400 degrees F.
3. Prepare a baking pan by greasing it with vegan butter or extra olive oil.
4. Add cauliflower florets to a large saucepan. Cover with water, add salt and place pan over medium heat. Bring to a boil and cook cauliflower until tender. Drain and set aside.
5. Place a large frying pan over medium heat and add 2 tablespoons of olive oil, carrots, onion, and celery. Cook until the vegetables become caramelized.
6. Add the cremini mushrooms in increments of 4. Ensure that each increment is cooked before adding the next.
7. Remove the wild mushrooms from the water. Reserve water. Roughly chop the mushrooms. Add to the frying pan.
8. Increase the heat from medium to high and add tomato paste and 1/4 cup of water. Cook until the liquid has almost evaporated before adding the wild mushrooms, liquid reserved from soaking the mushrooms, and vegetable stock.
9. Reduce heat to low and simmer for 10 minutes or until half of the liquid has evaporated. Remove the pan from the heat.
10. Add cauliflower to a food processor along with 2 tablespoons of olive oil, nutritional yeast, thyme leaves, nutmeg and salt. Blend until a smooth creamy consistency is achieved.

11. Pour mushroom mixture into the bottom of the prepared baking pan. Spread evenly on the bottom of the pan.
12. Top with the cauliflower mash. Smooth the top with a spatula.
13. Bake for 20 minutes or until the top is golden brown.
14. Allow to cool completely before dividing into serving plates.

Green Soup

Nutritional Information:

Total fat: 0.3g

Cholesterol: 0mg

Sodium: 200mg

Total carbohydrates: 11g

Dietary fiber: 3.6g

Protein: 3.6g

Calcium: 83mg

Potassium: 483mg

Iron: 2mg

Vitamin D: 0mcg

Time: 45 minutes

Serving Size: 6

Ingredients:

- 3 cups cauliflower, chopped
- 3 cups broccoli, chopped
- 1 large leek, chopped
- 3 cups water
- 2 cups kale
- 1 tbsp soy sauce
- ½ cup parsley
- 1 sprig of thyme
- 1 tsp turmeric
- 2 bay leaves
- 1 teaspoon garlic powder

Directions:

1. Cover chopped cauliflower and broccoli with water in a large pot and boil for 10 minutes over medium-high heat until just tender.

2. Add remaining ingredients and simmer for 10 minutes or until the kale is cooked.
3. Remove bay leaves and add mixture to blender. Blend until a smooth creamy consistency is achieved.
4. Divide into serving bowls and serve. Can be topped with roasted veggies.

Portobello Mushroom Tacos with Guacamole

Nutritional Information:

Total fat: 18.7g

Cholesterol: 3mg

Sodium: 131mg

Total carbohydrates: 12g

Dietary fiber: 4.9g

Protein: 4.4g

Calcium: 24mg

Potassium: 566mg

Iron: 1mg

Vitamin D: 0mcg

Time: 35 minutes

Serving Size: 7

Ingredients:

- 1 lb. portobello mushrooms, destemmed, rinsed and dried
- 3 tbsp olive oil
- 1 tsp ground cumin
- 1 tsp onion powder
- 1/4 cup harissa
- 7 lettuce leaves, rinsed and dried
- 2 ripe medium avocados
- 2 tbsp tomatoes, chopped
- 2 tbsp red onion, chopped
- 2 tbsp lime juice
- 1 tbsp cilantro, chopped
- A pinch of salt

Directions:

1. Mix half of olive oil, cumin, onion powder and harissa in a small bowl.

2. Brush each mushroom with cumin mixture, ensuring well coated. Allow to marinade for at least 15 minutes.
3. Prepare guacamole while mushrooms are marinating by halving and pitting avocados and scooping out the flesh. Add avocados, chopped tomatoes, red onions, lime juice, salt and cilantro to a bowl and mash to desired consistency.
4. When the mushrooms are done marinating, heat the remaining olive oil in a non-stick skillet over medium high. When the oil has become heated, place the mushrooms in the pan and cook for 3 minutes or until edges are browned. Flip and cook for another 3 minutes.
5. Turn off the heat and allow the mushrooms to rest for 3 minutes before slicing.
6. Fill each lettuce leaf with a few slices of portobello. Add guacamole and other desired toppings like more chopped tomatoes and cilantro. Serve.

Roasted Mushroom Burgers

Nutritional Information:

Total fat: 9.1g

Cholesterol: 5mg

Sodium: 316mg

Total carbohydrates: 6.5g

Dietary fiber: 2.9g

Protein: 6.5g

Calcium: 90mg

Potassium: 248mg

Iron: 3mg

Vitamin D: 189mcg

Time: 45 minutes

Serving Size: 4

Ingredients:

- 3 cups mushrooms, cooked and chopped
- 1 tbsp chia seeds
- ½ tsp salt
- ¼ tsp black pepper
- 3 tbsp protein powder
- ¼ tsp sweet paprika
- ¼ cup tahini

Directions:

1. Preheat your oven to 350 degrees F.
2. Prepare a baking sheet by lining it with parchment paper.
3. Add chopped mushrooms to food processor and pulse to a coarse consistency.
4. Transfer mushrooms to a mixing bowl and stir in chia seeds, salt, pepper, rosemary and tahini. Combine thoroughly. Allow mixture to stand for 5 minutes so that it thickens.
5. Stir in protein powder gradually until completely absorbed. If the protein powder stops being easily incorporated, stop adding protein powder so that the mixture does not become dry.
6. Form equally-sized patties and place them on the prepared baking sheet.
7. Bake for 25 minutes or until patties are firm.
8. Remove patties from oven and allow to cool for a few minutes before serving your favorite keto vegan bread topped with veggies and keto vegan friendly sauce.

Roasted Radishes

Nutritional Information:

Total fat: 5g

Cholesterol: 0mg

Sodium: 281mg

Total carbohydrates: 2g

Dietary fiber: 0.8g

Protein: 0.9g

Calcium: 28mg

Potassium: 88mg

Iron: 1mg

Vitamin D: 0mcg

Time: 30 minutes

Serving Size: 5

Ingredients:

- 25 medium radishes, washed, trimmed and quartered
- 2 green onions, sliced
- 1 ½ tbsp soy sauce
- 1 ½ tbsp peanut oil
- 3 tsp sesame seeds

Directions:

1. Preheat your oven to 425 degrees F.
2. Prepare a baking sheet by spraying it with nonstick spray.
3. Place the radishes on the baking sheet and brush with peanut oil. Arrange radishes cut side down so that it browns in the best manner.
4. Roast radishes for 20 minutes, stirring halfway through.
5. Mixed together soy sauce and any remaining peanut oil.
6. Remove radishes from the oven at the 20 minute mark and brush with the soy sauce mixture. Sprinkle with green onions. Bake for 5 more minutes.
7. Toast sesame seeds by placing in a hot dry pan and shaking pan for 1 minute over medium heat.
8. Sprinkle roasted radishes with toasted sesame seeds and serve hot. Can be served with your favorite keto vegan dipping sauce.

Roasted Pepper Zoodles

Nutritional Information:

Total fat: 16.8g

Cholesterol: 0mg

Sodium: 25mg

Total carbohydrates: 10.3g

Dietary fiber: 3.3g

Protein: 4.4g

Calcium: 27mg

Potassium: 428mg

Iron: 2mg

Vitamin D: 0mcg

Time: 25 minutes

Serving Size: 6

Ingredients:

- 2 red bell peppers, sliced
- ½ cup fresh arugula
- ½ cup fresh basil
- ¼ cup fresh cilantro
- 5 tbsp olive oil
- ¼ cup nutritional yeast
- 2 medium zucchini, spiralized into noodles

- 1 tbsp vegan butter
- 2 garlic cloves, minced
- 2 tsp lemon juice
- Salt and pepper to taste

Directions:

1. Preheat your oven to 300 degrees F.
2. Prepare a baking sheet by spraying it with nonstick spray. Place pepper slices skin side up in a single layer on prepared baking sheet. Place in oven broiler and broil for 10 minutes or until pepper skin chars.
3. Place peppers in food processor. Add arugula, basil, nutritional yeast, cilantro, salt and pepper. Process while streaming in 3 tablespoons of olive oil.
4. Place the rest of olive oil and vegan butter into a large skillet. Place over medium heat. Add garlic once the oil has heated and cook for 1 minute.
5. Add lemon juice and zucchini noodles and cook for 5 minutes or until the noodles soften slightly. Toss often.
6. Add pepper mixture and cook for 5 minutes.
7. Serve. Can be topped with nutritional yeast for a cheesier flavor.

Creamy Curry Zucchini Noodles

Nutritional Information:

Total fat: 16.5g

Cholesterol: 16mg

Sodium: 585mg

Total carbohydrates: 10g

Dietary fiber: 3.5g

Protein: 2.9g

Calcium: 42mg

Potassium: 569mg

Iron: 2mg

Vitamin D: 0mcg

Time: 20 minutes

Serving Size: 5

Ingredients:

- 2 large zucchini, spiralized
- 2 tbsp olive oil

- 2 cups cauliflower florets
- 1 red bell pepper, diced
- ¼ cup cilantro, chopped
- ¼ cup avocado mayonnaise (See recipe *Chapter 4: Sauces and Condiments: Spicy Avocado Mayonnaise*)
- 2 tbsp avocado oil
- 1 tsp ground ginger
- ½ tsp ground black pepper
- 1 tsp salt
- 1 tsp ground turmeric
- 1 tsp ground cumin
- 2 tsp curry powder
- 2 tbsp apple cider vinegar
- ¼ cup water

Directions:

1. Add olive oil to a large nonstick skillet and place over medium heat. Once the oil is hot, sauté zucchini noodles for 5 minutes, stirring occasionally.
2. Remove from heat and allowed to cool for 10 minutes.
3. Transfer zucchini noodles to a large mixing bowl. Add cauliflower, bell peppers and cilantro. Mix well.
4. To make creamy curry sauce, add the rest of the ingredients to a blender and blend until a smooth and creamy consistency is achieved.
5. Pour creamy curry sauce over zucchini and vegetable mixture and toss to coat.
6. Serve immediately or place in the refrigerator to chill for a few hours. Can be stored in an airtight container in the refrigerator for up to 2 days.

Creamy Spinach Shirataki

Nutritional Information:

Total fat: 6.9g

Cholesterol: 0mg

Sodium: 143mg

Total carbohydrates: 7.9g

Dietary fiber: 0.9g

Protein: 1.5g

Calcium: 23mg

Potassium: 60mg

Iron: 0mg

Vitamin D: 0mcg

Time: 25 minutes

Serving Size: 6

Ingredients:

- 1 package Shirataki noodles, drained and rinsed
- 2 oz vegan cream cheese
- 1 cup fresh spinach
- 1 yellow onion, chopped
- 1 tbsp olive oil
- 1 tsp garlic powder
- ½ cup full fat coconut milk
- Salt and pepper to taste

Directions:

1. Salt and pepper to taste
2. Add oil to a nonstick skillet and place over medium heat. When the heat oil is heated, add onions and sauté until onions are translucent.
3. Add spinach and sauté until leaves are wilted.
4. Add all the other ingredients and cook until liquid reduces, and a creamy texture is achieved. Serve.

Tempeh Broccoli Stir Fry Dinner

Nutritional Information:

Total fat: 5.9g

Cholesterol: 0mg

Sodium: 16mg

Total carbohydrates: 4.3g

Dietary fiber: 0.8g

Protein: 4.9g

Calcium: 42mg

Potassium: 210mg

Iron: 1mg

Vitamin D: 0mcg

Time: 25 minutes

Serving Size: 4

Ingredients:

- 3 oz tempeh, chopped
- 1 cup broccoli florets
- 1 cup frozen spinach
- 1 tbsp olive oil
- 1 tsp garlic powder
- Salt and pepper to taste
- Fresh chopped cilantro to garnish

Directions:

1. Add olive oil to a nonstick skillet and place over medium heat. Once the oil has become heated, add tempeh pieces and sauté for about 5 minutes or until the pieces begin to brown. Stir frequently.
2. Add the rest of the ingredients and sauté for about 2 more minutes or until spinach leaves have wilted. Stir occasionally.
3. Divide between serving plates and garnish. Serve.

Sautéed Brussel Sprouts Dish

Nutritional Information:

Total fat: 3.5g

Cholesterol: 0mg

Sodium: 109mg

Total carbohydrates: 9.2g

Dietary fiber: 3.4g

Protein: 4g

Calcium: 48mg

Potassium: 324mg

Iron: 1mg

Vitamin D: 0mcg

Time: 20 minutes

Serving Size: 2

Ingredients:

- 1 cup of Brussel sprouts, chopped
- ½ tsp olive oil
- 1 garlic clove, minced
- 1 tsp onion powder

- 1 cup frozen spinach
- Salt and pepper to taste
- 3 tbsp cauliflower hummus (See recipe *Chapter 4: Sauces and Condiments: Cauliflower Hummus*)

Directions:

1. Add olive oil to a skillet and place over medium heat to heat oil. Once oil is hot, add the Brussel sprouts and garlic and shake the pan so that all the cut sides of the Brussel sprouts settle down in a single layer in the pan.
2. Sauté undisturbed for 5 minutes the cut sides of the sprouts begin to caramelize.
3. Stir, add spinach and cook for 6 more minutes.
4. Add the rest of the ingredients. Stir and cook for 1 more minute.
5. Plate. Top with cauliflower hummus and serve.

Cauliflower Pizza Crust with Veggie Toppings

Nutritional Information:

Total fat: 7.2g

Cholesterol: 0mg

Sodium: 178mg

Total carbohydrates: 7.6g

Dietary fiber: 3.5g

Protein: 3.6g

Calcium: 51mg

Potassium: 50mg

Iron: 1mg

Vitamin D: 0mcg

Time: 1 hour

Serving Size: 5

Ingredients:

- 2 cups cauliflower rice, cooked
- ¼ cup tahini
- ¼ tsp salt
- ¼ cup whole psyllium husk

Directions:

1. Preheat your oven to 375 degrees F.
2. Prepare a baking sheet by lining it with parchment paper.
3. Mix all ingredients to form a uniform dough.
4. Roll the dough out into a 1/4 inch thick circle and place on the prepared baking sheet.
5. Bake for 15 minutes. Flip over and bake for an additional 10 minutes or until crust is golden brown.
6. Remove the dough from the oven and top with your favorite savory keto vegan sauce and fresh, sautéed or roasted veggies. Serve.

Tofu Tomato Stir Fry

Nutritional Information:

Total fat: 7.9g

Cholesterol: 0mg

Sodium: 336mg

Total carbohydrates: 5.5g

Dietary fiber: 1.1g

Protein: 3.1g

Calcium: 40mg

Potassium: 182mg

Iron: 1mg

Vitamin D: 0mcg

Time: 10 minutes

Serving Size: 2

Ingredients:

- ½ cup tomato, sliced
- ¼ block firm tofu
- 1 tbsp sesame oil
- 1 tbsp low-sodium tamari
- ½ cup cauliflower rice, cooked
- 2 green onions, sliced
- Salt and pepper to taste

Directions:

1. Add sesame oil and tamari to non-stick skillet and place over medium heat. Once oil heated, add green onions and sliced tomato. Toss then cover pan with lid and allow to cook for 5 minutes or until the tomatoes are soft.
2. Add tofu to pan and crumble with a fork. Stir so that the tofu is coated with the oil mixture. Cook for 2 minutes with the pan uncovered to allow the tofu to become warmed. This will allow the excess liquid to evaporate.
3. Remove the pan from the heat and seasoned with salt and pepper. Serve over cauliflower rice.

Walnut Zucchini Chili

Nutritional Information:

Total fat: 19.7g

Cholesterol: 0mg

Sodium: 58mg

Total carbohydrates: 15.1g

Dietary fiber: 5.3g

Protein: 12.5g

Calcium: 180mg

Potassium: 812mg

Iron: 3mg

Vitamin D: 0mcg

Time: 50 minutes

Serving Size: 8

Ingredients:

- 2 medium zucchini, diced
- 1 cup raw walnuts, minced
- 2 yellow bell peppers, finely diced
- 8 oz cremini mushrooms
- 4 celery stalks, finely diced
- 1 yellow onion, diced
- 2 garlic cloves, minced
- 1 tsp ground cinnamon
- 2 tsp chili powder
- 3 tsp ground cumin
- 1 tsp smoked paprika

- 1 tbsp tomato paste
- 2 large tomatoes, diced
- 1 tbsp unsweetened cocoa powder
- ½ cup coconut milk
- 3 cups water
- 2 tbsp olive oil
- 2 cups tofu, crumbled

Directions:

1. Add olive oil to a large pot and place over medium heat. Add celery and onion and cook for 4 minutes or until onion is translucent.
2. Add cinnamon, chili powder, cumin, paprika and garlic and sauté for 2 more minutes or until fragrant.
3. Add bell peppers, mushrooms and zucchini and cook for 5 more minutes.
4. Add tomato paste, tomatoes, coconut milk, tofu, water, walnuts and cocoa powder. Reduce heat to low and simmer for 25 minutes or until the sauce is thick and vegetables are soft.
5. Season with salt and pepper to taste. Serve.

Roasted Veggies on Broccoli Rice

Nutritional Information:

Total fat: 23.2g

Cholesterol: 0mg

Sodium: 117mg

Total carbohydrates: 16.9g

Dietary fiber: 6.7g

Protein: 6.5g

Calcium: 60mg

Potassium: 796mg

Iron: 3mg

Vitamin D: 0mcg

Time: 1 hour

Serving Size: 7

Ingredients:

- 1 head of broccoli
- 2 red bell peppers, chopped

- 2 cups cauliflower florets
- ⅓ cup olive oil
- 6 sun-dried tomatoes, chopped
- 1/2 cup pitted black olives
- 1 large avocado, sliced
- ¼ cup pumpkin seeds
- ¼ cup pine nuts
- ¼ cup sunflower seeds
- ¼ cup fresh parsley, finely chopped
- 1 tbsp fresh chives, finely chopped
- 1 tbsp fresh mint, finely chopped
- 1 tbsp nutritional yeast
- 1 tbsp coconut aminos
- ½ tbsp lime juice
- Salt and pepper to taste

Directions:

1. Preheat oven to 400 degrees F.
2. Placed chopped peppers and cauliflower florets on a baking sheet. Toss with 1 tablespoon of olive oil and a pinch of salt. Roast for 40 minutes or until veggies are soft.
3. While vegetables roast, add broccoli florets to a food processor and pulse until a rice like consistency is achieved.
4. Place all seeds and pine nuts on a baking tray. Toss with a pinch of salt and a small amount of olive oil. Roast for 5 minutes or until golden brown.
5. To make dressing, add remaining olive oil, coconut aminos, lime juice and a pinch of salt and pepper to a small bowl and whisk.
6. Fluff broccoli rice then add dressing, seeds, nuts, roasted veggies, sun-dried tomatoes, olives, avocado, herbs and nutritional yeast, and toss. Serve.

Keto Vegan Thai Curry

Nutritional Information:

Total fat: 14.6g

Cholesterol: 0mg

Sodium: 813mg

Total carbohydrates: 9.5g

Dietary fiber: 1.5g

Protein: 4.5g

Calcium: 50mg

Potassium: 255mg

Iron: 2mg

Vitamin D: 0mcg

Time: 25 minutes

Serving Size: 5

Ingredients:

- 1 block tofu, cubed
- 1 tsp Thai curry paste
- 2 tbsp coconut oil
- 1 tbsp peanut butter
- 1 tbsp tomato paste
- 2 ½ cup full fat coconut milk
- 2 tsp chili flakes
- 1 tsp ginger, grated
- 1 garlic clove, minced
- ¼ cup soy sauce
- 2 red bell peppers, cut into strips
- 1 stalk lemongrass, chopped

Directions:

1. Add coconut oil to a nonstick pan and place over medium heat. Add ginger and garlic and stir.
2. Add bell peppers and lemongrass. Stir for about 30 seconds then add coconut milk and chili flakes. Stir for 30 more seconds
3. Add the rest of the ingredients except for tofu cubes. Stir for 1 minute.
4. Add tofu cubes and allow curry cook for 10 minutes or until the sauce thickens.
5. Divide curry into serving bowls and serve.

Falafel with Tahini Sauce

Nutritional Information:

Total fat: 7.8g

Cholesterol: 0mg

Sodium: 299mg

Total carbohydrates: 7.1g

Dietary fiber: 4.1g

Protein: 2.9g

Calcium: 30mg

Potassium: 137mg

Iron: 1mg

Vitamin D: 0mcg

Time: 30 minutes

Serving Size: 8

Ingredients:

- 1 ½ cup cauliflower florets
- 2 tbsp olive oil
- 2 tbsp flax seeds
- 6 tablespoons water
- ½ cup slivered almonds
- 1 garlic clove, minced
- 2 tbsp fresh parsley, chopped
- 3 tbsp coconut flour
- 1 tbsp ground cumin
- 1/2 tbsp ground coriander
- 1 tsp salt
- ½ tsp cayenne pepper

Directions:

1. Create egg substitute by combining flaxseed and water in a small bowl. Set aside for 5 minutes.
2. Add cauliflower to a food processor and pulse until a grainy texture is achieved.
3. Add almonds to a food processor and pulse to a crumbly texture.
4. Combine cauliflower and almonds in a medium mixing bowl. Add the rest of the ingredients except for olive oil and stir to combine well.
5. Form 3 inch wide patties with the mixture. Press down until the patties are about 1/2 inch thick.
6. Add olive oil to a nonstick skillet and place over medium heat. When the oil is sizzling and add the panties and fry for 5 minutes or until the bottom edge browns.
7. Flip and fry for 5 more minutes. Remove patties and place on a paper towel lined plate to drain excess oil. Serve with tahini sauce or any other favorite keto vegan dipping sauce.

Chapter 8: Dessert and Snacks Recipes

Snacking is not the terrible villain it is made out to be. Not when it is done in the right way. In fact, snacking has a variety of benefits that include:

- Improving overall health
- Curbing cravings
- Regulating mood
- Boosting brain power
- Lowering the risk of developing heart disease
- Managing weight gain
- Providing energy throughout the day
- Help injects diet with nutrition that might have been missed during main meals

Snacking has gotten such a bad rap because most people reach for an unhealthy items such as those filled with sugar and unhealthy fats instead of healthy alternatives such as fruits and veggies. Not only do these contribute to negative health effects it also leads to overeating which can lead to excessive weight gain and even obesity.

The best way to avoid these negative consequences is to have healthy snacks on hand so that you can curb your cravings, eat smaller amounts, lower your blood sugar and keep your metabolism revved throughout the day. Below are 15 healthy keto vegan snack and dessert recipes you can keep on hand and indulge in when hunger strikes. Remember that moderation and careful planning are the keys to healthy snacking.

Baked Zucchini Chips

Nutritional Information:

Total fat: 1.5g

Cholesterol: 0mg

Sodium: 120mg

Total carbohydrates: 1.3g

Dietary fiber: 0.4g

Protein: 0.5g

Calcium: 6mg

Potassium: 103mg

Iron: 0mg

Vitamin D: 0mcg

Time: 2 hours 45 minutes

Serving Size: 10

Ingredients:

- 2 medium zucchini, sliced with a mandolin
- 1 tbsp olive oil
- 1/2 tsp salt

Directions:

1. Preheat your oven to 200 degrees F.
2. Prepare your baking sheets by lining with parchment paper.
3. Add all ingredients to a large mixing bowl and toss to thoroughly coat the zucchini with oil and salt.
4. Arrange the zucchini slices in a single layer on the baking sheet. They can touch but they should not overlap.
5. Bake for 2 and a half hours or until the zucchini chips are golden and crispy.
6. Turn off the oven and allow them to cool with the oven door cropped slightly open. This will allow the zucchini chips to crisp up even more as they cool.

Gluten-Free Nut-Free Red Velvet Cupcakes

Nutritional Information:

Total fat: 2.9g

Cholesterol: 0mg

Sodium: 93mg

Total carbohydrates: 4.9g

Dietary fiber: 2.4g

Protein: 1.8g

Calcium: 53mg

Potassium: 196mg

Iron: 2mg

Vitamin D: 0mcg

Time: 50 minutes

Serving Size: 8

Ingredients:

- 2 tbsp flax meal
- 4 tbsp cocoa powder
- ½ cup of almond butter
- ½ cup unsweetened almond milk
- 1 tbsp granulated erythritol
- 2 tbsp apple cider vinegar
- 4 tbsp ground flaxseed
- 1 tsp baking powder
- 1/2 tsp baking soda

Directions:

1. Preheat your oven to 350 degrees F.
2. Prepare a standard size muffin tin by lining it with paper liners.
3. In a small bowl, whisk together almond butter, almond milk and apple cider vinegar until a smooth combined mixture is achieved. Stir in flax seeds and erythritol and set aside.

4. In a large mixing bowl, sift together cocoa powder, flax meal, baking powder and baking soda. Mix to combine.
5. Pour the wet mixture into the dry ingredients and stir until there are no lumps. Do not overmix.
6. Divide the batter between the lined muffin wells. Ensure that each muffin is filled 3/4 of the way. Bake for 30 minutes or until the top of each muffin is firm to the touch.
7. Remove from the oven and allow to cool in pan for 10 minutes. Remove the cupcakes from the pan and allow to cool completely. Serve.

5-Ingredient Ice-cream

Nutritional Information:

Total fat: 10.1g

Cholesterol: 0mg

Sodium: 34mg

Total carbohydrates: 3.7

Dietary fiber: 0.9g

Protein: 4.7g

Calcium: 1mg

Potassium: 6mg

Iron: 2mg

Vitamin D: 0mcg

Time: 1 hour 10 minutes

Serving Size: 6

Ingredients:

- 1 ½ cup full fat coconut milk
- ⅓ cup natural peanut butter
- 2 tbsp vanilla extract
- ⅛ tsp stevia powder
- A pinch of salt

Directions:

1. Prior to starting this recipe, place a freezer-safe container in the freezer for at least 24 hours before to ensure that when the ice cream mixture is transferred no ice crystals are formed.
2. Add all ingredients to a blender and blend until a smooth and creamy consistency is achieved.
3. Chill this mixture by placing it in the refrigerator for 1 hour.
4. Transfer the mixture to an ice-cream maker and churn for 10 minutes or until it achieves a soft serve consistency.
5. Transfer the ice cream to the prepared freezer-safe container and freeze for at least one hour before serving. Can be served with caramel sauce (See recipe *Chapter 4: Sauces and Condiments: Keto Caramel Sauce*)

Peanut Butter Cups

Nutritional Information:

Total fat: 5.7g

Cholesterol: 0mg

Sodium: 33mg

Total carbohydrates: 3.2g

Dietary fiber: 0.9g

Protein: 2g

Calcium: 0mg

Potassium: 47mg

Iron: 1mg

Vitamin D: 0mcg

Time: 45 minutes

Serving Size: 18

Ingredients:

- ½ cup peanut butter
- 1 cup sugar-free dark chocolate chips
- 1 tbsp coconut oil

Directions:

1. Place the chocolate chips and coconut oil in a microwave-safe bowl. Microwave in 15 second bursts to melt the chocolate. Stir to combine the two ingredients.
2. Put a spoonful of chocolate into foil candy cups. Swirl so that the chocolate coats the sides of the cups. Pour excess chocolate back into the bowl.
3. Place the chocolate lined cups in the freezer for 10 minutes or until chocolate is set.
4. While the chocolate is setting, place the peanut butter in a microwave-safe bowl and microwave in 15 second bursts until the peanut butter becomes pourable.
5. Pour a spoonful of peanut butter into each of the chocolate-set cups. Tap the cups on a flat surface to smooth the tops of the peanut butter.
6. Pour a spoonful of melted chocolate on top of the peanut butter in each cup.
7. Place in the freezer for 10 minutes to set chocolate. Unmold and serve. Can be stored in the refrigerator in an airtight container for up to 3 days or in the freezer for up to 1 month.

Chocolate Avocado Mousse

Nutritional Information:

Total fat: 16.2g

Cholesterol:0mg

Sodium: 62mg

Total carbohydrates: 14.1g

Dietary fiber: 5.3g

Protein: 2.5g

Calcium: 24mg

Potassium: 402mg

Iron: 1mg

Vitamin D: 0mcg

Time: 10 minutes

Serving Size: 6

Ingredients:

- ½ cup dark chocolate chips
- 3 tbsp cocoa powder

- 2 large ripe avocados
- ¼ cup unsweetened almond milk
- 1 tsp vanilla extract
- ⅛ tsp salt
- Strawberries for topping

Directions:

1. Place chocolate chips in a microwave-safe bowl and microwave in 15 second bursts until the chocolate is melted but not burnt. Stir and set aside. Let cool until just barely warm.
2. Remove the pits from the avocados and scoop out the flesh. Place the flesh into a food processor. Add melted chocolate and the rest of the ingredients except for the strawberry topping. Blend until a smooth creamy consistency is achieved. Scrape down sides of bowl as necessary.
3. Spoon the mixture into serving glasses, top with sliced strawberries (or other preferred toppings) and serve as a pudding. To enjoy a mousse-like consistency, refrigerate for at least 2 hours. Can be stored in an airtight container in the refrigerator for up to 7 days.

Spiced Kale Chips

Nutritional Information:

Total fat: 3g

Cholesterol: 0mg

Sodium: 124mg

Total carbohydrates: 1.8g

Dietary fiber: 0.7g

Protein: 0.9g

Calcium: 30mg

Potassium: 100mg

Iron: 0mg

Vitamin D: 0mcg

Time: 30 minutes

Serving Size: 5

Ingredients:

- 1 bunch curly kale
- 1 tbsp olive oil
- ¼ tsp of salt
- ⅛ tsp garlic powder
- ⅛ tsp black pepper

Directions:

1. Preheat the oven to 300 degrees F.
2. Prepare a baking sheet by lining it with aluminum foil.
3. Rinse and dry kale thoroughly by spinning in a salad spinner or patting with paper towels.
4. Tear kale leaves off the stems and break into pieces the size of potato chips. Place into a large mixing bowl and add the rest of the ingredients. Toss so that the kale leaves are thoroughly coated with the spices and oil.
5. Place the coated kale leaves in an even layer that does not overlap on a wire baking rack. Place the wire baking rack atop the foil lined baking sheet.
6. Bake for 20 minutes or until the edges of the kale leaves are crispy.
7. Allow to cool and serve.

Coconut Fat Cups

Nutritional Information:

Total fat: 11.7g

Cholesterol: 0mg

Sodium: 4mg

Total carbohydrates: 2.5g

Dietary fiber: 1.7g

Protein: 0.7g

Calcium: 3mg

Potassium: 10mg

Iron: 1mg

Vitamin D: 0mcg

Time: 1 hour 15 minutes

Serving Size: 10

Ingredients:

- ¼ cup coconut butter, melted
- ¼ cup coconut oil, melted
- 3 drops liquid stevia
- ⅓ cup shredded coconut

Directions:

1. Add all ingredients to a medium mixing bowl and thoroughly combine.
2. Using a tablespoon, fill mini cupcake liners or an ice cube tray with the mixture.
3. Freeze for at least 1 hour and serve. Can be stored in the refrigerator for up to 3 days in an airtight container.

Almond Coconut Fat Cups

Nutritional Information:

Total fat: 4.7g

Cholesterol: 0mg

Sodium: 0mg

Total carbohydrates: 0.9g

Dietary fiber: 0.5g

Protein: 0.4g

Calcium: 4mg

Potassium: 29mg

Iron: 0mg

Vitamin D: 0mcg

Time: 1 hour 10 minutes

Serving Size: 16

Ingredients:

- 3 tbsp almonds, sliced
- 3 tbsp shredded coconut
- 2 tbsp cocoa powder
- ½ tsp almond extract

- ¼ tsp of vanilla extract
- 4 drops liquid stevia
- ¼ cup coconut oil, melted
- ¼ cup coconut butter, melted

Directions:

1. Combine coconut butter, coconut oil, cocoa powder, almond extract, vanilla extract and liquid stevia in a medium mixing bowl.
2. Fold in coconut flakes and sliced almonds.
3. Using a tablespoon, fill mini cupcake liners or an ice cube tray with the mixture.
4. Freeze for at least 1 hour and serve. Can be stored in the refrigerator for up to 3 days in an airtight container.

Candied Toasted Cashew Nuts

Nutritional Information:

Total fat: 3.3g

Cholesterol: 0mg

Sodium: 54mg

Total carbohydrates: 1.6g

Dietary fiber: 0.4g

Protein: 1.2g

Calcium: 3mg

Potassium: 2mg

Iron: 0mg

Vitamin D: 0mcg

Time: 15 minutes

Serving Size: 22

Ingredients:

- 3 cups unsalted cashew nuts
- 1 pack granulated monk fruit sweetener
- 1/2 tsp salt
- 1 tsp vanilla extract
- 1 tbsp cinnamon
- 1/4 cup water

Directions:

1. Place a large skillet over medium heat. When the pan is hot, add monk fruit sweetener, cinnamon, salt, water and vanilla extract. Stir to combine and allow to heat.
2. When the monk fruit sweetener has dissolved, add cashews and stir to ensure that all the cashews are coated with syrup mixture. Continue to stir the cashew mixture until the liquid begins to crystallize on the cashews.
3. Remove the pan from the heat and allow to cool. Stir occasionally to ensure that clusters do not form. Allow the candied cashews to cool completely before serving.

Almond Cookies

Nutritional Information:

Total fat: 1.1g

Cholesterol: 0mg

Sodium: 36mg

Total carbohydrates: 1.7g

Dietary fiber: 0.3g

Protein: 0.5g

Calcium: 19mg

Potassium: 36mg

Iron: 0mg

Vitamin D: 0mcg

Time: 35 minutes

Serving Size: 20

Ingredients:

- 1 cup almond flour
- 1 tbsp flax meal
- 4 tsp granulated erythritol
- ½ tsp almond extract
- ½ cup unsweetened almond milk
- 1 tsp almond extract
- ½ cup almond butter

- ¼ tsp salt
- 1 tsp baking powder

Directions:

1. Preheat your oven to 350 degrees F.
2. Prepare a baking sheet by lining it with parchment paper.
3. Sift almond flour, flax meal, erythritol, baking powder and salt into a large mixing.
4. In another mixing bowl, stir together the rest of the ingredients to form a wet mixture.
5. Fold in wet mixture into the dry ingredients to form a smooth, even batter.
6. Scoop spoonfuls of batter and place onto prepared baking sheet.
7. Flatten slightly and bake for 25 minutes or until cookies are golden brown.
8. Allow to cool then serve.

Coconut Protein Crackers

Nutritional Information:

Total fat: 3.7g

Cholesterol: 0mg

Sodium: 34mg

Total carbohydrates: 1.9g

Dietary fiber: 1.3g

Protein: 1.4g

Calcium: 33mg

Potassium: 22mg

Iron: 1mg

Vitamin D: 0mcg

Time: 1 hour 20 minutes

Serving Size: 20

Ingredients:

- ½ cup unsweetened shredded coconut
- ½ cup vanilla protein powder
- 3 tbsp ground flax seed

- 3 tbsp sesame seed
- 1 tbsp chia seed
- 1 tbsp coconut oil, melted
- ¼ tsp salt
- ½ cup water

Directions:

1. Preheat your oven to 300 degrees F.
2. Prepare a baking sheet by lining it with parchment paper.
3. Prepare egg substitute by combining flax seeds and water in a small bowl. Set aside for 5 minutes.
4. In a large mixing bowl, combine shredded coconut, sesame seeds, chia seeds, salt and protein powder. Mix well.
5. Add coconut oil and flax egg and fold into dry ingredients to incorporate well.
6. Transfer prepared dough onto prepared baking sheet. Spread the mixture as evenly as possible and score to form evenly sized crackers.
7. Bake for 1 hour.
8. Remove baking tray from oven and flip crackers. Place in the oven once more and bake for another 15 minutes.
9. Remove crackers from the oven and allow to cool completely before breaking into individual crackers. Serve.

Raw Strawberry Crumble

Nutritional Information:

Total fat: 15.7g

Cholesterol: 5mg

Sodium: 43mg

Total carbohydrates: 6.1g

Dietary fiber: 3.7g

Protein: 13.1g

Calcium: 216mg

Potassium: 320mg

Iron: 1mg

Vitamin D: 0mcg

Time: 5 minutes

Serving Size: 6

Ingredients:

- 4 cups fresh strawberries, hulled and sliced
- ¼ cup unsweetened coconut flakes
- ½ cup raw walnuts
- ½ tbsp ginger, grated
- ½ tbsp ground cinnamon

Directions:

1. Arrange sliced strawberries on the bottom of a pie dish or serving bowls.
2. Add all of the rest of the ingredients to a food processor and pulse until a crumble consistency is.
3. Arrange the crumble on top of the strawberries and serve.

Peanut Butter Energy Bars

Nutritional Information:

Total fat: 17g

Cholesterol: 0mg

Sodium: 6mg

Total carbohydrates: 13.8g

Dietary fiber: 4.9g

Protein: 9.1g

Calcium: 14mg

Potassium: 209mg

Iron: 1mg

Vitamin D: 0mcg

Time: 10 minutes

Serving Size: 8

Ingredients:

- 1 cup smooth peanut butter
- 4 tsp granulated erythritol

- ⅓ cup coconut flour
- 2 tbsp water

Directions:

1. Prepare a 9-inch loaf pan by lining it with parchment paper.
2. Mix erythritol, peanut butter and water in a medium bowl until a smooth consistency is achieved.
3. Stir in coconut flour and blend well to make a very thick but not dry mixture. If the mixture of appears dry, add a few more teaspoons of water.
4. Press mixture into prepared loaf pan.
5. Refrigerate for at least 2 hours or until set firm.
6. Remove the chilled bars from the loaf pan and cut into bars. Serve. Can be stored in an airtight container in the refrigerator for up to 1 month or in the freezer for up to 6 months.

Lemon Squares

Nutritional Information:

Total fat: 18.1g

Cholesterol: 0mg

Sodium: 2mg

Total carbohydrates: 4.6g

Dietary fiber: 2g

Protein: 1.5g

Calcium: 12mg

Potassium: 57mg

Iron: 0mg

Vitamin D: 0mcg

Time: 5 minutes

Serving Size: 10

Ingredients:

- ¼ cup lemon juice
- ¼ cup coconut oil, melted
- 1 cup unsweetened coconut flakes
- 1 cup macadamia nuts

- 2 tsp granulated erythritol
- 1 tsp vanilla extract

Directions:

1. Prepare a loaf pan by lining it with parchment paper.
2. Add all ingredients to a food processor and pulse for 2 minutes or until a smooth dough forms. It should resemble cookie dough. Scrape down sides of bowl as necessary.
3. Transfer the dough to the prepared baking pan and smooth.
4. Chill in the freezer for 15 minutes or until set.
5. Remove the squares from the loaf pan and slice. Serve. Can be stored in the refrigerator in an airtight container for up to 5 days.

Apple Cider Donuts

Nutritional Information:

Total fat: 17.6g

Cholesterol: 0mg

Sodium: 41mg

Total carbohydrates: 13.3g

Dietary fiber: 8g

Protein: 2.8g

Calcium: 20mg

Potassium: 78mg

Iron: 1mg

Vitamin D: 0mcg

Time: 45 minutes

Serving Size: 6

Ingredients:

- 1 tbsp apple cider vinegar
- 1 tsp vanilla extract
- ½ cup coconut butter
- ½ cup coconut milk

- 1 tbsp granulated erythritol
- 3 tbsp coconut flour
- ¼ tsp baking powder
- ¼ tsp ground cinnamon
- A pinch of salt
- A pinch of nutmeg
- ¼ tbsp psyllium husk

Directions:

1. Preheat your oven to 350 degrees F.
2. Grease a standard donut pan.
3. Combine coconut butter, coconut milk, apple cider vinegar, vanilla extract and erythritol in over a double boiler until the coconut butter is melted and an even, uniform mixture is formed. This will take approximately 5 minutes.
4. Combine the rest of the ingredients into a medium mixing bowl.
5. Pour coconut butter mixture into the dry ingredients. Mix well. Let mixture sit for about 5 minutes.
6. Evenly distribute the batter into 6 of the donut pan cavities. Smooth the top of each donut.
7. Bake for 30 minutes or until edges are golden brown and a toothpick comes how to clean when inserted into the thickest part of the donut.
8. Remove from the oven and allow to cool completely before removing from pan. Serve.

Chapter 9: Smoothies and Other Beverage Recipes

As part of choosing to follow a keto vegan diet, you will realize that most fruits are off limits. Fruits are typically a major ingredient in smoothies, juices and teas. The natural sweetness packs smoothies and juices with delicious flavor while they provide great nutrition in the form of vitamins, minerals and antioxidants.

Unfortunately, fruits are typically naturally high in sugar (carbohydrates). Consuming typical smoothies will kick your body out of ketosis. Therefore, most fruits need to be avoided.

While typical fruit-based smoothies are off limits, you can still indulge in delicious smoothies, juices and sweet teas. All you have to do is change your fruit choices to berries in moderate quantities and change your fruit pieces to vegetable bases. Cauliflower, zucchini and avocado are great fruit substitutes. Add ingredients like vanilla extract, coconut, cinnamon and cocoa and you've got a treat for your taste buds that is also great for your body.

Below you can find recipes for smoothies, juices and warm beverages that your taste buds with love and that will keep your body within ketosis limits.

Matcha Spinach Smoothie

Nutritional Information:

Total fat: 20.8g

Cholesterol: 1mg

Sodium: 19mg

Total carbohydrates: 10.6g

Dietary fiber: 3.6g

Protein: 4g

Calcium: 51mg

Potassium: 312mg

Iron: 1mg

Vitamin D: 0mcg

Time: 5 minutes

Serving Size: 3

Ingredients:

- ½ cup spinach
- ½ tsp matcha powder
- ½ medium avocado
- 1 tbsp MCT oil
- 1 tsp pure vanilla extract
- 1 tbsp granulated erythritol
- ½ cup coconut milk
- ⅔ cup water
- ⅓ cup ice cubes
- ¼ scoop vanilla protein powder

Directions:

1. Add all ingredients to a blender and blend until a smooth consistency is achieved. Serve.

Protein-Packed Blueberry Smoothie

Nutritional Information:

Total fat: 6.1g

Cholesterol: 3mg

Sodium: 73mg

Total carbohydrates: 6g

Dietary fiber: 0.8g

Protein: 6.4g

Calcium: 175mg

Potassium: 79mg

Iron: 1mg

Vitamin D: 0mcg

Time: 5 minutes

Serving Size: 2

Ingredients:

- ¾ unsweetened coconut milk
- ½ cup unsweetened almond milk
- ⅓ cup frozen blueberries
- 4 tbsp vanilla protein powder

Directions:

1. Add all ingredients to a blender and blend until a smooth consistency is achieved. Serve.

Chocolate Avocado Smoothie

Nutritional Information:

Total fat: 18.7g

Cholesterol: 0mg

Sodium: 12mg

Total carbohydrates: 8.1g

Dietary fiber: 4.7g

Protein: 4.3g

Calcium: 10mg

Potassium: 312mg

Iron: 2mg

Vitamin D: 0mcg

Time: 5 minutes

Serving Size: 2

Ingredients:

- 1 tbsp cocoa powder
- ½ medium avocado
- ¾ cup full-fat coconut milk
- ⅓ cup ice cubes
- 1 tbsp natural peanut butter
- 2 drops liquid stevia

Directions:

1. Add all ingredients to a blender and blend until a smooth consistency is achieved. Serve.

Mint Cauliflower Smoothie

Nutritional Information:

Total fat: 19.3g

Cholesterol: 5mg

Sodium: 123mg

Total carbohydrates: 8.8g

Dietary fiber: 5.1g

Protein: 13.7g

Calcium: 223mg

Potassium: 426mg

Iron: 1mg

Vitamin D: 0mcg

Time: 5 minutes

Serving Size: 2

Ingredients:

- ½ cup frozen cauliflower
- 1 tbsp mint, chopped
- ⅓ cup full fat coconut milk
- ⅓ cup ice cubes
- ½ small avocado

- 1 scoop vanilla protein powder
- 1 tbsp cocoa powder
- 1 tbsp coconut oil
- ⅛ tsp ground cinnamon
- A pinch of salt

Directions:

1. Add all ingredients to a blender and blend until a smooth consistency is achieved. Serve.

Strawberry Protein Smoothie

Nutritional Information:

Total fat: 14.2g

Cholesterol: 3mg

Sodium: 23mg

Total carbohydrates: 7.5g

Dietary fiber: 2.4g

Protein: 8.4g

Calcium: 116mg

Potassium: 178mg

Iron: 2mg

Vitamin D: 0mcg

Time: 5 minutes

Serving Size: 2

Ingredients:

- ½ cup frozen strawberries
- 1 tbsp almond butter
- ½ scoop vanilla protein powder
- ⅓ cup almond milk
- ½ cup ice

Directions:

1. Add all ingredients to a blender and blend until a smooth consistency is achieved. Serve.

Turmeric Avocado Smoothie

Nutritional Information:

Total fat: 27.3g

Cholesterol: 0mg

Sodium: 19mg

Total carbohydrates: 10.9g

Dietary fiber: 5g

Protein: 9.6g

Calcium: 65mg

Potassium: 685mg

Iron: 4mg

Vitamin D: 0mcg

Time: 5 minutes

Serving Size: 2

Ingredients:

- ¼ tsp turmeric powder
- 1/2 medium avocado
- 1 cup water
- 1 tbsp MCT oil
- ½ cucumber
- 3 kale leaves
- 2 tbsp of parsley
- 3 tbsp hemp seed
- 1 tbsp lemon juice

Directions:

1. Add all ingredients to a blender and blend until a smooth consistency is achieved. Serve.

Raspberry Avocado Smoothie

Nutritional Information:

Total fat: 19.8g

Cholesterol: 0mg

Sodium: 13mg

Total carbohydrates: 10.8g

Dietary fiber: 7.8g

Protein: 2.2g

Calcium: 21mg

Potassium: 531mg

Iron: 1mg

Vitamin D: 0mcg

Time: 5 minutes

Serving Size: 2

Ingredients:

- 1 small ripe avocado, peeled and pitted
- ¼ cup raspberries, frozen
- 2 tbsp lemon juice
- 1 cup water

Directions:

1. Add all ingredients to a blender and blend until a smooth consistency is achieved. Serve.

Vanilla Coconut Smoothie

Nutritional Information:

Total fat: 15.7g

Cholesterol: 5mg

Sodium: 43mg

Total carbohydrates: 6.1g

Dietary fiber: 3.7g

Protein: 13.1g

Calcium: 216mg

Potassium: 320mg

Iron: 1mg

Vitamin D: 0mcg

Time: 5 minutes

Serving Size: 2

Ingredients:

- 1 scoop vanilla protein powder
- ¼ cup full fat coconut milk
- ½ small avocado
- ½ tbsp of coconut oil, melted
- 1 tbsp sunflower seed
- ½ cup spinach
- ¼ tsp stevia powder
- ½ cup ice cubes

Directions:

8. Add all ingredients to a blender and blend until a smooth consistency is achieved. Serve.

Cleansing Green Spinach Juice

Nutritional Information:

Total fat: 3.7g

Cholesterol: 0mg

Sodium: 226mg

Total carbohydrates: 8.1g

Dietary fiber: 1.7g

Protein: 2.9g

Calcium: 92mg

Potassium: 456mg

Iron: 2mg

Vitamin D: 0mcg

Time: 5 minutes

Serving Size: 2

Ingredients:

- 6 kale leaves
- 2 cups spinach
- 1 inch fresh ginger piece, peeled
- 4 mint leaves

- ½ cucumber, peeled and chopped

Directions:

1. Ensure that vegetable pieces are cut into sizes that will fit into your juicer and juice all ingredients. Serve.

Lime Kale Juice

Nutritional Information:

Total fat: 0.2g

Cholesterol: 0mg

Sodium: 55mg

Total carbohydrates: 6g

Dietary fiber: 1.4g

Protein: 1.2g

Calcium: 54mg

Potassium: 297mg

Iron: 1mg

Vitamin D: 0mcg

Time: 5 minutes

Serving Size: 1

Ingredients:

- ½ tbsp lime juice
- 2 kale leaves
- 1/4 cup spinach
- 3 stalk celery
- ½ inch ginger piece, peeled

Directions:

1. Ensure that vegetable pieces are cut into sizes that will fit into your juicer and juice all ingredients. Serve.

Berry Spinach Juice

Nutritional Information:

Total fat: 0.3g

Cholesterol: 0mg

Sodium: 30mg

Total carbohydrates: 9.5g

Dietary fiber: 2g

Protein: 1.5g

Calcium: 46mg

Potassium: 365mg

Iron: 1mg

Vitamin D: 0mcg

Time: 5 minutes

Serving Size: 2

Ingredients:

- ¼ cup mixed berries, frozen
- ½ cup spinach
- 3 celery stalks
- 1 cucumber, peeled and chopped
- 1 tbsp lime juice

Directions:

1. Ensure that vegetable pieces are cut into sizes that will fit into your juicer and juice all ingredients. Serve.

Keto Vegan Hot Chocolate

Nutritional Information:

Total fat: 15.2g

Cholesterol: 0mg

Sodium: 48mg

Total carbohydrates: 4.8g

Dietary fiber: 2g

Protein: 1.3g

Calcium: 84mg

Potassium: 131mg

Iron: 1mg

Vitamin D: 0mcg

Time: 5 minutes

Serving Size: 2

Ingredients:

- 2 tbsp unsweetened cocoa powder
- ¼ tsp vanilla extract
- ½ tsp granulated erythritol
- ½ cup of hot water
- ½ cup unsweetened almond milk
- 2 tbsp coconut oil

Directions:

1. Add all ingredients to a blender and blend until smooth consistency is achieved. Serve.

Iced Coffee Latte

Nutritional Information:

Total fat: 13.3g

Cholesterol: 0mg

Sodium: 93mg

Total carbohydrates: 1.1g

Dietary fiber: 0.5g

Protein: 0.6g

Calcium: 153mg

Potassium: 126mg

Iron: 0mg

Vitamin D: 1mcg

Time: 15 minutes

Serving Size: 2

Ingredients:

- 1 cup unsweetened almond milk
- 1 tbsp MCT oil
- 2 tsp coconut oil, melted
- ½ cup strong brewed coffee
- ½ tsp vanilla extract
- ½ cup ice cubes

Directions:

1. To make strong brewed coffee, add 4 tablespoon of organic dark roast ground coffee blend and 1 cup or less of water to a small pan and bring to a boil on the stove top over high heat. Strain coffee then place in refrigerator to chill.
2. Once the coffee has cooled, remove from the refrigerator. Add remaining ingredients except for ice and vanilla extract to coffee. Add this mixture to a blender and blend until an extra frothy mixture is achieved.
3. Stir in vanilla extract and pour latte into serving cups. Add ice cubes on top. Pour in extra almond milk if desired and swirl to mix. Serve.

Keto Vegan Eggnog

Nutritional Information:

Total fat: 6.6

Cholesterol: 2mg

Sodium: 142mg

Total carbohydrates: 2.8g

Dietary fiber: 1.3g

Protein: 5.8g

Calcium: 266mg

Potassium: 151mg

Iron: 1mg

Vitamin D: 1mcg

Time: 5 minutes

Serving Size: 5

Ingredients:

- ¼ cup vanilla protein powder
- 3 cups unsweetened almond milk

- 1 tsp ground nutmeg
- 1 tsp vanilla extract
- 1 cup raw salted pecans
- A pinch of cinnamon

Directions:

1. Add all ingredients to a blender and blend until a smooth mixture is achieved.
2. Strain the resulting mixture and chill for at least 30 minutes before serving if a chilled beverage is desired. Can be warmed up on the stove top if a warm beverage is desired.

Creamy Golden Milk

Nutritional Information:

Total fat: 3.1g

Cholesterol: 0mg

Sodium: 8mg

Total carbohydrates: 1.6g

Dietary fiber: 0.4g

Protein: 0.4g

Calcium: 8mg

Potassium: 33mg

Iron: 1mg

Vitamin D: 0mcg

Time: 5 minutes

Serving Size: 1

Ingredients:

- 1 black tea bag
- ½ cup boiling water
- ¼ full fat coconut milk
- ½ tsp turmeric powder
- A pinch of cinnamon
- A pinch of ginger
- ½ tsp stevia powder

Directions:

1. Brew tea by placing tea bag and boiling water into a serving mug. Allow to sit until the tea reaches the desired strength. Remove and discard tea bag.
2. Add the resulting tea and all other ingredients to a blender and blend until a smooth consistency is achieved.
3. Warm in a saucepan over medium heat then serve.

Conclusion

We have come to the end of this book and you are likely wondering if this diet is right for you. Answer this:

Are you looking for a diet that is proven safe and effective?

Do you want to uphold the vegan principles of compassion for and nonviolence against animals, protecting the planet and sustaining human life while losing weight naturally and sustainably?

Do you want to lower your risk of developing chronic diseases like heart disease, obesity, and type 2 diabetes?

Do you want to have more energy everyday while improving your brain function?

Do you want to still enjoy delicious meals while improving your overall health and wellness?

I am assuming that you answered yes to all of these questions. If that is the case then the keto vegan diet is definitely the right choice for you. You have nothing to lose except for the unwanted pounds by giving this diet a try.

Thank you for downloading this book. I hope that it served its intended purpose of educating you on the keto vegan diet. Please try the recipes contained within and delight your taste buds as you start this journey to a happier, healthier, and improved you.

Printed in Great Britain
by Amazon